A Complete ABA Curriculum for Individuals on the Autism Spectrum with a Developmental Age of 3–5 Years

by the same authors

A Complete ABA Curriculum for Individuals on the Autism Spectrum with a Developmental Age of 1–4 Years
A Step-by-Step Treatment Manual Including Supporting Materials for Teaching 140 Foundational Skills
ISBN 978 1 84905 978 7
eISBN 978 0 85700 887 9

A Complete ABA Curriculum for Individuals on the Autism Spectrum with a Developmental Age of 4–7 Years
A Step-by-Step Treatment Manual Including Supporting Materials for Teaching 150 Intermediate Skills
ISBN 978 1 84905 980 0
eISBN 978 0 85700 889 3

A Complete ABA Curriculum for Individuals on the Autism Spectrum with a Developmental Age of 7 Years Up to Young Adulthood
A Step-by-Step Treatment Manual Including Supporting Materials for Teaching 140 Advanced Skills
ISBN 978 1 84905 981 7
eISBN 978 0 85700 890 9

A Complete ABA Curriculum for Individuals on the Autism Spectrum with a Developmental Age of 3–5 Years

A Step-by-Step Treatment Manual Including Supporting Materials for Teaching 140 Beginning Skills

JULIE KNAPP, Ph.D., BCBA-D AND
CAROLLINE TURNBULL, BA, BCaBA

Jessica Kingsley *Publishers*
London and Philadelphia

First published in 2014
by Jessica Kingsley Publishers
73 Collier Street
London N1 9BE, UK
and
400 Market Street, Suite 400
Philadelphia, PA 19106, USA

www.jkp.com

Library of Congress Cataloging in Publication Data
A CIP catalog record for this book is available from the Library of Congress

British Library Cataloguing in Publication Data
A CIP catalogue record for this book is available from the British Library

ISBN 978 1 84905 979 4
eISBN 978 0 85700 888 6

Printed and bound by Bell and Bain Ltd, Glasgow

FSC www.fsc.org MIX Paper from responsible sources FSC® C007785

Dedication

This book is dedicated to our youngest children, Devyn, Gillian and the little one yet to be born and named. Time with your mommies was sacrificed in order to write this book. We will forever make up this time and give you as much of the world as we can. We love you!

This book is also dedicated to all those wonderful parents and professionals who work with individuals with autism spectrum disorders (ASD) and developmental delays. The world is a better place because of you.

Acknowledgments

Many ABA insructors, Board Certified Behavior Analysts (BCBAs) and ABA interns on staff at the Knapp Center for Childhood Development deserve acknowledgment for their contributions to this curriculum. In providing ABA services to individuals with ASD through our center, they may have written a task analysis (TA) or provided suggestions for learning strategies contained within this manual. We extend a big thank you to (in alphabetical order) Jessica Campagna, Rene Edgell, Jennifer Gonda, Christa Homlitas, Ashley Krznar, Amy Lockney, Cecelia Maderitz, Carrie Snyder and Mary Vallinger.

In creating the supplementary CD that accompanies this curriculum, instructors on staff at the Knapp Center for Childhood Development, as well as patients treated by these instructors, stepped up and volunteered to be filmed. We would like to recognize these patients and their parents for volunteering to allow us to come into their home to record these videos or take pictures. We will not list your names here as we want to protect your confidentiality, but you know who you are, thank you! In addition, we would like to recognize the staff who participated. Our gratitude goes to Kara Kavitz-Voytko and Melanie Gregory. Some staff helped with editing parts of this book; thank you to Carolyn Fernberg, Jamie Siman and Megan Straub.

Finally, we would like to acknowledge Fotosearch (www.fotosearch.com) and Fotolia (www.fotolia.com) for permission to use their photos as program materials for this curriculum (photos found on the supplemental CD).

Contents

About the Authors

Dr. Julie Knapp, Ph.D., BCBA-D is a Pediatric Neuropsychologist and Board Certified Behavior Analyst-Doctorate. She is the Executive Director of the Knapp Center for Childhood Development located in Boardman, OH, which specializes in diagnostics and treatment of individuals with ASD. Dr. Knapp is also a Consultant for University Hospitals Rainbow Babies and Children's Hospital and holds an appointment at Case Western Reserve University. Previously, Dr. Knapp was a Staff Psychologist at Cleveland Clinic Center for Autism and she was a faculty member in psychology education forums for Duquesne University and Chatham University. She completed a two-year post-doctoral fellowship in neuropsychology and autism spectrum disorders at The Watson Institute, followed by completing additional training at Pennsylvania State University in behavioral analysis. Dr. Knapp was a committee member for two years for National Academy of Neuropsychology. Dr. Knapp currently holds certifications in both the Autism Diagnostic Observation Schedule (ADOS) and the Autism Diagnostic Interview –Revised (ADI-R). At the Knapp Center for Childhood Development, Dr. Knapp offers an International ABA Program assisting families from other parts of the world to traveling to the U.S. for ABA therapy. She also co-created and offers an ABA program for military families. She received a grant through Autism Speaks for seed money of her social skills program. She provides in-home ABA programs to individuals with ASD, as well as therapeutic summer camp programs, parent workshops and training to school districts. Dr. Knapp has published nine articles or abstracts on autism related topics in professional journals, presented numerous research posters at national conferences and she edited a resource guide for autism services in the state of Ohio (funded and published by the Cleveland Clinic). Dr. Knapp participated in multiple interviews or education forums through popular media (both television and magazine articles). Dr. Knapp was the primary investigator on a drug trial for toddlers with autism through the National Institute of Health (NIH) while on staff at Cleveland Clinic. She chaired the 1st and 2nd Mahoning Valley Walk Now for Autism Speaks in 2012 and 2013, raising over $100,000 for this organization. Dr. Knapp is on the Advisory Board and the Board of Directors for Autism Speaks Ohio Chapter and the Board of Directors for Autism Society of Ohio, Mahoning Valley Chapter. She reviews grant applications for Autism Speaks, Ohio Chapter. She has over 15 years of experience in working with children with developmental disabilities and has presented over 75 workshops or talks on autism-related topics at local, state, and national conferences or meetings.

Carolline Turnbull is a Board Certified Assistant Behavior Analyst at KidsLink Neurobehavioral Center in Twinsburg, Ohio. Carolline is a behavior consultant for home and school-based consultation and developed a dance class for children aged three to six with varying disabilities and their neuro-typical peers. She completed her Bachelor's degree in speech pathology and audiology at Kent State University and her course work for her BCaBA at Florida Institute of Technology (FIT). Carolline has worked in the area of behavioral management of children and young adults with developmental disabilities for the past 15 years. Prior to joining the team at KidsLink Neurobehavioral Center, Carolline worked at the Cleveland Clinic Center for Autism for eight years; during that time she held various positions including classroom behavior therapist and outreach behavior therapist, consulting in homes and school settings, and was the assistant director of the Social SPIES summer camp for two years.

PART I

CURRICULUM IMPLEMENTATION

Chapter 1

INTRODUCTION TO ABA CURRICULUM

The Journey of Development ABA Curriculum is designed to teach individuals with autism spectrum disorder (ASD) a variety of skills including attending skills, imitation (fine motor, gross motor and oral motor), visual spatial skills, receptive language, expressive language, pragmatic language, adaptive skills, academics, social/play skills and vocational abilities. This curriculum book is part of a four-book series in which the skills build upon each other, with this book representing the second book in the curriculum. Depending on the individual's skill sets, one might start out in the first, second, third or four book in the curriculum. However, it is important to ensure that the individuals you are teaching have the foundational skills presented in the first book in their repertoire before teaching more advanced skills found in the later books, as the individuals will likely have difficulty learning the more advanced skills if they have not yet mastered those foundational skills found in the first book. Although the title of the second book in the Journey of Development ABA Curriculum indicates that these programs are for individuals aged three to five years, this can be misleading. The programs in this book represent skills that most typically developing children obtain when they are between three and five years old. However, individuals with ASD present with developmental delays. Thus, the primary audience of this book may be children with ASD or other developmental delays who are chronologically between three and five years, but also individuals who are chronologically older than this but have a developmental age in this time frame. Finally, it is important to note that since individuals with ASD often do not present with even skill sets across domains (i.e. language, visual spatial skills, etc.), their specific ABA program is likely to include task analyses from two or more of the Journey of Development ABA Curriculum books at one time.

The Journey of Development ABA Curriculum offers over 550 specific programs to teach individuals with developmental delays, with this second book in the series offering approximately 140 of these programs. Each program or skill is presented as a task analysis (TA). We provide directions on how to read and implement the TA, how to collect and record data and how to graph the data. In addition, suggestions for teaching strategies are offered. Since this curriculum is designed as a workbook, an individual's progress can either be charted right onto the pages containing the TAs that will be used in the individual's ABA program, or TAs can be printed off the accompanying CD and placed into a binder that will comprise their individualized ABA curriculum. In addition to the TAs on the accompanying CD, there are three pages which you can download and print out. These include the daily data collection form and the two graphs (skill acquisition and prompt data). When using this workbook, these three pages will have to be printed in order to record the individual's data for each treatment session and graph the results. We recommend that you print out multiple copies of these three pages and place them into a binder, along with the TAs selected for the individual's individualized curriculum. In that binder, you may want to place the daily data collection forms on top since these will be used more frequently and make sections for each instructional domain (i.e. attending, visual spatial, receptive language, etc.). Within each section, you would include the TA(s), unless you are recording directly into the workbook, and a graph for each TA or program that is listed on the daily data collection form (you may be running 10–15 TAs per treatment session). That binder, along with the Journey of Development ABA Curriculum workbooks, will represent the individual's individualized ABA curriculum.

The Journey of Development ABA Curriculum also offers you a list of the programs that comprise the suggested skills to teach (this list is called the "curriculum guide"). This guide should be used to direct you in choosing specific curriculum programs for an individual and for marking off which programs are in the individual's current repertoire or which programs have been taught and archived. We conclude with offering approximately 140 programs that are designed to help your student achieve their optimal functioning and greatest level of independence.

Basic ABA Teaching Strategies

The content of the Journey of Development ABA Curriculum is based on the science and practice of Applied Behavior Analysis (ABA). It is largely recognized that ABA can alter the course of ASD with improvements in cognition, language, socialization and adaptive functioning. Using research as a guide and borrowing on our advanced training in behavioral analysis, we created a "how to" workbook for carrying out specific TAs to teach individuals with ASD. Each skill in this program is taught via a TA. A TA is the process of breaking a complex task down into smaller, simple steps. These simplified steps make learning an easier process for individuals and decreases frustration associated with learning complex tasks. The easier the learning process is for the individual, the easier it is to attain the targeted behavior. The easier it is to attain a targeted behavior, the greater the individual's success.

ABA is data driven. It is a dynamic approach to changing behavior and building skills that is based on analysis of the data. ABA is used to eliminate the maladaptive behaviors associated with ASD, attention deficit hyperactivity disorder (ADHD), learning disabilities, developmental delays and behavioral disorders. ABA is also used to increase desired adaptive behaviors through the use of reinforcement and prompting. ABA brings about comprehensive and enduring improvements in a wide range of skills for most individuals. Individuals with ASD may have great difficulty learning the way their peers do in traditional environments, but can learn a great deal when given the right kind of instruction. Two primary teaching tools in ABA are prompting and reinforcement. Both of the teaching tools are described below, as both tools are used consistently when implementing the TAs found in this curriculum.

Prompts and Prompting Hierarchy

Prompts are one of the primary teaching tools used in ABA. A prompt is assistance given to the individual designed to promote correct responding. Basically, if the individual is unable to perform the skill on their own, we provide prompts to teach them the skill. There is a hierarchy of prompts from most intrusive to least intrusive. You should always use the least intrusive prompt necessary to help the individual in responding correctly. It is important to fade your prompts so the individual does not become prompt dependent. Prompt dependency occurs when a individual becomes reliant on your prompt in order to correctly follow the directive or discriminative stimulus (S^D). To prevent this, you must fade your prompts and promote independent performance of the individual for each skill being taught.

In addition, when teaching the individual, be careful not to give inadvertent prompts. This occurs many times without the awareness of the instructor teaching the programs. This is one of the many reasons why it is important to work with a Board Certified Behavior Analyst (BCBA) to oversee the program, so more expert advice can be given regarding prompting and inadvertent prompts. Inadvertent prompts can lead to the individual being successful on a task not because they truly have mastered the task but because they are following the inadvertent prompts given from their instructor. For example, we suggest that the instructor always present teaching materials in a random fashion regarding placement of the targeted item or picture. For example, if working on a matching program and there is a field (this refers to the number of objects offered to the individual when they are expected to make a choice) of three objects, present the targeted item in varying locations during the instruction (i.e. to the left, right or center). This helps to avoid using an inadvertent prompt of placing the targeted object on the instructor's dominant side.

Figure 1.1 gives a description of some of the prompts most widely used in ABA. The hierarchy has the most intrusive prompts listed at the top and prompts become less intrusive as you move down the hierarchy.

Type of Prompt	**Description**	**Example**	**Picture of Prompt**
Full Physical (FP)	Individual requires full physical assistance to complete a task. The instructor provides "hand-over-hand" to the individual to ensure a correct response.	When teaching the individual to finger paint, the instructor places their hands on top of the individual's hands to show them how to dip their hands in the paint and place their hands on the art paper.	
Partial Physical (PP)	Individual requires partial physical assistance to complete a task.	When teaching the individual to request using the Picture Exchange Communication System (PECS) (Bondy and Frost 2002), the instructor takes the individual's hand and releases it right above the picture or touches the individual's forearm to guide them.	
Gesture (G)	Instructor makes some kind of gesture to prompt the desired response from the individual.	When teaching how to brush hair, the instructor and individual stand in front of a mirror while the instructor gestures toward parts of the head to indicate where to brush.	

Type of Prompt	**Description**	**Example**	**Picture of Prompt**
Positional (POS)	Instructor places a stimulus in a particular location.	When the individual is presented with a field of three pictures of familiar people and directed "Touch brother," the instructor places the correct response closest to the individual.	
Visual (VS)	Instructor provides a visual model of the response.	When presented with the S^D "What do we drink out of?" the instructor holds up a picture of a cup.	
Verbal (VB)	Instructor verbally models the desired response.	When teaching the expressive label of the color (the word) "purple" the instructor gives the following S^D immediately followed by the verbal prompt, "What color is it? Purple."	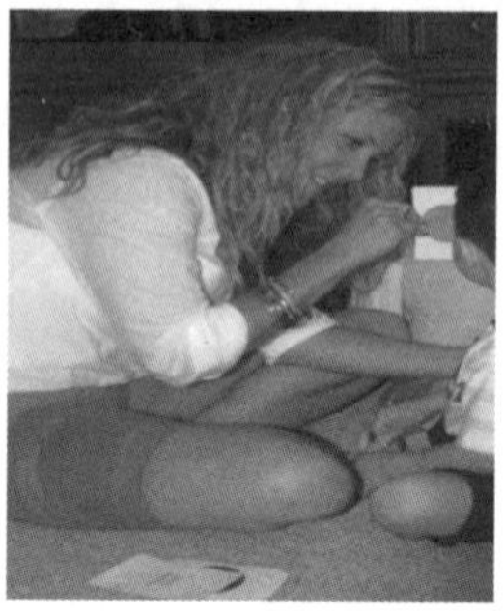

Figure 1.1 Descriptions of Frequently Used Prompts in ABA

Since all individuals can become prompt dependent, it is important to consider the level of prompting required to successfully complete the task and quickly try to fade the prompts to avoid prompt dependency. Generally, it is best to prompt from *least* to *most* intrusive. For example, if prompting an individual to touch a specific body part, you might use a gesture prompt and if the individual does not respond correctly you move up the hierarchy and use a partial physical prompt and finally a full physical prompt. This ensures that the instructor is trying to fade prompts and reduce the risk of prompt dependency. In addition, since verbal prompting is very difficult to fade, we recommend trying to use other prompting techniques when possible and only use verbal prompting when a verbal response is required.

Reinforcement

Reinforcement is the other primary teaching tool used in ABA. Reinforcement increases an individual's motivation to learn. Higher motivation often equates to increased interest in the skills being taught and thus, we are more likely to see improvement and progress with the skills. Below is a list of suggestions when delivering reinforcement in order to make reinforcement more successful:

- Reinforcers should be functional. In other words, reinforcers should be reinforcing to the individual being taught and have the desired effect on behavior. What is reinforcing to one person may not be reinforcing to another. For example, some individuals may want to work to earn popcorn whereas others may not like popcorn; thus, this would not be a functional reinforcer for that particular individual. In addition, reinforcers change over time. An individual may find something reinforcing at one time and then may not find it reinforcing at a later date. Thus, you continuously need to re-assess your functional reinforcers (preference assessments (a systematic presentation of potential reinforcers offered to the individual to determine which reinforcer would be the most effective) are often helpful with identifying new functional reinforcers).

- Continuously identify new functional reinforcers or help develop new functional reinforcers. Assess what your student likes to play with or what they gravitate toward when they are left to their own devices. Does the individual enjoy movement or objects that rotate? Do they enjoy objects that light up or prefer small tight spaces? Use the qualities of preferred toys and objects to determine other reinforcement ideas. For example, if the individual prefers toys that make sounds, they may also like musical books, a CD player, an app of musical videos on the iPhone or iPad, etc. To help continuously identify reinforcers, a reinforcement inventory (questionnaires used to identify effective reinforcers for the individual) can be very helpful.
- Reinforcement should be immediate when teaching a new skill. To be effective, when a new skill is emerging, reinforcement should immediately follow the expected response. After the skill is established, we can then consider delayed reinforcement (i.e. token economy (behavioral modification technique where individuals earn tokens to exchange for desired reinforcers)). You must be sure the individual associates their behavior with the reinforcement; this is why we want it to be immediate. To help them make this association, reinforcement is most effective when it occurs within one second following the expected response. They begin to learn that if they give the specific correct response, they will earn the reinforcement and this helps to facilitate the learning process.
- Reinforcers should only be available during treatment sessions or when teaching the skill in the natural environment. The individual should not have "free" access to the reinforcers at other times of the day as this will weaken the power of the reinforcer. For example, if a specific video is used for reinforcement during toilet training, the individual should not have access to the video at other times of the day. If they do have access to the video at other times, then they may not be motivated to eliminate in the toilet since they can gain access to the reinforcer when less effort is required of them.
- Use differential reinforcement. This means you provide the most favored reinforcement for unprompted correct responses during Discrete Trial Teaching (see p.31) and give moderately preferred reinforcement for prompted trials (see p.36). Incorrect responses should receive no reinforcement. Differential reinforcement will help the individual learn the skill more quickly.
- A wide range of reinforcers should be used to prevent against satiation of one specific reinforcer. This helps to ensure that the reinforcer will keep its value and continue to be functional for the individual. Using a variety of reinforcers also provides us with a way to give differential reinforcement. To help with this, you might want to create a reinforcement board with pictures of the reinforcers or reinforcers written out (for those individuals who can read), so the individual can choose what reinforcer they are working for. After a reinforcer has been selected, it should be removed from the board, to ensure other reinforcers are used for

the next programs and to avoid satiation of one specific reinforcer. Basically, you want to rotate the reinforcers.

- Save the reinforcers that are longer in duration or harder to remove from the individual to the end of the session. This way they can earn the longest or best reinforcement at the very end, and you do not have to worry about removing it from the individual. For example, if the individual enjoys watching a specific video or playing a videogame, save these highly motivating reinforcers that take a while to complete for the very end of your treatment session.
- It is critical to consistently pair secondary reinforcement (i.e. verbal praise) with primary reinforcers. Primary reinforcers are those things needed to live and survive, such as food and drink. Individuals with ASD often respond well to primary reinforcers, but not to secondary reinforcement such as social praise. However, primary reinforcers are not natural and are not likely to be used in a natural environment such as a classroom setting. For example, it is not natural for a school teacher to give a individual a sip from a favorite drink for correctly responding. It is natural for the teacher to tell the individual, "Good job." When we pair primary renforcers with secondary reinforcement such as social praise, the secondary reinforcement takes on the reinforcement properties of the primary reinforcer. In other words, the individual begins to be reinforced by social praise, so we can then decrease or stop using primary reinforcers.
- Reinforcement should be age appropriate (as long as it can also be functional). By using reinforcement appropriate to the individual's chronological age, this may help increase peer acceptance as peers may also find the particular object or activity reinforcing, and this can allow common bonds to form. By using reinforcers that are age appropriate, then you are also increasing the chances that the individual will encounter their reinforcers in their natural environment (i.e. school, community events).
- Reinforcement should be faded over time as an individual learns the new skill. Programs that are currently on a maintenance schedule or that the individual finds easier to perform should have a thinner schedule of reinforcement, meaning that delayed reinforcement is used. Using a token economy system helps fade the reinforcers or thin the reinforcement schedule. An individual might be required to complete several easier tasks or previously mastered skills that are on a maintenance schedule successfully prior to receiving the reinforcement. It is important to fade the reinforcers over time as this makes the reinforcement schedule more natural and one that the individual is likely to encounter in their natural environment.
- Timing of reinforcement is very important. You do not want to break the momentum of working in order to engage in reinforcement. After the individual understands the association of an expected response and reinforcement, then work toward completing several tasks or receive several correct responses before giving the individual their reward. Place reinforcement on a variable reinforcement schedule (a schedule where reinforcement is given at random successful times) so you do not break the momentum of working in order to provide reinforcement. You want to provide reinforcement at a natural stopping point during the work, such as when a task is completed or several tasks are completed. However, keep in mind that if the individual is just learning a new skill, then a more dense reinforcement schedule may be required and you may need to have a 1:1 ratio schedule for reinforcement, frequently stopping work to reinforce.

- Reinforcement schedules must be followed consistently. The more consistent the instructors are with applying the reinforcers as outlined in the reinforcement schedule then the more likely it is that the individual will consistently emit the correct response.
- Verbal reinforcement should be behavior specific, not global non-descript praise. Thus, do not say "Good job" or "Way to go" as this is non-descriptive and does not inform the individual what is a good job or what they did to receive the social praise. Ensure the verbal reinforcement is behavior specific such as "Good job sitting down."
- Do not bribe individuals with the reinforcement. Individuals should make a choice for a reinforcer at the beginning of a treatment session or at the beginning of a cluster of expected responses. Try to avoid reminding the individual of the reinforcer they will receive for working or completing a task, as this begins to bribe the individual as opposed to earning reinforcers for appropriate responding.

Chapter 2

CURRICULUM GUIDE

A curriculum guide containing a list of approximately 140 programs is offered in this workbook and can be found at the end of this chapter. This guide should be used to help you determine which programs you will teach first, second and so forth. The guide can also be used to check off which programs or skills the individual already has in their repertoire and which programs they have mastered and archived. You do not have to teach the programs in the order that is listed in the guide. In fact, we highly recommend that you teach a variety of the programs at one time from different sections or areas on the guide (and from different books in the curriculum series). We find, in general, that a individual with developmental delays can work through 10–15 programs in a two-hour treatment session. Upon initiation of an ABA program or using this workbook to teach a individual, it is recommended that you start off teaching a lower number of programs until you are comfortable with running and following the TAs listed in this curriculum and the individual is successfully working through the programs in the allotted time. As you become more proficient in carrying out the TAs and the individual is more fluent with completing tasks, then you should add more programs to your treatment session.

In choosing the programs to teach a individual, you want to choose a variety of the TAs from different skill areas (i.e. adaptive functioning, social/play, receptive language, etc.) so that the overall program is teaching a wide variety of skills. This will prevent boredom as well as frustration (frustration can easily occur if you only choose those programs that represent the individual's greatest struggle, such as only choosing expressive language programs). Finally, it is important that the individual has mastered or made progress toward the attending skills programs and imitation programs (TAs found in the first book of the Journey of Development ABA Curriculum series) prior to moving on to other more advanced skill areas. You can teach other skills while teaching the imitation and attending skills programs; it is simply recommended that if a individual does not have the ability to sit and attend, and the ability to imitate, you start off with teaching these programs since these programs are pre-requisite skills for many other skills listed in this curriculum. These skills also represent "readiness to learn," as the individual needs to be able to sit and attend to S^Ds to learn as well as have the ability to imitate in order to learn many other tasks. If the individual you are teaching is having difficulty learning a particular skill, it is important that you determine whether the pre-requisite skills have been learned. If not, the first book in this series may include those pre-requisite skills. For example, if teaching "Complex Fine Motor Imitation with Objects" and the individual is struggling with the concept, the instructor may first need to teach "Fine Motor Imitation with Objects" found in the first book of this series (this is simple imitation, not complex imitation). In addition, you should pay close attention to the "tips" offered at the end of the majority of the TAs, as these tips offer recommendations for pre-requisite skills for specific programs. For instance, if you are working with a nonverbal individual, you are going to want to teach the receptive language, verbal imitation and possibly even the TAs for the Picture Exchange Communication System (PECS) (Bondy and Frost 2002) prior to teaching the expressive language programs.

It is recommended that you start by teaching a program that involves the strength of the individual as you are more likely to gain quicker success, interest and motivation from the individual that will help you in teaching other programs.

When we developed the specific programs that comprise this workbook, we used a variety of standardized assessments to guide us, including the Assessment of Basic Language and Learning Skills—Revised (ABLLS-R (Partington 2006) and the Bracken Basic Concept Scale—Third Edition (Bracken 2006). These were used as a resource for determining the skill areas that need to be addressed in early learning. The ABLLS-R is an assessment tool and tracking system for monitoring progress with skills for individuals who have ASD or other developmental disabilities. It is recommended that you use the ABLLS-R at the beginning of the individual's program to identify deficiencies in the individual's motor skills, language abilities, academic skills, imitation, visual spatial skills and adaptive functioning. You can use the results from the ABLLS-R to choose the appropriate curriculum programs to teach. You will see that the skill areas on the ABLLS-R are very similar to the skill areas in this curriculum. The difference in this curriculum from the ABLLS-R is the specific targets to teach, and how to teach the targets. This curriculum also offers TAs showing how to teach each program to improve skills. The ABLLS-R can also be used to monitor the child's progress with this instructional program. We recommend that you re-administer the ABBLS-R every six months as a means to measure progress. Alternatively, if you do not have access to the ABLLS-R or you choose not to use the ABLLS-R system as a means to track progress, then you could follow the curriculum guide offered in this workbook and probe specific skill areas to determine which areas the individual struggles in and then teach those specific skills. For example, if you probe or present a specific S^D from a TA to a individual, and the individual can display the skill, then you would consider this skill already within their repertoire and move on to probing other skills until you find those skills with which the individual struggles. It would be these programs you would teach. To measure progress, you would use the baseline data (discussed later in this workbook) and graph the results (also discussed later in this workbook) to analyze the progress and learning trends.

An example of the specific programs that might be chosen for a younger nonverbal individual might include the following. (This is a list of programs from this book, but keep in mind that individuals with ASD have variable skills so a good list of programs would be likely to include TAs from multiple books.)

- Attending Skills: Appropriate Sitting during a Family Meal
- Imitation Skills: Complex Fine Motor Imitation with Objects
- Imitation Skills: Complex Gross Motor Imitation with Objects
- Visual Spatial Skills: Extending Sequence Patterns
- Receptive Language Skills: Receptive Instructions (Two-Step)
- Receptive Language Skills: Past Tense Verbs
- Play Social Skills: Duck Duck Goose
- Play Social Skills: Pretend Play: Detective
- Adaptive Skills: Applying Chapstick
- Adaptive Skills: Buttoning and Unbuttoning
- Academic Skills: Reading: Matching Letters Sounds to Pictures
- Academic Skills: Cutting
- In addition, the expressive language programs from the first book in this curriculum series might be used to teach expressive language skills (such as the PECS (Bondy and Frost 2002) TAs, verbal imitation TA, gestural language TA, etc.)

An example of the specific programs that might be chosen for an individual with verbal skills, ability to sit and attend, and ability to imitate but who struggles with answering questions, has delays in pre-academic skills, and deficits in play skills includes the following. (This is a list of programs from this book, but keep in mind that individuals with ASD have variable skills so a good list of programs would be likely to include TAs from multiple books.)

- Visual Spatial Skills: Sorting Objects by Function
- Receptive Language Skills: Receptive Instructions Delivered in a Group
- Expressive Language Skills: Answering Simple “When” Questions
- Expressive Language Skills: Answering Simple “Who” Questions
- Expressive Language Skills: Answering Social Questions
- Academic Skills: Receptive Labels of Three-Dimensional Shapes
- Academic Skills: Part/Whole Relationships
- Play/Social Skills: Pretend Play: Same Role—Pirates
- Play/Social Skills: Turn-Taking
- Adaptive Skills: Dressing and Undressing: Putting On and Taking Off Gloves
- Adaptive Skills: Snapping and Unsnapping

In addition to using this curriculum for young children, this curriculum can also be used for older children who have not yet mastered these skills, which are the pre-requisite skills required before learning more advanced concepts found in the third and fourth books in this curriculum series.

Chapter 3

ABA CURRICULUM—UNDERSTANDING THE TASK ANALYSES

This chapter describes how to read the TA associated with each skill area offered in this ABA curriculum. A TA involves the process of breaking a complex task down into smaller simple teachable steps. These simplified steps are chained together to teach an individual the complex skill. By teaching through a TA, learning becomes an easier process for individuals and decreases frustration associated with learning complex tasks. The easier the learning process is for the individual, the easier it is to attain the targeted behavior. The easier it is to attain a targeted behavior, the greater the individual's success.

The following is a description of how to read the TAs that comprise this curriculum, how to implement a TA and how to record data on the TA worksheet.

Header: Title and level

In the header of each TA is the title of the skill. These titles correspond with the titles listed on the curriculum guide. These are skills typically developing children may learn intuitively or with relative ease. For individuals with ASD or other developmental delays, these skills may need to be directly taught. To the right of the skill title is an area to check off the teaching level the individual is placed on. The Journey of Development ABA Curriculum suggests using a system which places individuals on a level specific to their learning rate in order to facilitate optimal learning and quicker acquisition of skills. This levels system is described in detail in Chapter 5 on teaching strategies. For now, note that this area on the TA is to check off the level the individual is on for that specific skill.

Top section of the task analysis

At the top of each TA, there are various sections describing the "rules" for how to implement a particular TA, including the discriminative stimulus (S^D), expected response, type of data collection, target criteria and the materials needed to run the TA. The S^D for each individual program is what the instructor says or does to evoke a response from the individual. This may include presenting materials and giving a verbal directive, such as presenting three objects representing different emotions to a individual and saying "Touch sad." It is recommended that instructors using this curriculum be consistent with the presentation of the S^D. In general, individuals with ASD or other developmental delays have language delays or language deficits. Thus, a short precise S^D is recommended. For example, if you are teaching the complex imitation programs, you will see that the S^D is simply "Do this" followed by demonstrating the actions that the individual should imitate. The instructor working with the individual should not change the S^D and say things such as "Do what I do" or "Copy what I do," as these S^Ds require a higher level of language comprehension. However, individuals are placed on levels based on their learning acquisition rate. For individuals on a higher level, changing the S^Ds may be recommended (please see the levels system guidelines in Chapter 5 on teaching strategies). However, as a general rule, do not change the S^D, unless definitely indicated to do so.

The next instructional area on the TA is the response. The response is what should be expected of the individual for each target on the TA or after the entire TA is completed. It is important that every instructor working with the individual expects the same response. A clear operational definition of the response behavior should be discussed and expected prior to implementing the TA and may need to be revisited, discussed and revised once the teaching begins. An operational definition is a clear description of the behavior that is observable and can be recorded. For example, for the "Appropriate Sitting during a School Activity" program, the response states "Individual will sit with a motionless body (hands on the table or their lap and feet still) and a quiet mouth." The adults running this program should determine beforehand what behavior is expected from the individual. Will the individual place their hands in their lap or place them on the table? Each instructor working with the individual should expect the same response so accurate data can be collected. Another example in which we often see errors is in programs where an instructor is expecting a higher-level response that would be associated with another skill. For example, in the program "Participation in Complex Songs and Games with Actions," the response expected should include the individual participating in the song or game (i.e. attempting to sing along, moving body or hands in close proximity of the movements associated with the song) and not include precise gross motor movements associated with the song. We have observed individuals demonstrate a stagnant learning trend (no learning for multiple consecutive days of teaching) because the instructor was expecting a precise gross motor movement to the target "I'm a Little Teapot" whereby the individual was expected to raise hand at shoulder length to form a teapot and then tip body sideways. The individual was attempting to engage in the song with raising hand at stomach level, but the instructor expected a response that was not associated with childhood songs and more expected with gross motor skills. It is important to discriminate the differences in expected responses and only require those associated with the particular skill.

Next on the TA is the data collection section. Data collection is the type of data that will be recorded by the individual implementing the TA. The Journey of Development ABA Curriculum utilizes two types of data collection: skill acquisition and prompt data. Skill acquisition data represents those programs which have a quick discrete beginning and end. For example, the S^D might be "What is your name?" and the response might be "Marleigh." This is a quick beginning and end to the discrete trial (discrete trial is a chaining or scaffolding method in ABA used to teach one step or target at a time). For skill acquisition, data is taken on every discrete trial presented. Data is recorded as correct (+), incorrect (-) or prompted trial (P) (a prompted trial is a discrete trial where the instructor delivers a prompt to the individual immediately following the S^D to ensure the individual responds correctly). If it is a prompted trial, the type of prompt is recorded (see description of prompts discussed in this workbook). For skill acquisition, data is taken on every trial presented. Data is recorded as correct (+), incorrect (-) or prompted trial (P)and would be recorded on the data sheet. If it is a prompted trial, types of prompts are recorded (see description of prompts in Figure 1.1). For skill acquisition programs, a skill is practiced multiple times each session. We recommend that data is collected on each target for the first ten times the S^D is presented. The skill should continue to be practiced in treatment sessions after your data collection is complete and if time permits. Prompt data represents those programs which use a chaining procedure to link all the steps together to form a larger skill. These programs generally take longer to complete. Examples include eating with a fork and spoon, sorting objects and tying shoes. For prompt data, the number and type of prompts are recorded for a particular step or target. Data will be recorded as FP, PP, G, POS, VS, VB (see description of prompts in Figure 1.1). We recommend for targets in those TAs for which prompt data is to be collected that the targets be practiced a minimum of one time per session, with data collected on the first presentation. The instructor may choose to practice this skill more times throughout the session to ensure sufficient practice for the individual to acquire this skill.

The section labeled "Target Criteria" tells us when the individual has met the specific criteria to move on to the next target. There are two specific sets of target criteria. For skill acquisition data, the target criteria will read "80% or above for 3 consecutive days across 2 people." This means that the individual must display the expected response accurately 80 percent or more of the time on their own (without any prompts) for three consecutive teaching days, with at least two different people giving the individual the S^D. Specifically, the S^D is presented ten times per teaching session as recommended. The individual must display the expected response accurately to the S^D eight, nine or ten times for three consecutive days. It is important that there are at least two adults presenting the S^D to the individual so we are generalizing this skill across people. The second set of target criteria is for prompt data. The criteria will read "0 prompts for 3 consecutive days across 2 people." This means that the individual must display independent performance of the skill, with zero prompts from the instructor, for three consecutive days with at least two people giving the S^D before the individual can move on to the next target or begin to fade the program to a maintenance schedule. This is very important as we want to promote optimal functioning and teach the individual to complete a given task on their own without help from an instructor. There are exceptions to the criteria expected. Later in this workbook, a levels system is discussed and recommended. Recommendations for individuals on Level 2 or 3 might include modifications to the target criteria in order to facilitate quicker completion of a skill program (see that section for specific recommendations on target criteria).

The last section in the top box of the TA is the materials section. This section lists the materials needed to run the specific program, as well as alternative materials that can be used. This section includes materials such as pictures, objects, timers, visual schedules and reinforcement. Some of the materials required for specific TAs are offered in the supplementary CD that accompanies this book.

Middle section of the task analysis labeled "fading procedure"

After the individual has met the target criteria (80% or above for three consecutive days across two people, or zero prompts for three consecutive days across two people) and generalized the skill into two new environments, the TA is moved into the fading procedure. On some TAs, the fading procedure may occur after only part of the program has been taught. This will be specifically listed on the TA. The fading procedure section includes the maintenance schedule and maintenance criteria, natural environment criteria and criteria for archiving a program. The program will first enter into the maintenance schedule. Maintenance of a TA ensures the retention of a skill over time. It is extremely important to place skills on a maintenance schedule as many individuals with ASD lose acquired skills once they are no longer exposed to the skill or have opportunity to practice the skill. Placing skills on a maintenance schedule helps maintain treatment gains after termination of daily teaching of the skill or TA.

Once the individual has met criteria for the targets in this program and the program has been generalized, it is ready to move into maintenance. It is imperative to have a plan to systematically fade the maintenance schedule of a previously acquired target. The recommended procedure that you use to fade the program includes a maintenance schedule of twice weekly (2W), one time weekly (1W) and monthly (M). This means that TAs that were being run in daily teaching (i.e. 5–7 times per week) will now be reduced to being run to two times per week, then faded to once per week and finally faded to once per month prior to moving the program into the natural environment.

The criterion for a maintenance schedule implemented two times weekly (2W) is four consecutive scores of 100 percent accuracy. Once this criterion is met, the program can move into once per week (1W) for implementation. When the individual responds with 100 percent accuracy for four consecutive therapy sessions, the program can be moved into the once per month (M) maintenance schedule. Probing the target once per month (M) should continue until the individual responds with three consecutive scores of 100 percent accuracy. If at any time during the maintenance schedule, an individual displays two consecutive scores lower than 100 percent, the individual's treatment should be moved back to the previous, more frequent maintenance schedule. For example, if you are at the 1W maintenance stage, but the individual receives two consecutive scores lower than 100 percent, then you should move the program into the 2W maintenance phase as the individual requires more exposure to the targets. Alternatively, if you observe a pattern of incorrect response(s), you can move back just those targets the individual continuously misses to a more frequent maintenance schedule or daily teaching schedule. For example, if you are running the program "Expressive Labels of Function of Body Parts" and the individual demonstrates a pattern of incorrectly labeling the function of eyes and mouth but correctly labels the other eight targets, then you can move the other eight targets forward in the maintenance schedule (less frequent exposure) and move the two continuously missed targets back to a more frequent maintenance schedule.

After the target has been successfully maintained at once per month maintenance, the program is then moved into the next phase of the fading procedure and assessed in the natural environment (NE). The whole purpose of teaching an individual a skill is to promote independence and optimal functioning. To reach the level of independence, an individual must be able to display the skill in naturally occurring activities in multiple environments. This does not include displaying the skill in the teaching environment, but rather displaying the skill within a novel activity in an environment that the individual might encounter (i.e. store, neighbor's house, church). An example of a natural environment situation for an acquisition program is after teaching an individual to create a pattern, the individual then displays the ability to create a pattern when working on a calendar task at school or a craft with beads at church. For a program that requires independence or zero prompts (i.e., washing hands, open-ended solitary toy play), the individual should display the target in naturally occurring settings with novel people and stimuli. An example of this would be the task of washing hands; the individual should display this skill in their classroom before snack, after using the bathroom in a public place or by washing their hands independently when they are sticky. The natural environment criterion is achieved when the target has been generalized in the NE across three novel naturally occurring activities.

Once the target criterion has been met, the maintenance criterion has been met and the natural environment criterion has been met, the program can be archived.

Middle section of the task analysis labeled "Suggestions for Targets and Probe Results"

The majority of the TAs listed in the Journey of Development ABA Curriculum offer suggestions for targets and an area to record probe results. Not all TAs will have this section. For example, most prompt programs will not have this section as there is only one target (i.e. wash hands, use a tissue, etc.). For the programs that do have this section, a list of targets is offered as suggestions to teach the individual. For example, if teaching the individual "Receptive Instructions (Two-

Step)," suggested targets include clap hands and touch head, stand up and turn around, walk across room and get [x], etc. It is important to note that the targets are not in any particular order. Targets you choose to teach should first and foremost be specific to the individual. For example, if you are teaching an individual this program and it is reported that the individual often gets out of their seat, then you might start off teaching targets that require the individual to sit before targets that require the individual to get out of their seat.

Under the area where suggested targets are listed is an area for recording probe results. These are targets already in the individual's repertoire. If you are beginning a new TA, you should start with probing all suggested targets on that TA under the suggested targets section. In addition, the instructor should probe additional targets that they deem specific to the individual that are not listed on the TA. If the individual can perform the skill upon your probe, then you would record this target in the probe results section, indicating that the skill is already in the individual's repertoire and does not need to be taught. If the individual cannot perform the skill, then this is listed as a target to teach under the target section of the TA.

Bottom section of the task analysis (where targets can be listed)

The final box on the TA is an area containing seven columns where an instructor can record the targets chosen to teach the individual, baseline accuracy, the date the target was introduced, the date the target criteria were met and an area for recording the fading procedure.

Target column

The column titled "Target" is the area in which the instructor records the ten targets that will be taught to the individual. More than ten targets can be chosen to teach the individual, the instructor will need two copies of the TA in order to have enough space to record the data. These targets are chosen only after a probe of targets has been conducted. If the individual can perform the target upon the probe, then the target is listed as in repertoire and not chosen as a target to teach. If the individual cannot perform the target on probe, then it can be listed as a target to teach. You may not automatically list it as Target 1, as it is important to list the targets you will teach in order of increasing complexity (use behavioral momentum with teaching easier skills first in order to facilitate learning) or in order of reinforcing properties. For example, if teaching "Complex Gross Motor Imitation with Objects" and the individual enjoys balls, then throwing balls or rolling balls might be chosen as one of the first targets to teach, as the reinforcing properties of the balls might increase the individual's interest and motivation, leading to quicker learning. Rolling balls might be chosen prior to catching balls as this skill is more complex than rolling the ball.

Baseline column

This area on the TA is for recording the baseline accuracy of the skill acquisition and prompt programs. Prior to each target being taught, a baseline score should be collected on the target (see the rules for collecting baseline data in Chapter 6 on data collection). This baseline score is listed in the baseline column next to its associated target. For example, if you are teaching the skill acquisition program "Receptive Labels of Rooms and Objects in a Room" and the target is "couch," the baseline score recorded might be 40 percent. However, if teaching the prompt program "Zipping a Connected and Unconnected Zipper," the baseline score would include number and type of prompts or 4 P (1 FP, 3 PP). Information on data recording is specifically detailed in Chapter 6 on data collection and recording.

Date introduced and date criteria met columns

After you have conducted the baseline, record the date that teaching begins in the Date Introduced column. Once the individual has met the target criteria for the current target (80% or above for three consecutive days across two people for skill acquisition programs or zero prompts for three consecutive days across two people for prompt data programs), write that date in the Date Criteria Met column.

Fading procedure columns

The vast majority of the programs in the Journey of Development ABA Curriculum only require maintenance of targets at the final step of the TA. In the final row of the TA, the instructor can chart and record the maintenance schedule. The TA lists 2W, 1W and M and you can simply circle the maintenance phase you are currently implementing. Once that has been achieved, you can cross it out and circle the next maintenance phase you are moving into. On some TAs, maintenance is recommended after specific targets instead of waiting until the final step of the program. For these TAs, the area will not be shaded out, but rather left blank to indicate that the instructor should implement the maintenance schedule sooner. This section of the TA also requires the instructor to list the date the individual begins working in the natural environment and the date the program is archived.

As with all suggestions in this workbook, we offer guidelines to follow in order to implement the Journey of Development ABA Curriculum. There is always room for therapy modifications specific to the individual. For example, in Chapter 5 on teaching strategies, we suggest that if an individual is having difficulty with generalizing skills in a new environment or maintaining a skill, then generalization or maintenance of that skill might occur after each target has been taught, and not at the end of the program.

Bottom of the task analysis

At the bottom of the majority of the TAs, tips for running that specific TA is offered. This is one of the most important areas on the TA as it gives suggestions for ensuring reliability of TA implementation. In addition, the tips may include pre-requisites skills that should be taught first, tips for prompting and tips for alternative teaching strategies.

Chapter 4

ABA CURRICULUM—IMPLEMENTING THE TASK ANALYSES

Choosing targets

When beginning to implement a TA procedure that includes targets that must be chosen, choose the targets and probe each one prior to starting the teaching process. When you probe a target, you are presenting the S^D one time to the individual to determine if it is already in their repertoire. If the individual correctly responds to the S^D, then it is suggestive that this is a target the individual has already reached and it should not be chosen for a target to teach. The instructor should write this target in the area on the TA marked "Probe Results (targets in repertoire)," found under the "Suggestions for Targets and Probe Results" section. If the individual responds incorrectly during the probe, then this target should become one of the targets to be taught. The instructor can write this target next to Target 1 on the TA. Alternatively, the instructor can wait until they find ten targets that the individual does not have in their repertoire (shown by their incorrect response to the S^D) during the probe, then choose the order to teach these ten targets, based on what targets may initially lead to a higher likelihood of success (i.e. targets associated with a individual's interest or targets the individual might find more reinforcing, targets the individual comes into contact with more frequently in their natural environment, etc.).

To illustrate the above concept, let's use the example of implementing the TA "Complex Gross Motor Imitation." The instructor would start off probing each target in the "Suggestions for Targets" section. The S^D for this program is "Do this" and the instructor would demonstrate the gross motor movement. The instructor should deliver this S^D and probe at least ten suggested targets. If the individual imitates a jumping jack and squatting but incorrectly responds to the other targets, then the instructor would write the two targets that received a correct response in the "Probe Results (targets in repertoire)" section and indicate which targets received an incorrect response (the instructor might circle these responses).

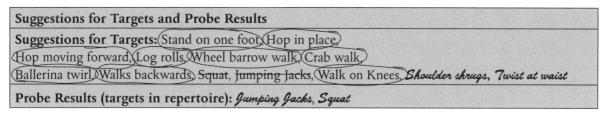

Suggestions for Targets and Probe Results
Suggestions for Targets: Stand on one foot, Hop in place, Hop moving forward, Log rolls, Wheel barrow walk, Crab walk, Ballerina twirl, Walks backwards, ~~Squat~~, ~~Jumping Jacks~~, Walk on Knees, Shoulder shrugs, Twist at waist
Probe Results (targets in repertoire): Jumping Jacks, Squat

Figure 4.1 Probing and choosing targets

The instructor needs to ensure that ten targets receiving incorrect responses are identified during the probe (as teaching ten targets is suggested). If only ten suggestions are provided in the "Suggestions for Targets" area and the individual correctly responds to two of these targets, then the instructor should identify additional targets to probe. In Figure 4.1, the instructor probed and the individual emitted an incorrect response for shoulder shrugs and twist at waist. Thus, these two targets were written in the area with suggestions for targets. Once incorrect responses are recorded on ten different targets in the probe phase, the instructor should determine which target will be taught first, second, third and so forth and place these in the "Target" area on the TA. In this example, the instructor might determine that the individual finds auditory stimulation to be reinforcing and so those targets which make a sound might be chosen as the initial targets (e.g. hop moving forward). Using targets which might have automatic reinforcement as the initial targets can lead to increased motivation and quicker acquisition of the overall skill (i.e. complex imitation).

Baseline of chosen targets

After probing and choosing targets, the instructor should then baseline Target 1. Refer to the rules for baselining targets which are found in Chapter 6. You baseline each new target before it is taught in order to compare treatment effectiveness. After you complete the baseline of a target for a skill acquisition program, write in the percentage for the baseline data in the Baseline column. The baseline percentage is the number of correct responses out of the number of trials. For example, if the TA "Expressive Labels of Gender" was being implemented, with the first target being "Boy" and the individual gave the correct response four out of ten times (with the other six trials being incorrect responses), then you would record "40%" in the Baseline column for Target 1. You would also record the date on which you completed the baseline under the Date Introduced column.

				Fading Procedure		
Target	**Baseline %**	**Date Introduced**	**Date Criteria Met**	**Maintenance**	**Date NE Introduced**	**Date Archived**
1. Target *1: Boy*	*40%*	*6-10-13*				

Figure 4.2 Baselining a target in a skill acquisition program

For programs in which prompt data is taken, record the number and type of prompts given during the baseline procedure. For example, if you were running the TA "Participation in Complex Songs and Games with Actions" and the target was "Musical Chairs," if the individual required four prompts during the song, then you would record the number four in the Baseline column along with the type of prompts used, such as 2 FP, 1 PP, 1G (see description of prompts in Figure 1.1).

Target	**Baseline: Number and Level of Prompts**	**Date Introduced**	**Date Criteria Met**	**Fading Procedure**		
				Maintenance	**Date NE Introduced**	**Date Archived**
1. Target *1: Musical Chairs*	*4 prompts (2 FP, 1PP, 1G)*	*11-12-13*				

Figure 4.3 Baselining a target in a prompt program

After completing the baseline of Target 1, you would then begin the teaching process of Target 1 through Discrete Trial Instruction (DTI), also known as Discrete Trial Teaching (DTT).

Discrete Trial Teaching (DTT)

DTT is one of the many teaching strategies used in ABA. There are multiple other instructional tools used in ABA such as chaining, shaping, incidental teaching, and behavior reduction strategies (i.e. extinction, over-correction, etc.). We often encounter individuals who equate DTT with ABA and this would be an incorrect assumption, as DTT is just one of many teaching strategies used within ABA. Nonetheless, this strategy is one of the primary strategies used in ABA and we recommend it is used when implementing this ABA curriculum.

DTT involves breaking a skill into smaller teachable steps. The instructor provides concentrated teaching of one step or one target at a time until the individual meets criteria for that target. Repetition and consistency of teaching any given step or target is a key ingredient to help the individual learn that particular target. Prompting and reinforcement would continue to be used and be two additional primary teaching tools used throughout DTT, but also, multiple additional teaching strategies can be used to help the individual learn the target (see teaching strategies in Chapter 5).

Basically, in DTT, the individual is given a S^D. To review, S^D stands for Discriminative Stimulus. This is a stimulus that signals to the individual that a given response will be reinforced. A S^D can be an object (e.g. handing the individual a puzzle piece to insert into the puzzle), a verbal directive, a picture or other visual item (e.g. showing the individual a letter that needs to be traced or a maze to complete), an action or part of a chain (e.g. in hand washing, the step of rubbing soap onto hands can act as an S^D for placing hands under water), or a cue from the natural environment (e.g. raining outside can act as a S^D to grab an umbrella before leaving the house). Some tips for delivering the S^D include: obtaining the individual's attention before delivering the S^D, ensuring the S^D is simple and clear (as written in the Journey of Development ABA Curriculum TAs), keeping the S^D consistent and using a fun intonation and inflection in your voice (as many individuals respond positively to this type of vocal characteristic).

After a S^D is given, the individual emits a response. An individual, after a period of time, learns or discriminates that under certain conditions, engaging in a behavior or correct response to the S^D will be followed by reinforcement. If the individual provides a correct response, then reinforcement is given. If the individual provides an incorrect response, the instructor ignores the incorrect response and records the response as incorrect (the trial is over). After the incorrect trial is complete, then an error correction procedure using prompting is provided. The instructor presents the S^D and provides the least intrusive prompt necessary to assist the individual in emitting the correct response. The instructor records the data for the prompted trial. Following each incorrect trial with one (or more) prompted trial(s) guarantees an environment of errorless learning, where the individual is reinforced for correct responses (even when prompted), and is not subject to being incorrect on two consecutive trials.

After a prompted trial, a new unprompted trial is given to the individual to determine if they have learned the correct response. The target should remain the same from the incorrect trial, prompted trial and the new unprompted trial. Once the individual has completed a correct unprompted trial, a new target can be worked on (if running random rotation) or a new program can be run. If the individual responds correctly, the instructor should move on to teaching another skill (even if ten trials were not yet implemented) in order to avoid practicing a target in a mass trial. Practicing a target in a mass trial (multiple presentations of the same target and S^D in consecutive trials) can lead to the individual giving a rote response and may lead to boredom. During the treatment session, the instructor would come back to presenting this S^D again until all ten trials are implemented; you simply want to rotate multiple TAs at once to keep the individual motivated with novel items. If the individual has not emitted a correct response on the probe after a prompted trial, the instructor would continue to use prompted trials and differential reinforcement to teach the individual. If the instructor implements the tenth trial for a particular program and the individual emits an incorrect response, it is recommended that one additional prompted trial be implemented (data does not need to be recorded) in order to end that particular TA for that treatment session with a correct response.

After any given trial, there is an inter-trial interval. This is a brief pause between the conclusion of one trial and the beginning of the next trial. This is the perfect time to administer highly preferred reinforcement to the individual if they emitted a correct unprompted response, moderately preferred reinforcement if they emitted a correct prompted response and/or record your data. Finally, we recommend clearing the teaching items after each trial during the inter-trial interval. This helps the individual learn that one trial is clearly over and the next trial will be presented.

To summarize DTT following our recommendations, Figure 4.4 outlines the procedural steps.

Once the individual has met criteria for Target 1 via DTT (the criteria of 80% or greater for three consecutive days across two people or zero prompts for three consecutive days across two people), then the instructor should baseline Target 2 followed by teaching Target 2 via DTT.

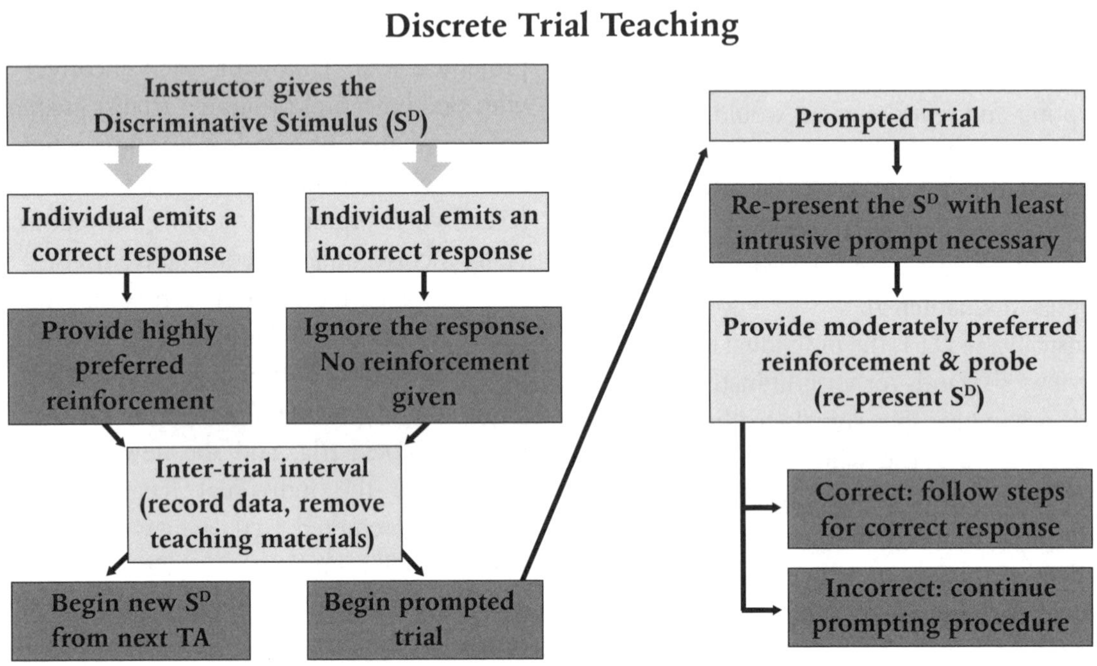

Figure 4.4 Procedural steps of Discrete Trial Teaching

Random rotation

On many of the TAs, the instructor is directed to complete a random rotation of the targets. Random rotation of the targets occurs after every two targets taught. Thus, the first random rotation will occur after the first two targets are taught and their criteria met.

Target	Baseline %	Date Introduced	Date Criteria Met	Fading Procedure		
				Maintenance	Date NE Introduced	Date Archived
1. Target 1:						
2. Target 2:						
3. Targets 1 and 2 random rotation	←					

Figure 4.5 Random rotation instruction on TA

Random rotation is an important step in the TA because it means that the skills previously learned by the individual are presented in a random order (random rotation) and the individual must learn to differentiate their responses for similar targets. For example, if an individual is learning to follow one-step commands, the first target might be "Stand Up," the second target might be "Sit Down" and the random rotation step would be the first and second targets presented in a random order (i.e. 1. Sit down; 2. Stand up; 3. Stand up; 4. Sit down; 5. Stand up, etc.).

When you get to the next random rotation step, all previously targeted skills would be presented randomly or all four targets are randomly rotated (i.e. 1. Sit down; 2. Stand up; 3. Come here; 4. Throw away; 5. Come here; 6. Sit down, etc.). During random rotation, it is important that there are not any predictable patterns in the presentation of previously mastered targets. Random rotation is important because it demonstrates true comprehension and differentiation of the targets.

Generalize to Other Materials/Stimuli

Prior to discussing the next two steps on the TA (Generalizing to another environment), generalization to other materials and stimuli needs to be addressed. During the first random rotation of targets and for every step on the TA following this first random rotation, it is recommended that instructors generalize materials for the targets. The TA is written to accommodate generalization of the skill across people, environment and time, but the TA does not have a specific place for generalization of materials. Thus, it is recommended that instructors automatically generalize to other materials beginning with the first random rotation of targets. Alternatively, for an individual on Level 2 or 3, generalization across materials and stimuli could begin with teaching Target 1 (refer to Systems of levels discussed in Chapter 5). An example of generalizing to other materials/stimuli includes teaching the receptive identification of a dog in which you should use multiple pictures of various dogs (e.g. beagle, poodle and pug).

Generalizing to another environment

After the individual meets the criteria of random rotation of ten targets, the next two steps on the TA are for generalization to another environment. Generalization is the ability to apply learned skills with other people, across varying materials, in different environments and over time. By the time you reach the generalization to another environment step, the individual should already be generalizing to other people since the target criteria require the skill to be displayed for three consecutive days across two people. In addition, when implementing DTT, instructors should automatically rotate teaching materials to ensure the individual is generalizing across materials. On the materials CD that accompanies this book, the majority of targets are offered three times each to allow for generalization of materials. For example, the "Receptive Labels of Function of Body Parts" TA includes a suggested target of "Eyes (see with eyes)." The varying materials include different color and shape of eyes. This ensures that the individual generalizes the skill of identifying eyes across different colors and shapes of eyes.

In each TA, steps are taken to ensure that the individual can generalize the task or demonstrate the skill across multiple environments. If the individual is learning at home in a formal home program with the primary teaching area being the kitchen, the individual should demonstrate the skill in other areas of the home or outside of the home before the TA is moved to a maintenance schedule. Generalized environments in the home include other areas besides where the primary treatment takes place such as the front porch, kitchen, backyard, family room, basement, etc. If the individual primarily receives their ABA treatment at school, generalized environments may be other classrooms, library, cafeteria, recess, outside, etc. The environments should be written on the TA and on the graph, indicating the name of the environments that the individual is generalizing to as well the date generalization to Environment 1 and Environment 2 was initiated and mastered. If generalization across environments does not take place, the skill should not be considered mastered.

Target	**Baseline %**	**Date Introduced**	**Date Criteria Met**
Generalize to another environment Environment 1: *Living room*	*80%*	*1-7-14*	*1-30-14*
Generalize to another environment Environment 2: *Outside patio*	*50%*	*2-02-14*	

Figure 4.6 Generalizing to other environments, as shown on TA

Fading procedure

After the individual meets criteria for ten targets presented in random rotation and they have generalized the skill into two other environments at 80 percent or greater (or zero prompts for prompt programs), then the instructor should begin the fading procedure. The fading procedure fades the daily teaching of the skill while ensuring the skill is maintained over time and regression or loss of skill is avoided. The fading procedure involves two instructional tools before archiving the program. These include the Maintenance and Natural Environment teaching phase. Both of these instructional methods were discussed in the previous chapter under "Middle Section of the Task Analysis Labeled 'Fading Procedure.'" When following the recommended fading procedure (i.e. DDT instruction is first moved into a maintenance schedule of twice weekly probing followed by once per week probe and ending with one per month probe), the instructor can mark on the TA which step they are implementing simply by circling or crossing out that specific area on the TA.

Target	**Baseline %**	**Date Introduced**	**Date Criteria Met**	**Fading Procedure**		
				Maintenance	**Date NE Intro-duced**	**Date Archived**
14. Generalize to another environment Environment 2:	60%	12/14/13	12/20/13			
15. Maintenance: Assess in varied environments				~~2W~~ (1W) M		

Figure 4.7 Fading procedure in progress, as shown on TA

In this illustration, the individual met criteria for generalizing this specific program into the second environment on 12/20/13 and then the program was moved into the twice weekly (2W) fading procedure. The instructor circled 2W to indicate this is the step of the TA they were implementing. Once criteria were met on 2W, the instructor crossed out 2W and circled 1W to indicate the individual is now working on the skill only once per week. The instructor should also include results of each fading procedure on the graph (please see Chapter 7 for specific information on graphing).

When the instructor is implementing the maintenance procedure, it is suggested that the probe occur in varied environments to ensure the individual continues to generalize the skill in multiple settings. The instructor should follow the recommended fading procedure prior to archiving the program to ensure the individual maintains the skill over time and generalizes the skill into the natural environment.

Chapter 5

TEACHING STRATEGIES

Every individual learns at different rates and may present with different difficulties in learning new skills. Although our books are designed to offer a systematic curriculum to implement with individuals with developmental delays, the curriculum is not meant to be a cookie-cutter approach to teaching. The curriculum is designed to be a guide and those adults teaching the individuals with delays should individualize the teaching strategies for each person's needs in order to facilitate learning and quicker acquisition of new skills. Individuals with ASD and other developmental delays have the potential to learn, but they may require different teaching strategies that are optimized to help them reach their full potential. This chapter offers valuable information and solutions for implementing a variety of teaching strategies to accelerate an individual's learning and to troubleshoot learning difficulties that may arise.

The Journey of Development ABA Curriculum recognizes that prompts, reinforcement and repetitive presentation of the programs are the fundamental aspects of an ABA program that should be implemented with every new skill taught. However, it should be recognized that many individuals with ASD will continue to struggle with learning a skill, even with prompting and reinforcement in place. Thus, a variety of behavioral teaching strategies are offered here to help the instructor in educating the individual who might be struggling with learning a skill.

Levels system

Since every individual learns at a different rate, we offer the following levels system as a guide for modifying the ABA programs within this curriculum to individualize teaching to the person's learning rate. By individualizing teaching strategies to each person's needs, we are more successful in increasing an individual's ability to learn and learn at a quicker rate. The system is comprised of three levels that include modifications to the TA, including presentation of the S^D, criteria to be met, when to add in teaching strategies and modifications to the fading schedule, natural environment teaching and archiving a program. These suggestions are a guide and are not meant to be a replacement for a Board Certified Behavior Analyst (BCBA), but can offer some solutions to increase learning acquisition.

Level 1

Level 1 is suggested for individuals who are very young, acquire skills more slowly, may be new to ABA therapy, considered lower functioning, nonverbal or regress when there is a period of time without intervention. A Level 1 individual would follow the TA as written (i.e. learn one target at a time with random rotation after every two targets). This individual would start the Journey of Development ABA Curriculum with approximately 10–12 new programs. You add in new programs when behavioral control is established (i.e. individual sits and attends to the instructor and follows basic instructions), the individual becomes fluent in completing additional work (i.e. it initially took two hours to complete 10–12 programs and now the individual is completing these same 10–12 programs in 105 minutes), or programs go into maintenance. For a Level 1 individual, if no learning trend, variable learning trend or stagnant learning trend (see Interpreting graphs in Chapter 7) is observed within the data across five consecutive therapy days, then the instructor should add in a teaching strategy to facilitate learning.

To summarize, for Level 1 individuals:

- Follow TAs as they are designed.
- Start with 10–12 programs.
- Add in programs when behavioral control is established, the individual becomes more fluent in completing more work, or programs go into maintenance.
- If there are five consecutive days of no learning trend, variable learning trend or a stagnant learning trend, then add in a teaching strategy.

Level 2

Level 2 is suggested for individuals who have demonstrated a quicker learning curve. These individuals may have already been engaged in ABA therapy, and analysis of graphs showing learning trends indicate that the individual is quickly mastering the targets or that when the individual reaches 80 percent or zero prompts across one day, they tend to stay at this level and continue to master at 80 percent or zero prompts across other successive days (no drop/decrease in accuracy).

Modifications to the TAs to facilitate quicker acquisition of the skills and completion of the TAs include teaching two targets at once (as opposed to teaching one target at a time) and reducing the target criterion from three consecutive days of a skill being displayed at 80 percent or zero prompts to two consecutive days of a skill being displayed at this level prior to moving on to the next two targets.

This level also includes modifications to receptive language TAs whereby the instructor should initially baseline all receptive language programs with a field of three (FO3), as opposed to a baseline with a field of one (FO1) as written on the TA. If the response is accurate at 50 percent or higher, then teaching should continue with a FO3. If the response is accurate at 30–40 percent, then the instructor should drop back to a FO2 to teach the skill and move on to FO3 once FO2 is mastered. If the accuracy is below 30 percent, then the instructor should drop back to a FO1 to begin teaching the skill. By using this modification, if an individual can learn starting at a FO3, then precious time and energy is saved by not focusing on teaching within a FO1 or FO2.

We have found that individuals following the Journey of Development ABA Curriculum who are on Level 2 are less likely to lose skills once they have been acquired. Thus, for individuals on Level 2, after the final step of the TA has been achieved (generalization to a second environment), before the fading procedure begins, instructors should probe the skill in the natural environment. If the individual can generalize the skill into the natural environment (at least three naturally occurring activities/environments) at that time, then the program can be archived (no maintenance required). If the individual cannot generalize the skill into the natural environment at the probe, then the maintenance schedule should be implemented for additional practice prior to probing once again in the natural environment. If the individual can demonstrate the skill in one or two natural environments, then continue teaching in the natural environment until the individual can display the skill in at least three naturally occurring activities/environments.

Level 2 also includes modifications to TAs that involve more than one S^D (those TAs where there is a S^D A, S^D B, and so forth). For these TAs, when you get to the second S^D (S^D B), probe the last step of that S^D. If the individual has 50–70 percent accuracy, continue teaching at this step. If their accuracy is lower than this (40% or below), then drop back to the beginning of S^D B and begin teaching at this step. For example, if teaching the individual the "Simple Requests" program from the first book on the Journey of Development ABA Curriculum series,

S^D A includes showing the individual a desired item and saying "What do you want?" After the individual meets criteria for the first 16 steps of this TA (ten targets plus generalization into two environments), then the instructor should probe Step 31 which includes random rotation of showing the individual ten different desired items and then hiding them, and saying "What do you want?" If the individual responds with an accuracy rate of 50 percent or higher, then the instructor can make the decision to stay at this step in the teaching process. This allows the individual to skip concentrated teaching of Steps 17–30 which saves valuable time but also allows the individual to still learn the skill. It should be noted that jumping to the final step of the second S^D (S^D B) may not always be appropriate so the instructor should use their best judgment. For example, if teaching the program "Rote Counting" (program from the first book on the Journey of Development ABA Curriculum series), S^D A includes telling the individual to "count" whereas S^D B includes directing the individual to count to a specific number. In this TA, it is suggested that all S^D B targets are probed to ensure the individual can count and stop at various desired numbers.

For Level 2 individuals, when randomly rotating Targets 1–4, complete the teaching in a different environment. If the individual displays a 50 percent or higher accuracy, then continue to teach the targets and all upcoming targets in different environments. If the individual displays 40 percent or lower accuracy, then teach in the one therapy environment for this and all upcoming targets until you get to the generalization to another environment step. By adding in this modification, if the individual can generalize to another environment at random rotation of Targets 1–4 and so forth, then the instructor can skip the two steps of generalizing to another environment at the end of the TA, as this already occurred in the teaching of the targets.

Finally, at this level, since individuals generally display a quicker acquisition rate, if the individual displays three consecutive days (instead of five) of no learning trend, variable learning trend or stagnant learning trend, then add in a teaching strategy.

To summarize, for Level 2 individuals:

- To meet target criteria, the response required (80% or zero prompts) only needs to be displayed across two consecutive days as opposed to three consecutive days.
- Teach two targets at once as opposed to teaching one target at a time. When you teach two targets at once, you randomly present them so they are in random rotation; thus you can skip random rotation of Targets 1 and 2, since you already addressed this. You should also only graph one line.
- In TAs involving receptive language, the instructor can initially baseline FO3 (as opposed to FO1):
    - If the response accuracy is 50 percent or higher, remain teaching at FO3.
    - If the response accuracy is 30–40 percent, drop back to FO2 to begin teaching the target.
    - If the response accuracy is lower than 30 percent, drop back to FO1 to begin teaching the target.
- Probe the natural environment (NE) before initiating the maintenance procedure. If the individual can demonstrate the skill in the NE at that time, then archive the program; there is no need to implement the maintenance procedure.
    - If the individual can demonstrate the skill in one or two NE, continue teaching in NE.
    - If the individual can demonstrate the skill accurately in three or more NE, then archive the program.

    - If the individual cannot demonstrate the skill in any of the three NE probes, drop back to the maintenance schedule.
- For those TAs that have multiple S^Ds, when the individual meets criteria for all targets under S^D A, probe the last step in S^D B:
    - If the response accuracy is 50–70 percent, stay and teach at this level, if not drop back to teaching the initial targets in S^D B.
- Generalization to new environment: after meeting criteria of Targets 1–4, when you randomly rotate Targets 1–4, complete this step in a different environment:
    - If the response is 50 percent or higher accuracy, continue to teach these targets and all upcoming targets in different environments. The instructor can then skip the two steps at the end of the TA which is generalization to another environment.
    - If the response is 40 percent or lower accuracy, then teach in one therapy environment for these targets and all upcoming targets until you get to the generalization to another environment step.
- If there are three consecutive days of no learning trend, variable learning trend or stagnant learning trend, then add in a teaching strategy.

Level 3

Level 3 is suggested for an individual who is higher functioning, has average to above average cognition and has demonstrated quick learning acquisition. These individuals have succeeded at Level 2, maintenance was not required and skills were not lost. Level 3 individuals would follow all the same modifications of a Level 2 individual with the following exceptions: a Level 3 individual would be taught five targets at once and would skip the steps of maintenance and go straight into natural environment teaching. In addition, targets should be frequently changed. The five targets taught might follow the same theme but not be the same exact target. For example, if teaching the individual how to tell time, the instructor would not present the exact time as a target but rather present themes, for example Target 1 is time on the hour, Target 2 is time by the 30-minute increment, Target 3 is time by 15-minute increments, and so forth. When teaching the second set of five targets, teach them in a new environment so generalization to different environments can occur and the instructor can skip the steps at the end of the TA of generalizing to another environment if the individual succeeded learning random rotation of Targets 5–10 in different environments. Finally, when conducting a baseline of the targets, only present the targets one time (not five times as indicated in the baseline rules).

To summarize, for Level 3 individuals:

- Follow the same modifications as Level 2 individuals with the following exceptions.
- Teach five targets at once.
- Change targets frequently—do not use the exact same target requiring the same response to be emitted.
- For the second set of five targets—teach in new environments.
- No maintenance teaching, go straight to NE teaching.
- When conducting a baseline of targets, only run one trial (not five trials).

90/10 teaching strategy

If an individual is having difficulty grasping a new program or a new target, or if they have demonstrated a stagnant/variable/no learning trend for multiple consecutive treatment sessions, then the instructor might want to implement the 90/10 teaching strategy in order to facilitate learning. This means that an individual would be prompted to display the skill for the first nine of ten trials; then the tenth trial is probed to see if they learned the response. Once the individual can show they learned the response, then the instructor would drop to 80/20, meaning they would prompt the response for the first eight of ten trials then probe the final two trials. The criterion to move to the next level of prompt/probe would be achieving 20 percent on the probed trials for 80/20. The instructor would prompt the first eight trials and the individual would need to emit a correct response for the final two trials, then the teaching strategy can be faded to 70/30 prompt/probe. This would continue until the instructor reaches a 50/50 prompt/probe; then the instructor would go back to typical teaching of presenting all ten trials for the individual to do on their own.

Decreasing immediate echolalia with verbal programs

Another teaching strategy to use if the individual presents with immediate echolalia (i.e. the instructor gives a S^D and the individual echoes whole or part of the S^D) includes the instructor presenting the S^D (i.e. question) in a lower voice followed by immediately giving the prompted response (within one second of the question) in a louder voice. By changing tone in voice, it helps the individual discriminate the S^D from the desired response. It is then important to fade the change in tone by stating the S^D more loudly and prompted response lower until both have the same variation in tone. If the individual imitates you and changes their tone of voice while providing a response, it is important to determine what tone will be expected for a correct response. This helps the individual to learn that the correct response is reinforced and not the particular tone in voice.

Modifying the S^D

When an individual is being taught a more advanced TA (TAs from books later in the series), the complexity of the S^Ds on these TAs increases. Also, at times, with the S^Ds on the TAs that represent the foundational skills in the first book in the series, an individual may have difficulty with the language associated with the S^D. A teaching strategy that may be used is to modify the S^D by simplifying the language that is used or using a built-in prompt with the S^D (visual or gestural prompt) to ensure correct responding. For example, if running the TA "Receptive Instructions (Two-Step)" and the S^D includes providing two directions, the instructor could write down the instructions as a visual prompt or reminder, or the instructor might have the individual repeat the S^D or instructions before providing a response. This ensures that the individual comprehends the complex instructions. It is important to remember when using a built-in prompt or simplifying the S^D, that the target is not considered mastered until the individual can demonstrate the skill with the original more complex S^D, so the prompt will need to be faded.

Modifying the field size

Another teaching strategy is modifying the field size or number of teaching targets introduced at one time. More advanced individuals are able to work on multiple targets at a time or a larger field size can be used. However, some individuals may become distracted by a larger field size or have difficulty learning when too many distractor items are presented. The instructor should make informed decisions about when to reduce the field size or decrease the number of targets.

Modifying backward chains via over-practice

There are multiple TAs in this curriculum book that are taught via a backward chain. The traditional backward chaining procedure is a teaching strategy whereby the instructor completes all steps in the chain with the exception of the final step. The instructor would teach the final step and collect data on the individual's performance with displaying this step. Once the individual can independently complete the final step of the chain, the instructor would complete all steps of the chain with the exception of the final two steps. These two steps would be taught to the individual, with data collected on those two steps. We suggest using a modification to the traditional backward chain at times, whereby over-practice is also used. Here, the instructor would prompt the individual through all steps of the chain but only collect data on the final step. The individual completing all steps with instructor prompting allows the individual to over-practice each step even though data is only collected on the step currently being taught. The major difference between the traditional backward chain and the Journey of Development ABA Curriculum modification is that in the traditional backward chain, the instructor is initially completing the majority of steps, but in the Journey of Development ABA Curriculum modification, the individual is prompted through all steps immediately. The use of over-practice may lead to quicker skill acquisition.

On the TAs in this curriculum book, when a backward chain is used, the description offered in the tips section on the TA will be the description of the modification to the traditional backward chain. For example, the TA may state "the task analysis is taught in reverse order (last step first) until all steps are completed independently. Thus, for Target 1, prompt individual through all steps of the chain with the exception of the last step. For Target 2, prompt through all steps with the exception of the final step and Step 8. For Target 3, prompt through all steps with the exception of the final step, Step 8 and Step 7. Continue to follow this procedure until independent mastery of entire chain has been achieved." The instructor may want to consider prompting through all steps with the exception of the final step; on this step, the instructor would teach the individual the step using prompts and collect data on the number and type of prompts. The instructor would then work to fade prompts until the individual masters the step. The instructor would then proceed to prompt through all steps but the final two steps. We have found that this backward chain modification has been successful with higher-functioning individuals and individuals without problematic behaviors. However, for some individuals who may have cognitive impairment and/or problematic behaviors, the traditional backward chain may be optimal as this requires less effort from the individual and may reduce the probability of problematic behaviors.

Choosing less distracting materials

Another teaching strategy is using materials with fewer distractions to teach the skill and more distracting materials for generalization of the skill. On the CD that accompanies this book, three pictures are offered for each target within a program. In most cases, one of the pictures will be of just the target with a solid white background. This offers no distractions and often helps the individual learn the skill. The other two pictures may involve more distractions, such as a social scene and these pictures should be used in the random rotation or generalization steps.

Inadvertent prompts

Inadvertent prompts can lead to a individual emitting the correct response not because they have acquired the skill but because they are following an instructor's prompt without the instructor being aware they are giving such a prompt. We have observed this to occur with the most advanced instructors. Thus, to self-monitor our behaviors and ensure instructors are not providing inadvertent prompts, here are a few suggestions:

- If part of the S^D is giving materials to the individual, the instructor can hand the individual an object, picture or item with their nondominant hand each time and use their dominant hand for recording data. For example, if working on a matching program and there is a field of three objects, using the same hand to give the individual an object to match helps to avoid using an inadvertent prompt of handing the individual the object with the hand that is closest to the expected response. We have seen examples where instructors have inadvertently used their left hand to give an individual an object when an expected response was on the left side and so on.

- Videotape some of your sessions and observe your own behaviors to ensure you are not emitting inadvertent prompts. Many instructors without being aware often give silent verbal prompts whereby they silently give the response. For example, if teaching "Expressive Labels of Beginning Sounds of Letters," we have seen instructors show the individual a letter and say "What sound does this letter make?" followed by silently pursing their lips in a position to say "Ba" for B or the expected response.
- Keep your eyes on the individual, not the objects, as this will decrease the inadvertent prompt of looking at the correct response.

Difficulty with generalizing skills

If an individual has significant difficulty generalizing skills to another person, environment or other materials, then increase the generalization steps (as opposed to waiting until the end of the program for generalization). For example, teach Target 1 then immediately generalize to another environment and/or another person/materials before teaching Target 2. After teaching Target 2, immediately generalize to another environment and/or another person/materials before random rotation of Targets 1 and 2, and so forth. By increasing opportunities for generalization, the individual may begin to generalize into other environments and generalize spontaneously without direct teaching. When generalizing to other materials, you may want to wait until the individual is at 80 percent or above with one material before introducing another.

Difficulty with maintenance or maintaining the skill over time

There are many options for teaching during the maintenance phase when individuals consistently respond incorrectly. One option when an individual misses a few targets in a program is for the instructor to continue to use DTT and error correction procedures during the maintenance schedule and review the missed targets multiple times during the probe (data is taken only on the first response). For example, if the individual is working on "Expressive Labels of Attributes" and misses the target "tall" the first time it was presented, the instructor should present this target multiple times during the day to teach the correct response.

Another option for teaching targets which an individual misses frequently during the maintenance phase is to remove the particular target(s) that the individual continues to miss and place only those targets on a more frequent maintenance schedule. For example, if the individual is working on "Receptive Labels of Function of Body Parts" once weekly during the maintenance schedule and produces an incorrect response when directed to "Point to what you scratch with" across multiple probes, the target (fingers) should then be moved to the previous more frequent schedule twice weekly (2W) while the targets which the individual got correct continue to be faded at 1W. Once the individual meets criteria for those targets that were frequently missed, they should systematically move along the maintenance schedule. The other targets from that particular program can be moved along the maintenance schedule to monthly (M).

Just as our program is not "cookie cutter," our maintenance schedule can be adjusted too, especially for those individuals who need extended repetition. The maintenance schedule can be adjusted to a more frequent schedule. For example, three times weekly (3W) or four times weekly (4W) maintenance schedule where the individual is running mastered targets in random rotation with other programming may be needed before moving to a (2W) schedule.

Delay in responding

Some individuals with ASD miss out on social or emotional opportunities due to their delay in providing a social or verbal response. In order to decrease their response latency (the time that elapses from the S^D to the individual responding), try using Fluency Based Training. Here, the individual engages in repetitive practice and over-learning, even after the response is learned and accurate, in order to help them learn to respond more quickly. In other words, overlearning involves repeated practice to the point where the response becomes automatic to the individual, and therefore also more fluent to the individual.

Fading teaching strategies

It is important to note that when using any of the teaching strategies offered in this chapter, the instructor leading the program should review the individual's graphs in order to make informed decisions about when to implement a teaching strategy or when to use a different teaching strategy. Each individual is different and acquires skills at different rates. When a teaching strategy is put in place, use the key on the graph to indicate that a teaching strategy was introduced and label the strategy on the graph. This will help in determining if the strategy is effective. Once the individual demonstrates the skill using the teaching strategy, meeting the specified criteria, the teaching strategy may need to be faded and the original S^D and presentation should be re-introduced.

Chapter 6

DATA COLLECTION AND DATA RECORDING

This chapter describes in detail how to utilize the data collection form (offered on the accompanying CD) for both skill acquisition and prompt data. Readers are given suggestions for how to collect baseline data and how to collect daily data.

There are two types of data collection and graphs for the TAs in this book. For skill acquisition programs, a target is practiced multiple times each session. Data is taken on every trial presented. Data is recorded as correct (+), incorrect (-) or as a prompted trial (P). The benefits of programs that are skill acquisition are: the individual receives repeated practice on a particular target (we recommend a minimum sample of ten trials per session); and the instructor can review data and prompt levels to further analyze and troubleshoot teaching strategies for the individual. Data is summarized as a percentage and graphed, requiring the individual to respond with 80 percent accuracy or above before the particular target is considered mastered or in their repertoire. When providing reinforcement for skill acquisition, it should be delivered after every correct or prompted trial (unless the skill is a familiar program for the individual and the instructor does not want to break the momentum of work to reinforce so the individual is on a variable reinforcement schedule).

Prompt data represents those programs which uses a chaining procedure to link all the steps together to form a larger skill. Targets that require prompt data collection allow the individual to work towards independent responding or independently completing a skill. Typical prompt programs include leisure skills (pretend play, board games, independent play schedule, playing videogames, etc.) and activities of daily living (chores, exercise, employment activities, etc.). This type of TA should be run a minimum of one time per session, with data collected on the first presentation. When running a prompt data program, the data should be recorded as the number and type of prompts used for the targeted step in the TA. The prompting hierarchy we suggest is as follows: Full Physical (FP), Partial Physical (PP), Gestural (G), Positional (POS), Visual (VS) and Verbal (VB). Data is summarized on the graph as the number and type of prompts used. When providing reinforcement for prompt data, it should be delivered after the targeted step is complete.

Data collection form

The daily data collection form should be filled out and updated daily as targets, steps or teaching strategies can change. At the top of the daily data collection form is an area to complete pertinent information such as the individual's name, the day and date (including the year) of the treatment session, and the instructor's name (this information is important for when the lead ABA instructor or BCBA reviews the accuracy in data or identifies patterns of inconsistency in scoring from one instructor to the next. The individual may respond differently on certain days/times of the week, due to fatigue, etc.).

The headings and key areas of the data collection form are now explained. In addition, an illustration of these concepts is provided.

Individual: Sara
Day & Date: ____________
Instructor: ____________
Time of session: ____________

Data Key:
+ correct, independent **−** incorrect, no response **P** prompted

Prompt Type:
FP full physical **PP** partial physical **G** gestural
POS positional **VS** visual **VB** verbal

Implementation Schedule	Curriculum Program	Curriculum Category	S^D	Response	Data	% Correct OR Number and Type of Prompts
Baseline DTT Maintenance 2W 1W M	Appropriate Sitting	Attending Skills	"Sit Nicely"	Sara will respond by sitting with a motionless body and quiet mouth	+ − P (FP PP G POS VS VB) + − P (FP PP G POS VS VB) + − P (FP PP G POS VS VB) + − P (FP PP G POS VS VB) + − P (FP PP G POS VS VB) + − P (FP PP G POS VS VB) + − P (FP PP G POS VS VB) + − P (FP PP G POS VS VB) + − P (FP PP G POS VS VB) + − P (FP PP G POS VS VB)	60%
Baseline DTT Maintenance 2W 1W M	Eye Contact (in response to name)	Attending Skills	SD A: "Sara, look at me." SD B: "Sara"	Sara will respond to name by giving eye contact to instructor and giving a verbal response (i.e. "yes")	+ − P (FP PP G POS VS VB) + − P (FP PP G POS VS VB) + − P (FP PP G POS VS VB) + − P (FP PP G POS VS VB) + − P (FP PP G POS VS VB) + − P (FP PP G POS VS VB) + − P (FP PP G POS VS VB) + − P (FP PP G POS VS VB) + − P (FP PP G POS VS VB) + − P (FP PP G POS VS VB)	20%
Baseline DTT Maintenance 2W 1W M	Receptive Instructions (One-Step)	Receptive Language	Give a one-step verbal directive	Sara will respond by following the directive	+ − P (FP PP G POS VS VB) + − P (FP PP G POS VS VB) + − P (FP PP G POS VS VB) + − P (FP PP G POS VS VB) + − P (FP PP G POS VS VB) + − P (FP PP G POS VS VB) + − P (FP PP G POS VS VB) + − P (FP PP G POS VS VB) + − P (FP PP G POS VS VB) + − P (FP PP G POS VS VB)	100%
Baseline DTT Maintenance 2W 1W M	Gross motor imitation with Objects	Imitation Skills	"Do this" and show a model of a gross motor movement with an object	Sara will respond by imitating the motor action with the object	+ − P (FP PP G POS VS VB) + − P (FP PP G POS VS VB) + − P (FP PP G POS VS VB) + − P (FP PP G POS VS VB) + − P (FP PP G POS VS VB) + − P (FP PP G POS VS VB) + − P (FP PP G POS VS VB) + − P (FP PP G POS VS VB) + − P (FP PP G POS VS VB) + − P (FP PP G POS VS VB)	30%
Baseline DTT Maintenance 2W 1W M	Participation in complex songs and games with actions	Play/Social Skills	Sing song/ play game with individual and prompt the actions that accompany the song or game	Sara will participate in the song/game by demonstrating the accompanying actions and singing along with instructor	FP PP G POS VS VB FP PP G POS VS VB FP PP G POS VS VB FP PP G POS VS VB FP PP G POS VS VB FP PP G POS VS VB FP PP G POS VS VB FP PP G POS VS VB FP PP G POS VS VB FP PP G POS VS VB	6 prompts (1 FP, 3 PP, 1 POS and 1G)

Figure 6.1 Daily data collection form

- Implementation Schedule: the implementation schedule should reflect the current stage of therapy the program is in. When "Baseline" is circled, this means the instructor is baselining a new target and the instructor should follow the baseline rules for that particular target. When "DTT" is circled, the instructor should teach daily using DTT. When the particular maintenance schedule is circled (2W, 1W or M), the instructor should run this program/target on the specified schedule.
- Curriculum Program: this corresponds with the title of each TA.
- Curriculum Category: this section corresponds with the Journey of Development ABA Curriculum Guide sections. This is helpful because at a quick glance at the data collection form, you want to see various programs being run from various categories (so as not to bore the individual with programs being taught all from the same one or two categories).
- S^D: the S^D is what the instructor will say or present to the individual. It is important to record any changes that the team makes to the S^D or presentation the individual sees.
- Response: the response is what is expected for the individual to demonstrate in order for a correct response to be recorded.
- Data: the data collection section represents that data the instructor collects during DTT. This information is the data from ten trials in skill acquisition programs or one trial in prompt programs that tell the ABA instructor how the individual responded across all teaching trials or what prompts were needed for the individual to be correct/independent.
- Percentage correct or Number and Type of Prompts: this section of the form is the tally of the data (percentage correct for skill acquisition programs or number and type of prompts for prompt programs). This is the section that will be transferred to the graphs. The percentage would be recorded on a skill graph and the number and type of prompts would be recorded on a prompt graph.

Collecting and recording data

ABA programs are data driven. This means that data should be taken on every task the individual is directed to complete. The data from these tasks are analyzed to determine treatment progress and whether teaching strategies should be implemented to increase skill acquisition. Prior to beginning a new program or TA, baseline data should be collected to determine the individual's abilities or skills that may have spontaneously generalized from the initial probe (this is when, on probe, the individual did not accurately respond but after teaching several targets within a program, the individual may begin to spontaneously generalize the skill to other targets and may baseline out of the target). Once teaching begins, data should be taken on each response to a S^D in order to determine treatment effectiveness.

Collecting baseline data

It is essential to conduct a baseline procedure at the inception of each program and when teaching a new target within the program. A baseline is data that is collected in the absence of treatment. Think of a baseline as a "pop quiz," where we test the knowledge of the individual prior to teaching the target or skill. Baseline data helps us determine if a particular target should be taught. For example, if you present a new target using skill acquisition data to an individual and the individual gives the correct response 80 percent or more of the time, then we would consider this skill to be within the person's repertoire (perhaps because it generalized from teaching other targets). There is no need to teach this target and another target should be baselined. Baseline data is also critical as it provides us with the individual's current skill level in which we compare treatment effectiveness.

During baseline, there is no prompting or reinforcement for the particular skill you are assessing. For example, when conducting a baseline for the skill of "Receptive Labels of Function of Body Parts," the instructor will not reinforce or prompt the response of touching the "body part function." The instructor could and should reinforce for appropriate behaviors such as sitting nicely, making appropriate eye contact, being a good listener, etc. Alternatively, the instructor can intermix maintenance programs for which reinforcement can be offered. When taking baseline data for skill acquisition programs, the instructor would only mark + (correct response) or – (incorrect response) on the data sheet. The prompting section on the data sheet would not be utilized, since prompting is not used while collecting baseline data. When the baseline for a particular target is 80 percent or above, that skill is in the individual's repertoire and the next target should be baselined.

When taking a baseline for skill acquisition programs, run five trials of the specific target. Do NOT prompt, reinforce or correct the individual in any way. Simply present the S^D and record the individual's response (+ or -). If the individual is correct for four of the five trials, you can stop the baseline for that particular target. Mark that target as "80%" in the area "Baseline" on the TA (4/5 = 80%). Since the individual has obtained 80 percent with no teaching, then we consider this target as spontaneously generalizing from other targets which were taught. For example, at the beginning of implementing the TA "Expressive Labels of Community Helpers," the instructor probed multiple targets and determined which targets the individual did not know. Once teaching commenced, the individual might learn several targets (e.g. doctor, dentist and fireman) and then when a new target (e.g. policeman) is baselined, the individual may score 80 percent or higher but at probe they could not label a policeman. In this case, the individual is spontaneously generalizing the program to other non-taught targets.

If the individual misses two or more of the five baseline trials, then the instructor should go on to collect a total of ten trials for that specific target. Once you run ten trials for a specific target, calculate the baseline percentage (total correct/10). For example, if the individual displayed the expected response four times, then 4/10 would be 40 percent. Mark this percentage in the area "Baseline %" on the TA.

Data collection for a baseline of a skill acquisition target is depicted in Figure 6.2.

Implementation Schedule	Curriculum Program	S^D	Response	Data	Percentage Correct OR Number and Type of Prompts
Baseline (circled)	Receptive Labels of Function of Body Parts	"Touch what you smell with"	Individual touches body part.	(+) -- P (FP PP G POS VS VB)	50%
DTT				+ (--) P (FP PP G POS VS VB)	
				+ (--) P (FP PP G POS VS VB)	
Maintenance				(+) -- P (FP PP G POS VS VB)	
2W 1W M				(+) -- P (FP PP G POS VS VB)	
				(+) -- P (FP PP G POS VS VB)	
				+ (--) P (FP PP G POS VS VB)	
				(+) -- P (FP PP G POS VS VB)	
				+ (--) P (FP PP G POS VS VB)	
				+ (--) P (FP PP G POS VS VB)	

Figure 6.2 Data collection for a baseline of a skill acquisition program

In this example, the individual incorrectly responded to two of the first five trials, so the instructor went on to present all ten trials. The individual responded correctly 5/10 times for a baseline of 50 percent.

To summarize, when collecting baseline data, follow these rules:

- Run five trials of the specific target. Do NOT prompt, reinforce or correct the individual in any way. Simply present the S^D and record the response (+ or -). If the individual is correct for four of the five trials, you can stop the baseline for that particular target. Mark that target as 80 percent in the area "Baseline" on the TA (4/5 = 80%).
- If the individual obtained 80 percent for baseline of a target, then introduce another target and collect baseline data for this target.
- If the individual misses two or more of the five trials, then go on to collect a total of ten trials for that specific target. Once you run ten trials for a specific target, calculate the baseline percentage (total correct/10). For example, if the individual displayed the expected response four times, then four out of ten would be 40 percent. Mark this percentage in the area "Baseline %" on the TA.
- It is important not to reinforce the individual during baselining for a specific target. This includes verbal praise, smiles, high fives, pats on the shoulder, etc. It is equally important not to teach during baselining. This includes not telling the individual the answer, and not giving facial responses that would indicate that the individual got the answer correct or incorrect. However, during baselining, to keep the individual motivated, you can reinforce behaviors not associated with the target such as "Good job sitting nicely" or "Nice working."

When conducting a baseline for targets in a prompt program, the instructor should run the program one time and record the number and type of prompts it took for the individual to complete the specific step/target. Be sure to indicate which prompt worked and which were attempted but did not work. For example, if the instructor gives the S^D "Dry hands" and prompts the individual to get the towel for drying hands using a partial prompt (PP) and the individual touches the towel then stops, then you deliver a full physical prompt to help the individual grasp the towel, you should indicate for your baseline data two prompts (<u>1 FP</u>, 1 PP) with circling or marking the "1 FP" indicating that this was the prompt that worked in helping the individual get the towel.

Baseline is taken at the inception of the program or when targeting a new step/target in the TA. When the individual's responds with zero prompts, this skill/step is in the individual's repertoire and the next step should be baselined. Baseline data for a prompt program is depicted in Figure 6.3.

Implementation Schedule	Curriculum Program	S^D	Response	Data	Percentage Correct OR Number and Type of Prompts
Baseline DTT Maintenance 2W 1W M	Closed Ended Solitary Toy Play with Cause and Effect Toys	Present Puzzle, say "Play"	Individual completes 5 piece puzzle	FP PP G POS VS VB FP PP G POS VS VB FP PP G POS VS VB FP PP G POS VS VB FP PP G POS VS VB FP PP G POS VS VB FP PP G POS VS VB)	4 Prompts (1 FP, 1 PP, 2 G)

Figure 6.3 Data collection for a baseline of a prompt program

General rules/recommendations for baseline of targets

- Rotate the programs you present to the individual when collecting baseline data. Do not keep things consistent as the individual may respond based on the routine or pattern you created. For example, if you are collecting baseline data on five programs, then present S^Ds for first trial of programs 1, 2, 3, 4, 5 followed by S^Ds for second trial of programs 3, 5, 2, 1, 4 followed by S^Ds for third trials of programs 5, 2, 4, 3, 1 etc.
- Only collect baseline data for a specific target when you are ready to begin teaching that target. For example, let's say you are working on "Expressive Labels of Categories." Then only collect baseline for Target 1 (i.e. animals) followed by teaching that category. Once this target has met criteria, then you collect baseline for Target 2 (i.e. food) followed by teaching that target, etc.
- When collecting baseline data, you do not offer reinforcement for the correct response. Since lack of feedback may become frustrating for an individual, make sure that you reinforce the individual for other behaviors (sitting appropriately, eye contact or participation). Alternatively, you can intermix maintenance programs in which you can offer reinforcement.

Collecting daily data

When collecting data on the responses emitted during DTT, it is important that the trials are clear and discrete. There should be a clear beginning (S^D), a response and a consequence (reinforcement or ignoring the incorrect response). Each trial begins with a S^D. Each of the individual's responses should be recorded as a separate trial. A plus (+) is recorded when the individual responds correctly. A minus (-) is recorded when the individual responds incorrectly or doesn't respond. A prompt (P) is used after an incorrect trial. The type of prompt is recorded on the data sheet. The instructor should circle the prompt that was effective in evoking the correct response. If other prompts are used and are ineffective in achieving the desired outcome, a slash should be marked through those types of prompts. Figure 6.4 gives an example of data collection for a skill acquisition program.

Implementation Schedule	Curriculum Program	S^D	Response	Data	Percentage Correct OR Number and Type of Prompts
Baseline DTT Maintenance 2W 1W M	Receptive Labels of Function of Body Parts	"Touch what you smell with"	Individual touches body part.	+ -- P (FP PP G POS VS VB) + -- P (FP PP G POS VS VB) + -- P (FP PP G POS VS VB) + -- P (FP PP G POS VS VB) + -- P (FP PP G POS VS VB) + -- P (FP PP G POS VS VB) + -- P (FP PP G POS VS VB) + -- P (FP PP G POS VS VB) + -- P (FP PP G POS VS VB) + -- P (FP PP G POS VS VB)	60%

Figure 6.4 Data collection for a skill acquisition program

Implementation Schedule	Curriculum Program	S^D	Response	Data	Percentage Correct OR Number and Type of Prompts
Baseline DTT Maintenance 2W 1W M	Playground: Swing	"Play on the Swing"	Individual will play on swing.	FP PP G POS VS VB FP PP G POS VS VB FP PP G POS VS VB FP PP G POS VS VB FP PP G POS VS VB FP PP G POS VS VB FP PP G POS VS VB)	5 Prompts (1 FP, 1 PP, 2 G, 1 POS)

Figure 6.5 Data collection for a prompt program

When taking prompt data on a skill/step, data should be recorded with the number and type of prompts needed to achieve the targeted skill/step. Run the program one time. You only need to run the program once (not five or ten times as in skill acquisition programs) since you are prompting the individual through the TA (when prompting, this is teaching). The type of prompt(s) that was effective in evoking the correct response should be circled. Figure 6.5 gives an example of data collection for a prompt program that is in daily DTT.

Collecting maintenance data

During the maintenance schedule, the instructor will run a probe trial of each target in random rotation for the program. This consists of probing random rotation of all targets if it is a skill acquisition program or probing the final step/target of the prompt programs. The instructor records the individual's first response for the target(s) on the data sheet. A plus (+) should be given if the individual displays the correct response for the target the first time it is presented and a minus (-) if the individual was incorrect on the first trial of any of the targets. If the individual is incorrect in their response, the instructor should follow the guidelines for DTT (i.e. re-present the target with a prompt, then present it again to determine if the individual learned the target) but recording of the response should only include the initial presentation. For example, let's say you taught the program "Expressive Labels of Emotions." There are ten targets that go into maintenance. When presenting the individual with the targets during maintenance, you randomly rotate the ten emotions that the individual learned. If the individual correctly labels nine emotions, they receive a response accuracy of 90 percent and for the one emotion they incorrectly labeled, the instructor should use the prompting procedure to teach the target. In order to move to a less frequent maintenance schedule, the individual needs to have a response accuracy of 100 percent for four consecutive treatment sessions when at the 2W level, 100 percent for four consecutive treatment sessions when at the 1W level, and 100 percent for three consecutive treatment sessions when at the M level. Please refer to Chapter 5 on teaching strategies regarding individuals who have difficulty maintaining the accuracy of targets in the maintenance phase.

Collecting natural environment data

Data collection in the natural environment (NE) is important because it tells us that our teaching was effective for the individual to learn the concept of what was taught through the TA, and can now generalize this skill into real-world activities and environments. When collecting NE data, the program materials, possibly the S^D, teacher and environment should be different. This is where the individual will demonstrate true learning and understanding of the concept. Data is collected on the entire concept of the TA, using other materials then previously generalized with during the teaching portion of the TA. For example, when taking data on completing patterns in the NE, the data can be collected on a center-based activity (e.g. stringing beads in a pattern) or during the morning calendar activity (e.g. creating a pattern that corresponds with the days of the month).

Another example is collecting data in the NE for prompt data programs. When collecting the data in NE, the instructor would collect data only on the last step of the chain on the TA. For example, if implementing the TA "Appropriate Sitting during a Family Meal," the last step would be sitting for entire duration of the meal. You would not need to probe or teach the previous steps since they are smaller increments of time (i.e. ten minutes). Examples of NE teaching for "Appropriate Sitting during a Family Meal" could include sitting at a restaurant, at another family member's home or at a church picnic. Another important tip for data collection in the NE is to individualize this skill to areas that the individual may come across within their daily lives. For example, if the family does not attend church, this should not be targeted for NE teaching. However, if the family does attend an older brother's soccer games, eating hotdogs while sitting in the stands might be targeted.

Recording programs that are archived

Once the individual has met criteria for NE teaching (i.e. demonstrating the skill in the NE across three novel naturally occurring activities), the program can be archived. When a program is archived, this means that the individual successfully maintained and generalized this skill across materials, environments, people and possibly S^Ds. The archive date should be recorded on the front of the TA and the program should be removed from the teaching schedule. In addition, the graphs can be removed from the program book and placed in a separate archived binder for future reference if needed. It is important to keep all archived graphs in one place for quick reference to see what the individual demonstrated during the teaching phase. When an individual progresses through the different volumes of the Journey of Development ABA Curriculum, the number of archived programs will grow and the people working with the individual may change. It is important for future ABA instructors working with the individual to have all the information about what the individual has achieved throughout the course of their therapy.

Chapter 7

GRAPHING

Graphing is an integral part of any ABA program. Graphing the data helps make large data sets coherent and easier to interpret. It is recommended that graphing occurs after each treatment session (not saved and graphed a week or month at one time). By immediately graphing after the session, the ABA instructor has ongoing access to a complete record of the individual's skills and can immediately assess treatment effectiveness. This allows for changes or treatment modifications to occur more quickly.

The following is a description of how to use the two different graphs associated with the Journey of Development ABA Curriculum, the graphing symbols that are placed on the graphs and interpreting the data. There are two different types of graphs that are used to record data with this curriculum. The first is a skill acquisition graph that matches up with skill acquisition programs and results in percentage correct. The second is a prompt graph which matches up with prompt programs and results in the number and type of prompts recorded. When setting up your ABA program book, refer to the TA for what type of graph should be utilized with each TA.

Graphing symbols

Below is a key of the symbols used on the graphs and a brief definition of each.

Skill acquisition programs/graphs

X *(Baseline):* Conduct a baseline before each new target or each new step in the TA and record with an '**X**'. A baseline score and the daily data points should not be connected on the data path.

● *(Data Point to indicate Daily Percentage):* Place a ● to represent the data point at the appropriate intersection of squares on the graph to record the daily percentage or response accuracy. Draw a line connecting daily percentages (this line is known as the Data Path).

// *(Break in Therapy):* Record breaks in treatment on the graph with **//** (i.e. weekend, holiday, vacation, sick, etc.). For a break in therapy, do not connect the preceding percentage point with the percentage point following the break.

| *(Condition Line to represent Target Criteria have been Met):* Mark a vertical line after target criteria have been met. This separates the targets on the graph and allows for quick review and analysis of the data.

¦ *(Phase Line to indicate Change in Treatment Strategy):* Mark a broken line when there is a change in a teaching strategy, such as a change in the reinforcement schedule or implementation of a new teaching strategy. Along the broken line, it is often helpful to write what the teaching strategy is that is being implemented. This allows for improved analysis of effective and ineffective teaching strategies for the individual.

Figure 7.1 gives an example of a skill acquisition graph.

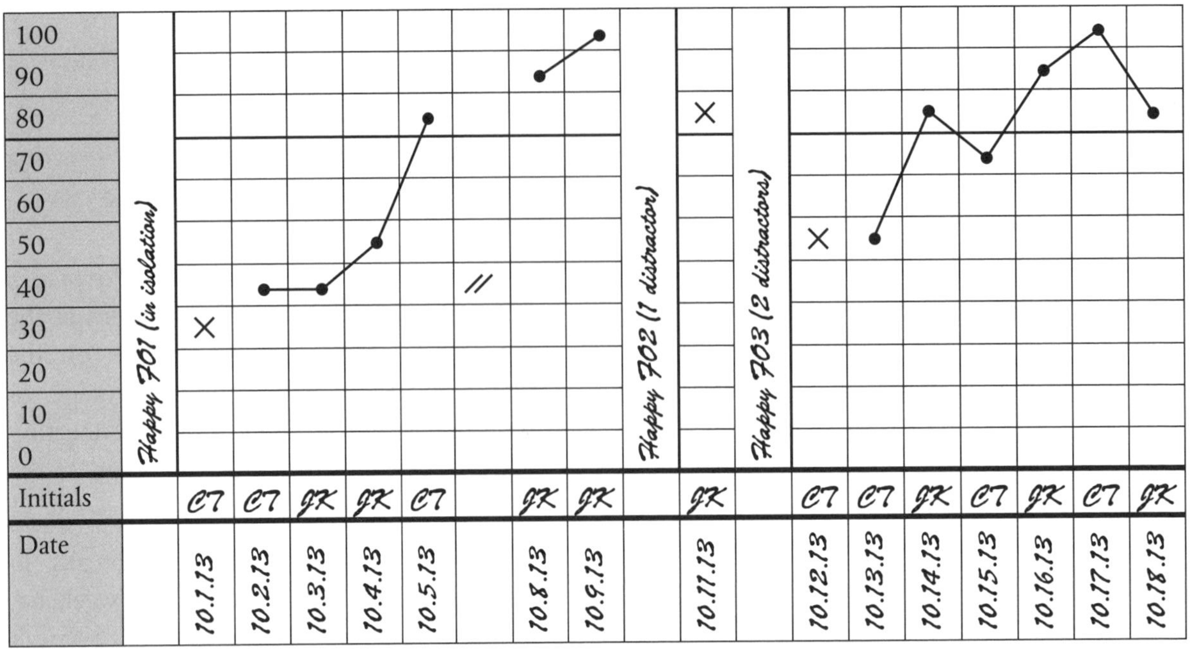

Figure 7.1 Example of skill acquisition graph

The TA in the provided example is "Receptive Labels of Emotions." The first target on the graph is identifying "happy" in isolation. The solid vertical line indicates a new target is beginning. On October 1, 2013, the ABA instructor CT conducted a baseline and the individual scored 30 percent. The score is indicated on this graph with an X. This score of 30 percent should also be marked in the baseline column on the TA. The next day, October 2, 2013, CT began teaching the target ("happy" in FO1). This date should also be recorded on the TA under the column 'Date Introduced'. The program continued to be taught through October 5, 2013 by various instructors (CT and JK). From October 6 to 7, 2013 the individual did not receive ABA therapy, so a break in treatment is indicated on the graph and the data points from 10.5.13 and 10.8.13 do not get connected. The following consecutive scores were then recorded on the graph: 80 percent (10.8.13) and 100 percent (10.9.13). The individual has met criteria (80% or above for three consecutive days across two people); thus, a solid vertical line to indicate the target met criteria is drawn (this date should also be recorded in the 'Date Criteria Met' line on the TA) and a new target is written on the graph (after the solid condition line). The second target is "happy" in a field of two items (FO2). Baseline was conducted at 80 percent. This indicates that the skill spontaneously generalized without teaching from a FO1 to FO2. The baseline percentage and the date introduced and date mastered (date of baseline 10.11.13) should be recorded on the TA. The final target in the example is "happy" in a field of three (FO3). The baseline is recorded with an X at 50 percent on 10.12.13. Teaching of the target began on 10.13.13. On 10.18.13, the individual met criteria for "happy" in a FO3. The same procedure continues for all other targets.

Prompt programs/graphs

X *(Baseline):* Conduct a baseline before each new target or each new step in the TA and record with an '**X**'. The baseline score (X) should not be connected to the data points. If the individual scores zero prompts (independent performance) at baseline, that target is considered to be in repertoire and you can move on to the next step in the TA (baselining the next target).

● *(Data Point to Indicate Number of Prompts):* Place a ● at the appropriate intersection of squares on the graph to record the number of prompts required for the individual to complete the current step/skill in the TA. Draw a line connecting prompts used each treatment session (this line is known as the Data Path).

// *(Break in Therapy):* Record breaks in treatment on the graph with **//** (i.e. holiday, vacation, sick, etc.). For a break in therapy, do not connect the preceding percentage point with the percentage point following the break.

| *(Condition Line to represent Target Criteria have been Met):* Mark a vertical line after target criteria have been met.

¦ *(Phase Line to indicate Change in Treatment Strategy):* Mark a broken line when there is a change in a teaching strategy.

Figure 7.2 gives an example of a prompt graph.

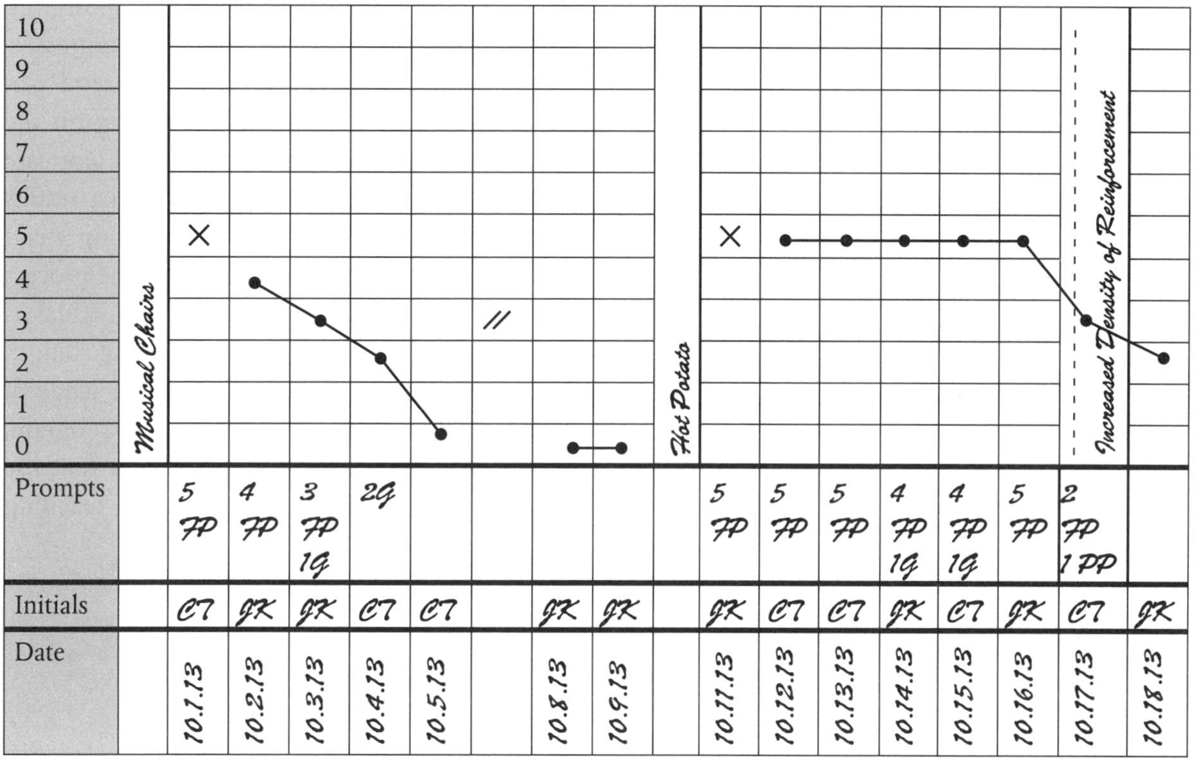

Figure 7.2 Example of a prompt graph

In the provided example, the individual is working on the program "Participation in Complex Songs and Games with Actions." This TA requires the ABA instructor to record prompt data (number and type of prompts). The target is written on the graph (musical chairs) and a baseline was conducted on 10.1.13. When conducting a baseline for prompt data, the number and type of prompts are recorded on the graph. A baseline (**X**) is recorded as the total number of prompts that are required for the individual to successfully complete the step/task. On 10/1/13, it took five prompts for the individual to be successful with completing the target. The data recorded on the graph is marked with an **X** in Row 5 and the type of prompts used (full physical prompts, 5 FP) in the prompt row. In the provided example, the date teaching was introduced was 10.2.13 and the individual required four prompts to complete the task. From

October 6 to 7, 2013, the individual did not receive therapy, a break in treatment is indicated on the graph and the data points from 10.5.13 and 10.8.13 do not get connected. The criteria for prompt data is three consecutive days of zero prompts across two people for the step/target. In the example, the criteria have been met on 10.9.13 with three consecutive treatment days at zero prompts. This date in recorded in the 'Date Criteria Met' column on the TA. A second target (hot potato) was introduced on 10.11.13. The individual required five prompts to complete this target. From 10.12.13 to 10.16.13, the individual required five prompts each day demonstrating no learning across these five days. Thus, a treatment strategy (increasing the density of reinforcement) was implemented on 10.17.13. This is marked with a phase change line (broken line) that indicates the target stayed the same, but a teaching strategy was introduced. The teaching strategy was labeled along this broken line for future reference of what strategy was implemented.

Interpreting graphs

Allow the data to guide treatment decisions. Data is objective and visual analysis of the data should be the primary method for determining treatment effectiveness (not a subjective opinion). Data should be evaluated daily and compared to the baseline rates in order to determine if progress is being made, how quickly and when teaching strategies should be implemented. There are four main types of learning trends that data displays. Trend lines refer to the direction taken by the data points/data path.

Positive stable learning trend

This is the trend line we strive for, indicating that the individual is learning and progress is being made. This type of learning trend can be ascending or descending depending on the type of program you are running. If you are running a skill acquisition program that results in percentage correct, then an ascending trend line indicates that the behavior is in the process of increasing or improving. The individual is successfully acquiring the skill being taught and manipulations do not need to be made at this time. If you are running a prompt program, then a descending trend line indicates that the individual is acquiring the skill and teaching strategies are not required.

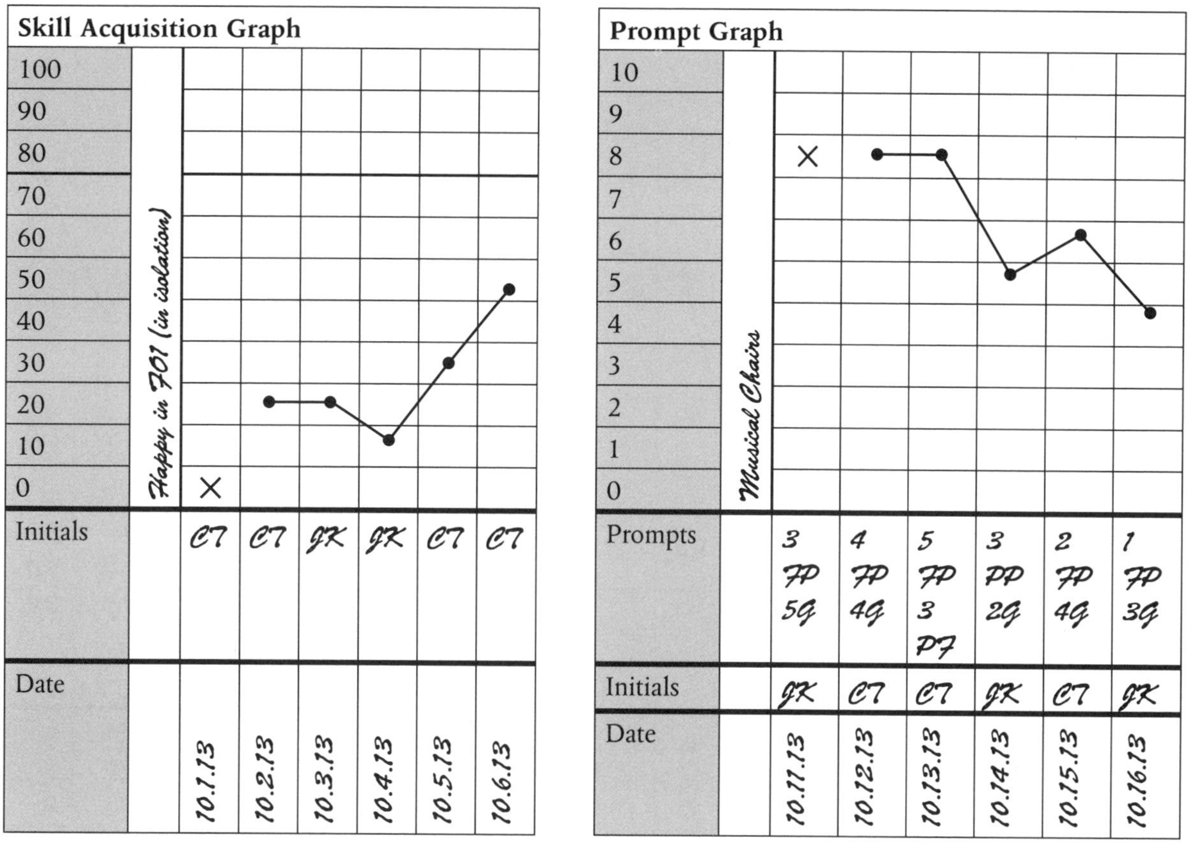

Figure 7.3 Graphs showing positive stable learning trends for skill acquisition program and prompt program

Variable learning trend or sporadic learning trend

This is a trend line when there are varying ranges in the data plots or varying ranges in the individual's rates for learning a particular skill/step. When an individual exhibits a sporadic learning trend, this indicates that implementation of teaching strategies will need to be made at this time and further observations will need to be made to determine the cause of this type of learning trend. Variable learning trends can result from a variety of sources including but not limited to problems with execution of the reinforcement (i.e. reinforcement is not dense enough), materials used to teach the skill, change in instructor, problems with consistency of treatment implementation and individual's illness.

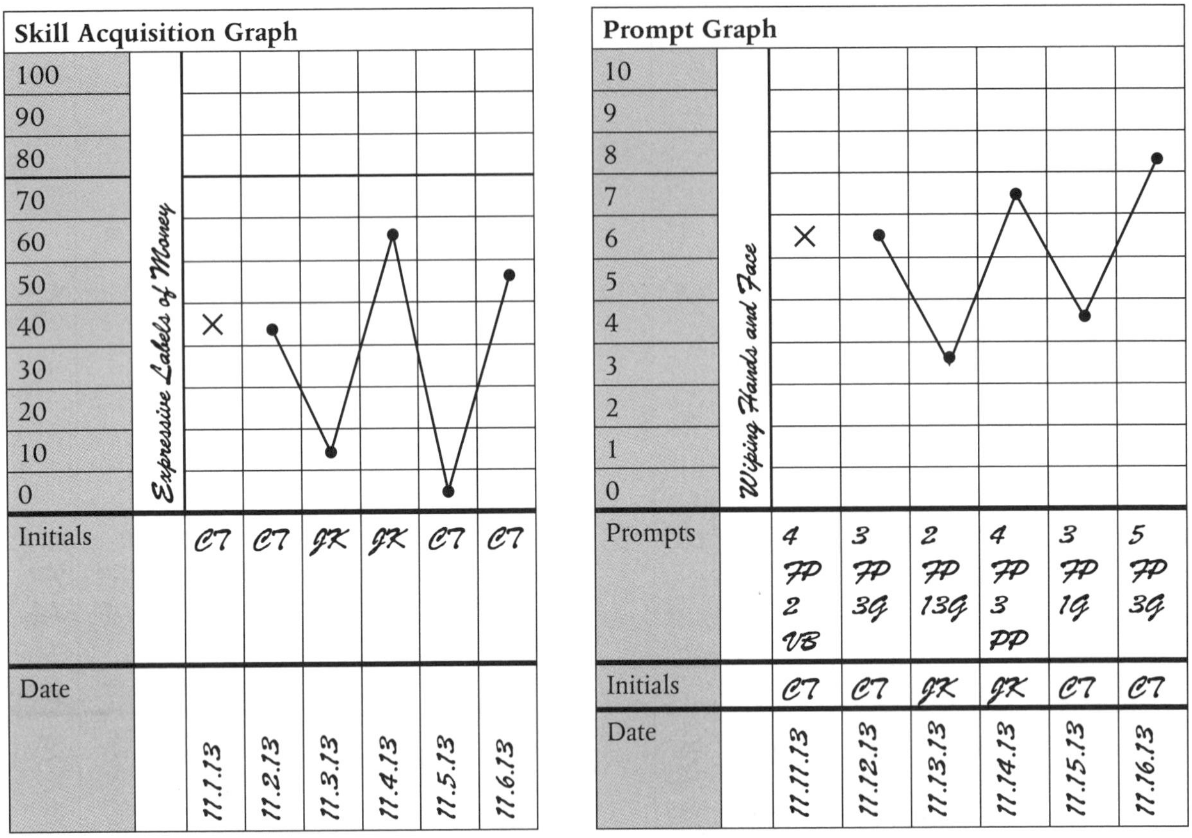

Figure 7.4 Graphs showing variable learning trends

Static learning trend

Static learning or stagnant learning trend is a lack of movement in the data plots or lack of movement in the individual's rates for learning a particular skill. When an individual exhibits a static learning trend, this indicates that the individual has reached a plateau and teaching strategies need to be made at this time to help the individual continue learning the skill and overcome the plateau.

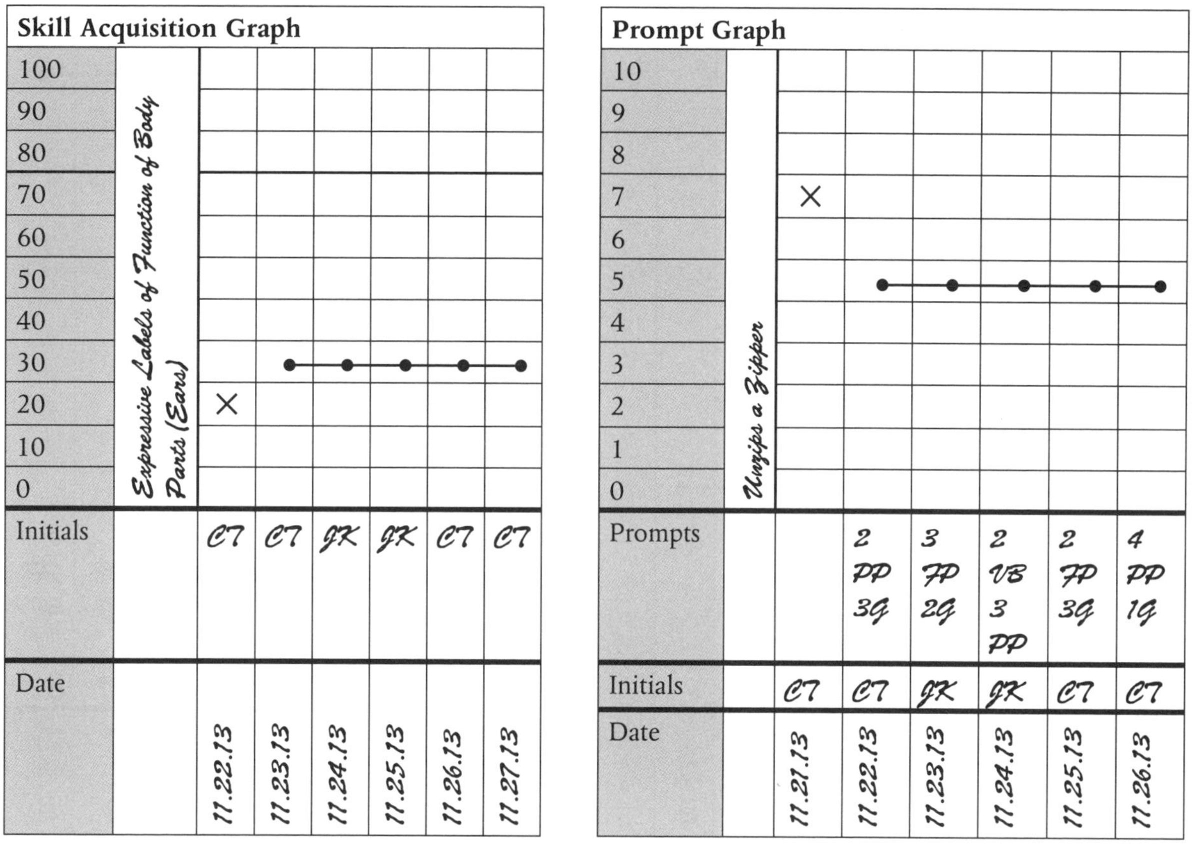

Figure 7.5 Graphs showing static learning trends

No learning trend

No learning trend occurs when the individual consistently requires full physical prompts or is consistently attaining zero percent accuracy. When a individual exhibits no learning trend, this indicates that they are not learning and teaching strategies need to be made at this time. Further observations need to occur to determine the cause of this type of learning trend. As with a variable learning trend, there are multiple reasons no learning trend could occur, from reinforcement to materials to an individual's illness.

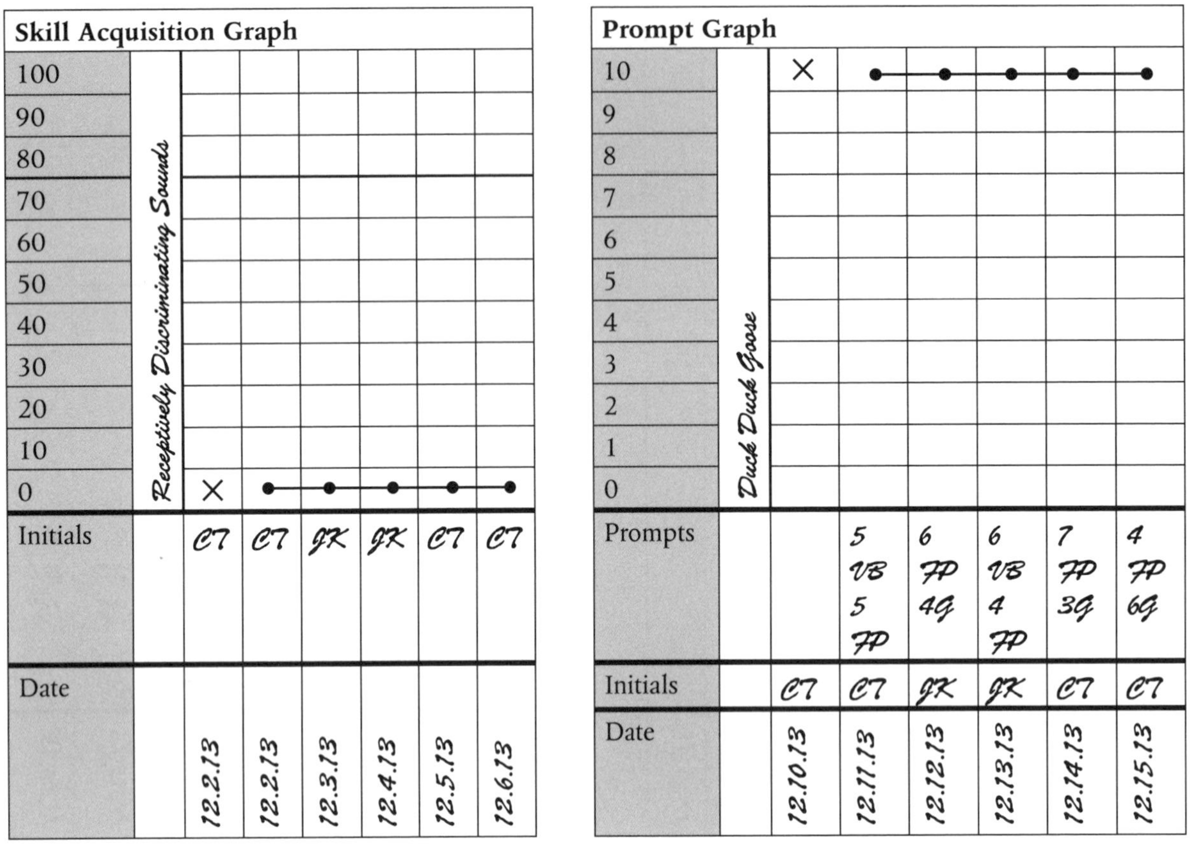

Figure 7.6 Graphs showing no learning trends

We recommend that if an individual demonstrates a variable learning trend, static learning trend or no learning trend for three to five consecutive treatment sessions (the number depends on the level the individual is on), then a teaching strategy should be implemented. In Chapter 5, we offered a variety of teaching strategies that can be considered. In addition to those teaching strategies, the ABA instructor could consider other treatment modifications such as breaking down the step or skill into smaller parts, changing treatment materials, ensuring pre-requisite skills have been acquired, manipulating the therapy environment to be more conducive for learning, assessing the consistency of treatment implementation or adding a visual prompt. Once you have made changes to treatment and added in a new strategy, continuous assessments are necessary. In addition, it is equally important to determine how you will fade some of your teaching strategies, such as visual cues. Working with a BCBA is very helpful when troubleshooting learning difficulties and determining strategies to put into place.

Chapter 8

CREATING AN ABA ENVIRONMENT

This chapter describes in detail how to set up an ABA therapy environment in your home or classroom. Information offered in this chapter includes recommendations for appropriate types of furniture, how to arrange the furniture in the room and how to organize materials to best suit the learning environment for the individual. Pictures are provided as examples of an ideal therapy space. Finally, suggestions for reinforcing toys and activities are offered.

The ABA therapy room

The individual's therapy room should be located in a place where distractions can be controlled to a minimum (i.e., not a lot of traffic walking throughout the room, limited distractions on the wall/window, etc.). The therapy area should be a place where the individual feels comfortable working. We recommend that the therapy space is not located in the individual's bedroom. Ideally, the room should have a door so it can be closed if needed. This will limit noise and distraction from the rest of the house as well as create a natural barrier if the individual has maladaptive behavior of trying to escape or avoid a task by engaging in tantrum behavior or running away from the therapy area.

The room should have two separate areas: one for teaching and one for break/play. The teaching area of the room should be organized with various types of furniture used for storage as well as teaching purposes. A table and chair appropriate to the size of the individual should be used for table activities such as academic tasks or independent tasks and should be large enough for a minimum of two people to sit. The table and chairs need to be stable and sturdy and not easily tipped. The chair should have a back without arms to more easily promote and teach appropriate sitting.

Shelving/small storage containers should be labeled with the program name or use (e.g. "Receptive Labels of Categories," Reinforcers, etc.). It is important that the room be organized for easy access to needed teaching materials as well as for the instructor to know where toys or needed materials are located for easy retrieval. Some other common types of furniture to utilize in the therapy area would be a shelf large enough to hold bins of required materials for the individual's program (e.g. receptive or expressive labels of community helpers, etc.). Tupperware/bins/accordion files should also be labeled with the program name and hold program materials or reinforcement items.

A dry erase board/chalk board for teaching use and/or for team use can be beneficial. This can hold important meeting notes, reminders for treating behavior or questions for other ABA instructors working with the individual. A bookshelf can be added for displaying books that can be read or looked at independently during break time or facilitated play. Books should be rotated periodically to maintain reinforcing qualities.

The break/play area should be an area where the individual can sit and play comfortably. Depending on the age and size of the individual, this area may include another table and chairs or carpeted area so they can sit and play on the ground comfortably. A shelf that holds various games and leisure items is often helpful. The break area can be set up with pictures of where specific toys are to be kept and easily identified for the individual. Toys should be rotated periodically to promote expanding play repertoire and avoid satiation. A closet should be used for storage of larger items, as well as items to be used in the future.

Figure 8.1 offers several pictures of a therapy space created for two young individuals.

Example	Description of Room
	This ABA therapy space has a small table and chairs appropriate to the size of the individual. There is a dry erase board on the wall that is used as a teaching tool and communication log between instructors. There are minimal distractions.
	This ABA therapy space has a small carpeted area to indicate the space the individual can sit in to engage in play TAs, enjoy reinforcement or take a break. Reinforcing toys and activities are on the wall and in bins next to the wall. The closet holds extra therapy supplies and can easily be locked.
	This ABA therapy space has a table and chairs suitable to the size of this older individual. The bins behind the table are numbered to match the various TAs being run. This makes it easy and convenient for the instructor to quickly grab the materials required for specific programming.
	This ABA therapy space has a calendar on the wall, similar to what you would find in school circle time areas. This individual was working on the TAs "Calendar," "Pledge of Allegiance," "Weather" and other circle time activities. In addition, this space shows rules and visual reminders for the individual.
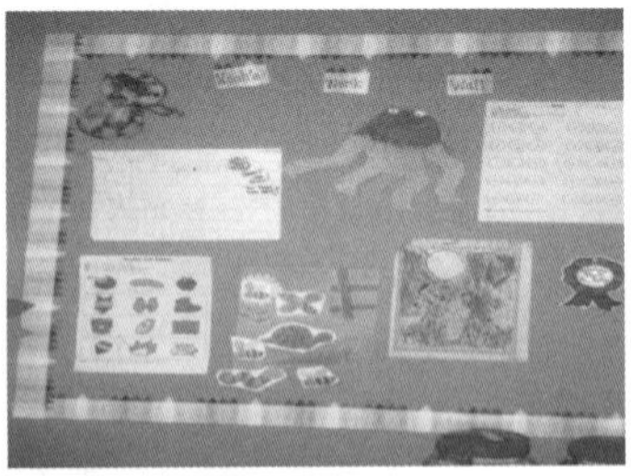	This area in the ABA therapy space is a designated spot where the individual's work samples are displayed. In addition, his art work is a reinforcement for him and is displayed here.

Figure 8.1 Therapy spaces

Parent involvement

Parent involvement is an extremely important part of an individual's ABA program. The parent's initial responsibilities when setting up a home ABA program is purchasing teaching materials and furniture for the therapy space, organizing the therapy room and determining who will be their child's treatment team. The parents will need to work out a schedule with the instructors that allow for consistent days and times for treatment to take place. Parents are also responsible for withholding specified reinforcement that is strictly used for therapy time only.

Parents are responsible for reading about and receiving training on ABA. Most treatment teams will provide this directly to the parents while implementing the ABA program with their child. However, parents are encouraged to read reputable books (such as Cooper, Heron and Heward 2007; Leaf and McEachin 1997; Lovaas 2003) on ABA programming to learn about ABA theories, teaching strategies, behavior reduction strategies, etc. In addition, parents should receive training on the child's specific individual ABA program, such as the targets that are being used and how they can help teach the targets with incidental teaching in the NE.

Once ABA therapy is initiated, it is important for the parent to be home for all team meetings. The parent should be aware of the targets/teaching procedures for each program. The parents play a large role in individualizing their child's ABA curriculum. The parents work alongside the ABA instructor and/or BCBA in choosing targets/skill areas that the individual does not display. Without the parents' help, the ABA instructor will possibly only see a portion of the individual's day.

The parents are also part of the team that teaches their child. They work on generalizing skills to another person, place and across materials. Parents are encouraged to observe their child's ABA program being implemented so they can learn the different teaching strategies (e.g. prompting hierarchy) so they can be reliable with implementing the teaching strategies. The parents also ensure that therapy supplies and reinforcers are stocked.

One of the most important roles of the parents is to communicate with all team members (ABA instructor, BCBA, pediatrician or other doctor, teacher, etc.). It is very important that the parents notify the ABA instructor with any concerns or questions regarding therapy or current targets. It is also important to notify the treatment team with any changes in the individual's daily routine (i.e. sleep cycle, medication changes, other medical conditions, etc.) as this may have an effect on treatment outcomes. Having an open and honest relationship will only help the treatment team make the most informed decision for treatment.

To summarize parent involvement:

- Be aware of the procedures for each program.
- Follow through with what has been taught during therapy.
- Keep reinforcements for therapy only for therapy.
- Make sure supplies and reinforcers are stocked.
- Have the therapy room ready and organized.
- Attend all team meetings.
- Be home during all therapy sessions.
- Receive training on ABA; read and learn ABA strategies.
- Observe ABA sessions to become reliable with the strategies.
- Keep the communication network open with the treatment team.
- Notify the treatment team with any concerns or questions.
- Organize the work schedule (days/times) for consistent ABA treatment sessions.

Suggestions for reinforcing toys and activities

In the first chapter of this book, a list of rules for reinforcement was offered. Using reinforcers effectively is very important for learning to take place and skills to be acquired. Instructors should refer to this list frequently to ensure that reinforcers are used to their maximum capabilities. In this section, we offer suggestions for reinforcers that can be used in treatment. These suggestions are not meant to be a replacement for preference assessments or reinforcement inventories (as these are very helpful in ABA therapy in identifying potential reinforcers), but simply a list of potential reinforcers that individuals with ASD might find reinforcing and can be used in treatment sessions.

Primary reinforcers

Primary reinforcers are those items that are required for an individual to live and survive, such as food and drink. Primary reinforcers are not natural reinforcers to use in the daily life of a individual. For example, teachers typically offer praise to a individual for a job well done, not offer a sip of a drink or a snack. However, individuals with ASD often respond very well to this type of reinforcement and may not respond as well to secondary reinforcers such as praise or a toy. Thus, primary reinforcers may be needed at the beginning of treatment in order to teach the individual the skills and how to respond to secondary reinforcers. The ABA instructor should pair primary reinforcement with secondary reinforcement so secondary reinforcers begin to take on the reinforcing properties of the primary reinforcers. When this occurs, the primary reinforcers should be faded from treatment. The following is a short list of common primary reinforcers that can be considered to use in treatment; the most important factor is that the reinforcement is functional or reinforcing for the individual.

Look for those primary reinforcers that do not take a long time to consume (e.g. bite-size snack), so more time is allotted for learning/working, such as:

- sip of a preferred drink
- popcorn
- candy such as M&Ms, Reece's Pieces, or Skittles
- slice of fruit, carrots, celery sticks
- fruit gummies/fruit snacks
- potato chip, pretzel, other crunchy snack
- tater tots
- piece of cookie, bite of cake, other bakery items
- raisins
- nuts.

Secondary reinforcers

Secondary reinforcers are also called conditioned reinforcers because they are items the individual may not find naturally reinforcing (like primary reinforcers), but after a conditioning process whereby the secondary reinforcer is paired with the primary reinforcer, the individual associates the secondary reinforcer with the primary reinforcer and the secondary reinforcer becomes reinforcing. ABA instructors are advised to pair these items with the primary reinforcers so the primary reinforcers can eventually be faded from treatment.

The suggestions for secondary reinforcers we offer are ordered by qualities of sensory experiences, as this may offer a built-in automatic reinforcement for the individual. For example, if the individual enjoys objects that make sounds, then it is suggested the instructor attempt to use other objects that make sounds as the auditory stimulus may be automatically reinforcing for the individual and the conditioning process might be able to be eliminated or occur more quickly. Following is a list of suggested reinforcement items that can be used in ABA programming:

For individuals who are reinforced by objects that move or have a cause/effect quality, try:

- balls (light up balls, stress balls that can be squeezed, vibrating balls)
- light chaser toy
- toys that light up
- flashlights where the lights spins or blinks
- Jack-in-the-box
- pop-up toys
- see and say toys/games
- rain stick.

For individuals who are reinforced by gross motor movement, try:

- trampoline
- rocking toys
- swings
- therapy balls
- Sit-and-spin
- scooter boards
- seesaws
- bicycle/tricycle
- sliding board
- tickles
- hula-hoop.

For individuals who are reinforced by auditory stimuli, try:

- sound puzzle
- musical books
- musical instruments
- sound machines
- music sticks
- toys that talk/make noise
- echo microphone
- songs/music.

For individuals who are reinforced by tactile stimuli/different textures, try:

- books and toys that have different textures to feel
- sand table
- water table
- table/bins filled with rice or beans
- Play-Doh
- finger-painting activities
- playing with shaving cream or Funny Foam.

For individuals who are reinforced by deep pressure, try:

- being squished between pillows or couch cushions
- hugs
- hammocks
- tickles
- bean bag chairs
- ball pits
- wrapping in blankets
- sleeping bags
- massagers
- rolling over carpets
- vibrating pillows.

For individuals who are reinforced by visual stimuli, try:

- Lite-Brite
- electronic games, computer games
- flashlights
- strobe lights
- lava lamps
- glow-in-the-dark stickers
- toys that light up
- View master

- light chaser toys, light chaser necklaces
- glitter wands or wands that when turned upside down, material floats to the other side.

For individuals who are reinforced by olfactory stimuli (i.e. strong smells), try:

- seasonings
- Scratch and Sniff stickers
- aromatherapy machines
- scented markers
- lotion
- scented Play-Doh.

For individuals who are reinforced by small spaces/small areas, try:

- tents
- tunnels
- boxes big enough to sit in/fit into
- small play houses
- storage bins.

For individuals who are reinforced by watching things fall or dangle, try:

- bubbles
- long silk flags
- liquid motion toys
- water sprinkler
- foam airplanes
- stomp rockets
- parachute toy
- rubber poppers
- material wind chimes.

Making therapy fun

It is important that individuals are motivated in therapy sessions so learning occurs; so, as ABA therapists, we need to strive to make therapy fun and as natural as possible. In turn, this will help with compliant behaviors, interest in therapy and generalization of skills. Below is a list of suggestions that ABA instructors are encouraged to use in order to ensure that ABA therapy sessions are fun and enjoyable, and learning occurs:

- Use enthusiastic tones when presenting the S^Ds and reinforcement.
- Language used in sessions should be as natural as possible.
- Treatment sessions should occur in various environments (different rooms of the house, outside, and community settings). This will keep things novel and help with generalization to different environments. Get creative; if the individual is motivated by jumping on a trampoline or riding on a swing, place the individual on the apparatus and, when they earn a reward, let the reward be jumping on a trampoline for a specific duration of time or several pushes in the swing.
- Vary the instructions you give the individual as their language improves.
- Pair yourself with highly enjoyable activities, thus making yourself a reinforcer for the individual.
- Teach concepts (i.e. colors, shapes, counting, etc.) using favorite toys or objects.
- Constantly vary the objects you are using to teach a skill. For example, shapes can be taught using flashcards, large beads, pattern blocks, or by drawing and tracing shapes on paper. This not only promotes generalization across materials but also keeps activities novel for the individual.
- Be sure to place TAs that met criteria into maintenance (or the fading procedure recommended), so you do not bore the individual with continuing to practice mastered skills.

- Use an ABA therapy schedule whereby you work for 15–20 minutes followed by taking a 5–10-minute reinforcement break/play break. Breaks are important to maintain the fun. Do not punish the individual by trying to extend the 15–20 minutes of teaching when the individual is being cooperative.
- Maintain a high success rate and be sure to end therapy sessions on a success.
- Intersperse tasks or TAs. It is important that you are constantly working on several TAs at one time and continuously rotating them so not to bore the individual.
- Vary the reinforcers; try to make reinforcers as natural as possible.
- Incorporate music into the therapy session, even making up silly songs to teach concepts such as body parts.

PART II

CURRICULUM PROGRAMS

Chapter 9

TASK ANALYSES FOR ATTENDING SKILLS

- Appropriate Sitting during a Family Meal
- Appropriate Sitting during a School Activity
- Sustained Eye Contact

APPROPRIATE SITTING DURING A FAMILY MEAL

LEVEL: □ 1 □ 2 □ 3

S^D: Say "Sit nicely"	**Response:** Individual will sit still (remaining in seat, quiet feet) for family dinner
Data Collection: Prompt data (number and type of prompts used)	**Target Criteria:** 0 prompts for 3 consecutive days across 2 people
Materials: Chair, family having dinner (or contrived situation) and reinforcement	

Fading procedure

Maintenance Criteria: 2W = 4 consecutive scores of 0 prompts; 1W = 4 consecutive scores of 0 prompts; M = 3 consecutive scores of 0 prompts	**Natural Environment (NE) Criterion:** Target has been generalized in NE across 3 novel naturally occurring activities	**Archive Criteria**: Target, maintenance and NE criteria have been met

Target list

Target	Baseline: Number and Type of Prompts	Date Introduced	Date Criteria Met	*Fading Procedure*		
				Maintenance	**Date NE Introduced**	**Date Archived**
Backwards chaining procedure						
1. Target 1: Last step in the chain Last 10 minutes of meal time.						
2. Target 2: Step 4 of the chain Last 12 minutes of meal time.						
3. Target 3: Step 3 of the chain Last 15 minutes of meal time.						
4. Target 4: Step 2 of the chain Last 20 minutes of meal time.						
5. Target 5: Step 1 of the chain Sit for entire duration of meal.						
6. Generalize to another environment Environment 1:						

7. Generalize to another environment Environment 2:						
8. Maintenance: Assess in varied environments				2W 1W M		

Specific tips for running this task analysis

- Ensure pre-requisite skills have been taught for this TA. Examples of pre-requisite skills for "Appropriate Sitting during a Family Meal" include "Appropriate sitting" and progress made toward "Receptive Instructions (One-Step)" (TAs found in the first book of the Journey of Development ABA Curriculum series).
- When working on this TA, serve foods that the individual enjoys. The purpose of this TA is to teach sitting during meal time, not expand food preferences.
- When generalizing to another environment, if you choose to generalize sitting for dinner in a restaurant, start with a fast food restaurant where there is less waiting, move on to a diner where food may be served quickly and then on to other elaborate restaurants where there may be increased waiting time before the food arrives.
- This program is designed to teach the individual how to sit during meal time using the backward chaining procedure whereby the TA is taught in reverse order (last step first) until all steps are completed independently. Thus, for Target 1, have the individual attend meal time for the last 10 minutes of the dinner. This will allow the individual time to eat and complete the meal at the same time as the other members of the family, with everyone concluding the meal and leaving the table at the same time. For Target 2, bring the individual to the table for the last 12 minutes of the meal and continue the process until the individual is sitting for the entire duration of the meal.

APPROPRIATE SITTING DURING A SCHOOL ACTIVITY

LEVEL: □ 1 □ 2 □ 3

S^D: Say "Sit nicely"	**Response:** Individual will sit with a motionless body (hands on table or lap and feet still) and a quiet mouth
Data Collection: Skill acquisition	**Target criteria:** 0 prompts for 3 consecutive days across 2 people
Materials: Chair (or alternatively carpet square if individual is sitting during circle time) and reinforcement	

Fading procedure

Maintenance Criteria: 2W = 4 consecutive scores of 0 prompts; 1W = 4 consecutive scores of 0 prompts; M = 3 consecutive scores of 0 prompts	**Natural Environment (NE) Criterion:** Target has been generalized in NE across 3 novel naturally occurring activities	**Archive Criteria:** Target, maintenance and NE criteria have been met

Target list

Target	Baseline: Number and Type of Prompts	Date Introduced	Date Criteria Met	*Fading Procedure*		
				Maintenance	Date NE Introduced	Date Archived
1. Target 1: 1 minute						
2. Target 2: 3 minutes						
3. Target 3: 5 minutes						
4. Target 4: 10 minutes						
5. Target 5: Sit for entire duration of activity						
6. Generalize to another environment Environment 1:						

7. Generalize to another environment Environment 2:						
8. Maintenance: Assess in varied environments				2W 1W M		

Specific tips for running this task analysis

- Ensure pre-requisite skills have been taught for this TA. Examples of pre-requisite skills for "Appropriate Sitting during a School Activity" include "Appropriate Sitting" and progress made toward "Receptive Instructions (One-Step)" (TAs found in the first book of the Journey of Development ABA Curriculum series).

SUSTAINED EYE CONTACT

LEVEL: □ 1 □ 2 □ 3

S^D: Engage the individual in a conversation	**Response:** Individual will respond by giving eye contact to the instructor during the duration of the conversation
Data Collection: Prompt data (number and type of prompts used)	**Target criteria:** 0 prompts for 3 consecutive days across 2 people
Materials: Reinforcement	

Fading procedure

Maintenance Criteria: 2W = 4 consecutive scores of 0 prompts; 1W = 4 consecutive scores of 0 prompts; M = 3 consecutive scores of 0 prompts	**Natural Environment (NE) Criterion:** Target has been generalized in NE across 3 novel naturally occurring activities	**Archive Criteria:** Target, maintenance and NE criteria have been met

Target list

Suggestions for targets and probe results

Suggestions for Conversation Length: 30 seconds, 1 minute, 2 minutes, 3 minutes, 4 minutes, 5 minutes, 6 minutes, 7 minutes, 8 minutes, 9 minutes and 10 minutes.
Probe Results (targets in repertoire):

Target	Baseline: Number and Type of Prompts	Date Introduced	Date Criteria Met	*Fading Procedure* Maintenance	Date NE Introduced	Date Archived
1. Target 1:						
2. Target 2:						
3. Targets 1 and 2 random rotation						

4. Target 3:						
5. Target 4:						
6. Targets that met criteria: random rotation						
7. Target 5:						
8. Target 6:						
9. Targets that met criteria: random rotation						
10. Target 7:						
11. Target 8:						
12. Targets that met criteria: random rotation						
13. Target 9:						
14. Target 10:						
15. Targets that met criteria: random rotation						
16. Generalize to another environment Environment 1:						
17. Generalize to another environment Environment 2:						
18. Maintenance: Assess in varied environments				2W 1W M		

Specific tips for running this task analysis

- Ensure pre-requisite skills have been taught for this TA. Examples of pre-requisite skills for “Sustained Eye Contact” include mastering the attending skills programs in the first book of the Journey of Development ABA Curriculum series and progress toward “Receptive Instructions (Two-Step)” (TA found in this curriculum book).
- The response should appear natural with the individual looking at the speaker for the majority of the time and brief glances away permitted. When the individual stops looking for longer than a ten-second interval, the instructor should prompt the individual to give eye contact to the conversational partner.

Chapter 10

TASK ANALYSES FOR IMITATION SKILLS

- Complex Fine Motor Imitation
- Complex Fine Motor Imitation with Objects
- Complex Gross Motor Imitation
- Complex Gross Motor Imitation with Objects
- Imitation: Mirror, Speed, Intensity, Sequence
- Pretend Actions Imitation (No Objects Used)

COMPLEX FINE MOTOR IMITATION

LEVEL: □ 1 □ 2 □ 3

S^D: Say "Do this" and demonstrate a complex fine motor movement	**Response:** Individual will imitate the complex fine motor movement
Data Collection: Skill acquisition	**Target Criteria:** 80% or above for 3 consecutive days across 2 people
Materials: Reinforcement	

Fading procedure

Maintenance Criteria: 2W = 4 consecutive scores of 100%; 1W = 4 consecutive scores of 100%; M = 3 consecutive scores of 100%	**Natural Environment (NE) Criterion:** Target has been generalized in NE across 3 novel naturally occurring activities	**Archive Criterion**: Target, maintenance and natural environment criterion has been met

Target list

Suggestions for targets and probe results

Suggestions for Targets: Cross fingers for good luck, make a peace sign, make OK sign, drum fingers on table, make church steeple with fingers, do a butterfly with both hands, make a telescope hole with fingers to look out of, fold hands in prayer, touch thumb to pinky/ring/middle/index finger, and put thumb out over shoulder for "Get out of here."
Probe Results (targets in repertoire):

Target	Baseline %	Date Introduced	Date Criteria Met	*Fading Procedure*		
				Maintenance	Date NE Introduced	Date Archived
1. Target 1:						
2. Target 2:						
3. Targets 1 and 2 random rotation						
4. Target 3:						

5. Target 4:						
6. Targets that met criteria: random rotation						
7. Target 5:						
8. Target 6:						
9. Targets that met criteria: random rotation						
10. Target 7:						
11. Target 8:						
12. Targets that met criteria: random rotation						
13. Target 9:						
14. Target 10:						
15. Targets that met criteria: random rotation						
16. Generalize to another environment Environment 1:						
17. Generalize to another environment Environment 2:						
18. Maintenance: Assess in varied environments				2W 1W M		

Specific tips for running this task analysis

- Ensure pre-requisite skills have been taught for this TA. Examples of pre-requisite skills for "Complex Fine Motor Imitation" include mastering "Fine Motor Imitation" (TA located in the first book in the Journey of Development ABA Curriculum series).

COMPLEX FINE MOTOR IMITATION WITH OBJECTS

LEVEL: □ 1 □ 2 □ 3

S^D: Demonstrate a fine motor movement using an object while saying "Do this"	**Response:** Individual will imitate the motor action with the object
Data Collection: Skill acquisition	**Target Criteria:** 80% or above for 3 consecutive days across 2 people
Materials: Common objects that require fine motor movements and reinforcement	

Fading procedure

Maintenance Criteria: 2W = 4 consecutive scores of 100%; 1W = 4 consecutive scores of 100%; M = 3 consecutive scores of 100%	**Natural Environment (NE) Criterion:** Target has been generalized in NE across 3 novel naturally occurring activities	**Archive Criteria:** Target, maintenance and NE criteria have been met

Target list

Suggestions for targets and probe results

Suggestions for Targets: String small beads, shoot marbles with fingers, build with blocks (e.g. tower, 3-D objects such as house and train), build with toys (e.g. Mr. Potato Head, train track), and create with Play-Doh (e.g. roll and cut out with cookie cutter, make a snowman, make an animal).
Probe Results (targets in repertoire):

Target	Baseline %	Date Introduced	Date Criteria Met	*Fading Procedure*		
				Maintenance	Date NE Introduced	Date Archived
1. Target 1:						
2. Target 2:						
3. Targets 1 and 2 random rotation						
4. Target 3:						
5. Target 4:						

6. Targets that met criteria: random rotation						
7. Target 5:						
8. Target 6:						
9. Targets that met criteria: random rotation						
10. Target 7:						
11. Target 8:						
12. Targets that met criteria: random rotation						
13. Target 9:						
14. Target 10:						
15. Targets that met criteria: random rotation						
16. Generalize to other environment Environment 1:						
17. Generalize to another environment Environment 2:						
18. Maintenance: Assess in varied environments				2W 1W M		

Specific tips for running this task analysis

- Ensure pre-requisite skills have been taught for this TA. Examples of pre-requisite skills for "Complex Fine Motor Imitation with Objects" include mastering "Fine Motor Imitation with Objects" (TA located in the first book in the Journey of Development ABA Curriculum series).
- Use objects the individual has around the home in order to reduce cost of program materials for the family.
- Be vigilant of the individual while using small objects that can be easily swallowed. If the individual displays mouthing of objects, until mouthing is extinguished, then you might want to consider not running this program due to choking hazards.

COMPLEX GROSS MOTOR IMITATION

LEVEL: □ 1 □ 2 □ 3

S^D: Say "Do this" and demonstrate a complex gross motor movement	**Response:** Individual will imitate the complex gross motor movement
Data Collection: Skill acquisition	**Target Criteria:** 80% or above for 3 consecutive days across 2 people
Materials: Reinforcement	

Fading procedure

Maintenance Criteria: 2W = 4 consecutive scores of 100%; 1W = 4 consecutive scores of 100%; M = 3 consecutive scores of 100%	**Natural Environment (NE) Criterion:** Target has been generalized in NE across 3 novel naturally occurring activities	**Archive Criteria:** Target, maintenance and NE criteria have been met

Target list

Suggestions for targets and probe results

Suggestions for Targets: Stand on one foot, hop in place, hop moving forward, log rolls, wheelbarrow walk, crab walk, ballerina twirl, walk backwards, squat, Jumping Jacks, and walk on knees.
Probe Results (targets in repertoire):

Target	Baseline %	Date Introduced	Date Criteria Met	*Fading Procedure* Maintenance	Date NE Introduced	Date Archived
1. Target 1:						
2. Target 2:						
3. Targets 1 and 2 random rotation						
4. Target 3:						
5. Target 4:						

6. Targets that met criteria: random rotation						
7. Target 5:						
8. Target 6:						
9. Targets that met criteria: random rotation						
10. Target 7:						
11. Target 8:						
12. Targets that met criteria: random rotation						
13. Target 9:						
14. Target 10:						
15. Targets that met criteria: random rotation						
16. Generalize to other environment Environment 1:						
17. Generalize to another environment Environment 2:						
18. Maintenance: Assess in varied environments				2W 1W M		

Specific tips for running this task analysis

- Ensure pre-requisite skills have been taught for this TA. Examples of pre-requisite skills for "Complex Gross Motor Imitation" include mastering simple "Gross Motor Imitation" (TA located in the first book in the Journey of Development ABA Curriculum series).
- This TA should be run on a soft mat to prevent injury in case the individual falls.

COMPLEX GROSS MOTOR IMITATION WITH OBJECTS

LEVEL: □ 1 □ 2 □ 3

S^D: Demonstrate a gross motor movement using an object while saying "Do this"	**Response:** Individual will imitate the motor action with the object
Data Collection: Skill acquisition	**Target Criteria:** 80% or above for 3 consecutive days across 2 people
Materials: Common objects or toys and reinforcement	

Fading procedure

Maintenance Criteria: 2W = 4 consecutive scores of 100%; 1W = 4 consecutive scores of 100%; M = 3 consecutive scores of 100%	**Natural Environment (NE) Criterion:** Target has been generalized in NE across 3 novel naturally occurring activities	**Archive Criteria:** Target, maintenance and NE criteria have been met

Target list

Suggestions for targets and probe results

Suggestions for Targets: Lie on large ball and rock back and forth and side to side, sit on large ball and rock back and forth and side to side, climb up stairs, walk down the stairs, pedal a tricycle, ride scooter board, catch a ball, throw a ball, kick a ball, spin on a Sit-and-Spin, climb steps to sliding board, and jump on trampoline.
Probe Results (targets in repertoire):

Target	Baseline %	Date Introduced	Date Criteria Met	*Fading Procedure*		
				Maintenance	**Date NE Introduced**	**Date Archived**
1. Target 1:						
2. Target 2:						
3. Targets 1 and 2 random rotation						
4. Target 3:						

5. Target 4:						
6. Targets that met criteria: random rotation						
7. Target 5:						
8. Target 6:						
9. Targets that met criteria: random rotation						
10. Target 7:						
11. Target 8:						
12. Targets that met criteria: random rotation						
13. Target 9:						
14. Target 10:						
15. Targets that met criteria: random rotation						
16. Generalize to another environment Environment 1:						
17. Generalize to another environment Environment 2:						
18. Maintenance: Assess in varied environments				2W 1W M		

Specific tips for running this task analysis

- Ensure pre-requisite skills have been taught for this TA. Examples of pre-requisite skills for "Complex Gross Motor Imitation with Objects" include mastering simple "Gross Motor Imitation with Objects" (TA located in the first book in the Journey of Development ABA Curriculum series).
- Use objects the individual has around the home in order to reduce costs of program materials for the family.

IMITATION: MIRROR, SPEED, INTENSITY, SEQUENCE

LEVEL: □ 1 □ 2 □ 3

S^D: Say "Do this" and demonstrate motor movements depicting a sequence (touch fork then cup), speed (tapping table fast vs. tapping table slow), intensity (clapping hard vs. clapping soft) and actions in a mirror	**Response:** Individual will imitate the motor movement in sequence, speed, accuracy or in a mirror
Data Collection: Skill acquisition	**Target Criteria:** 80% or above for 3 consecutive days across 2 people
Materials: Mirror, everyday items and reinforcement	

Fading procedure

Maintenance Criteria: 2W = 4 consecutive scores of 100%; 1W = 4 consecutive scores of 100%; M = 3 consecutive scores of 100%	**Natural Environment (NE) Criterion:** Target has been generalized in NE across 3 novel naturally occurring activities	**Archive Criteria:** Target, maintenance and NE criteria have been met

Target list

Suggestions for targets and probe results

Suggestions for Targets: *Motor imitation in the mirror:* clap, touch head, wave, touch nose, stick tongue out, open mouth, smile, and tongue lateralization (side to side). *Sequence:* two or three actions in a row that involve and do not involve objects. *Speed of gross motor movement:* (fast/slow) clapping, stomping, tapping lap, knocking, and walking/running. *Intensity of gross motor movement:* (hard/soft) clapping, knocking, tapping lap, stomping/marching, and shaking maracas.

Probe Results (targets in repertoire):

Target	Baseline %	Date Introduced	Date Criteria Met	*Fading Procedure*		
				Maintenance	**Date NE Introduced**	**Date Archived**
1. Target 1: Gross motor imitation in a mirror.						
2. Target 2: Gross motor imitation in a mirror.						

3. Targets 1 and 2 random rotation						
4. Target 3: Oral motor imitation in a mirror.						
5. Target 4: Oral motor imitation in a mirror.						
6. Targets that met criteria: random rotation						
7. Target 5: Imitation of 2 actions in a sequence.						
8. Target 6: Imitation of 3 actions in a sequence.						
9. Targets that met criteria: random rotation						
10. Target 7: Speed of gross motor movement.						
11. Target 8: Speed of gross motor movement.						
12. Targets that met criteria: random rotation						
13. Target 9: Intensity of gross motor movement.						
14. Target 10: Intensity of gross motor movement.						
15. Targets that met criteria: random rotation						
16. Generalize to another environment Environment 1:						
17. Generalize to another environment Environment 2:						

18. Maintenance: Assess in varied environments				2W 1W M		

Specific tips for running this task analysis

- Ensure pre-requisite skills have been taught for this TA. Examples of pre-requisite skills for "Imitation: Mirror, Speed, Intensity, Sequence," include mastering gross motor, fine motor and oral motor imitation programs in the first book of the Journey of Development ABA Curriculum series and progress toward imitation of "Complex Gross Motor Imitation" (TA in this curriculum book).

PRETEND ACTIONS IMITATION (NO OBJECTS USED)

LEVEL: □ 1 □ 2 □ 3

S^D: A. Say "Do this" and demonstrate a pretend action B. "Pretend to [action]" and demonstrate the pretend action	**Response:** Individual will imitate the pretend action
Data Collection: Skill acquisition	**Target Criteria:** 80% or above for 3 consecutive days across 2 people
Materials: Reinforcement	

Fading procedure

Maintenance Criteria: 2W = 4 consecutive scores of 100%; 1W = 4 consecutive scores of 100%; M = 3 consecutive scores of 100%	**Natural Environment (NE) Criterion:** Target has been generalized in NE across 3 novel naturally occurring activities	**Archive Criteria:** Target, maintenance and NE criteria have been met

Target list

Suggestions for targets and probe results

Suggestions for Targets: Blow bubbles, brush hair, wash hands, brush teeth, cut paper, swim in water, ride horse, blow nose, eat, drink, hammer, knock on door, and rock a baby.
Probe Results (targets in repertoire):

Target	Baseline %	Date Introduced	Date Criteria Met	*Fading Procedure*		
				Maintenance	Date NE Introduced	Date Archived
1. S^D A: Target 1:						
2. S^D A: Target 2:						
3. Targets 1 and 2 random rotation						
4. S^D A: Target 3:						

5. S^D A: Target 4:						
6. Targets that met criteria: random rotation						
7. S^D A: Target 5:						
8. S^D A: Target 6:						
9. Targets that met criteria: random rotation						
10. S^D A: Target 7:						
11. S^D A: Target 8:						
12. Targets that met criteria: random rotation						
13. S^D A: Target 9:						
14. S^D A: Target 10:						
15. Targets that met criteria: random rotation						
16. S^D B: Target 1:						
17. S^D B: Target 2:						
18. Targets 1 and 2 random rotation						
19. S^D B: Target 3:						
20. S^D B: Target 4:						

21. Targets that met criteria: random rotation						
22. S^D B: Target 5:						
23. S^D B: Target 6:						
24. Targets that met criteria: random rotation						
25. S^D B: Target 7:						
26. S^D B: Target 8:						
27. Targets that met criteria: random rotation						
28. S^D B: Target 9:						
29. S^D B: Target 10:						
30. Targets that met criteria: random rotation						
31. Generalize to another environment Environment 1:						
32. Generalize to another environment Environment 2:						
33. Maintenance: Assess in varied environments				2W 1W M		

Specific tips for running this task analysis

- Ensure pre-requisite skills have been taught for this TA. Examples of pre-requisite skills for "Pretend Actions Imitation (No Objects Used)" include gross motor imitation with and without objects and fine motor imitation with and without objects (TA can be found in the first book of the Journey of Development ABA Curriculum series).
- Use the same targets for S^D A and S^D B as this will lead to quicker skill acquisition and understanding of "pretend."

Chapter 11

TASK ANALYSES FOR VISUAL SPATIAL SKILLS

- Arranging by Series or Sequence
- Building Block Formations
- Extending Sequence Patterns
- Matching Block Formations to Pictures of Block Formations
- Matching Object Association
- Matching Uppercase to Lowercase Letters
- Matching Lowercase to Uppercase Letters
- Mazes
- Puzzles (Square Border and Jigsaw)
- Sorting Objects by Feature
- Sorting Pictures by Feature
- Sorting Objects by Function
- Sorting Pictures by Function
- What Doesn't Belong?

ARRANGING BY SERIES OR SEQUENCE

LEVEL: □ 1 □ 2 □ 3

S^D: Present individual with 4 objects or pictures varying by 1 quality and say "Put in order from X to Y" (e.g. smallest to biggest)	**Response:** Individual will put the objects or pictures in the correct order
Data Collection: Skill acquisition	**Target Criteria:** 80% or above for 3 consecutive days across 2 people
Materials: Objects or pictures of objects that can be ordered by size, color, sequence of completion, quantity or order, reinforcement (picture cards can be found on accompanying CD)	

Fading procedure

Maintenance Criteria: 2W = 4 consecutive scores of 100%; 1W = 4 consecutive scores of 100%; M = 3 consecutive scores of 100%	**Natural Environment (NE) Criterion:** Target has been generalized in NE across 3 novel naturally occurring activities	**Archive Criteria:** Target, maintenance and NE criteria have been met

Target list

Suggestions for targets and probe results

Suggestions for Targets: *Sequence of completion—3 in series*: Circle, circle with eyes, happy face. *Sequence of completion—4 in series*: 1 part of square, 2 parts of square, 3 parts of square, 4 parts of square. Also arrange by number, letter, shades of color, size and quantity.
Probe Results (targets in repertoire):

				Fading Procedure		
Target	**Baseline %**	**Date introduced**	**Date Criteria Met**	**Maintenance**	**Date NE Introduced**	**Date Archived**
1. Target 1: Order numbers lowest to highest						
2. Target 2: Order numbers highest to lowest						
3. Targets 1 and 2 random rotation						
4. Target 3: Order by quantity						

5. Target 4: Order by letters						
6. Targets that met criteria: random rotation						
7. Target 5: Order by size (smallest to biggest)						
8. Target 6: Order by size (biggest to smallest)						
9. Targets that met criteria: random rotation						
10. Target 7: Order by shades of color (lightest to darkest)						
11. Target 8: Order by shades of color (darkest to lightest)						
12. Targets that met criteria: random rotation						
13. Target 9: Order by sequence of completion—in series						
14. Target 10: Order by sequence of completion—in series						
15. Targets that met criteria: random rotation						
16. Generalize to another environment Environment 1:						
17. Generalize to another environment Environment 2:						
18. Maintenance: Assess in varied environments				2W 1W M		

Specific tips for running this task analysis

- When teaching targets that involve sequence of completion, use pictures depicting objects (not social scenes). The idea of this TA is to sequence and arrange by series, not interpret social scenes and determine order of socialization.

BUILDING BLOCK FORMATIONS

LEVEL: □ 1 □ 2 □ 3

S^D: A. Present a pre-built block structure and blocks required to replicate the structure and say "Build this" B. Present a picture of a pre-built block structure and blocks required to replicate the structure and say "Build this"	**Response:** Individual will build with the blocks to replicate the structure
Data Collection: Skill acquisition	**Target Criteria:** 80% or above for 3 consecutive days across 2 people
Materials: Colored blocks, pictures of pre-built structures and reinforcement	

Fading procedure

Maintenance Criteria: 2W = 4 consecutive scores of 100%; 1W = 4 consecutive scores of 100%; M = 3 consecutive scores of 100%	**Natural Environment (NE) Criterion:** Target has been generalized in NE across 3 novel naturally occurring activities	**Archive Criteria:** Target, maintenance and NE criteria have been met

Target list

Suggestions for targets and probe results

Suggestions for Targets: 2-block, 3-block, 4-block and 5-block structures of same-color blocks and different-color blocks
Probe Results (targets in repertoire):

Target	Baseline %	Date Introduced	Date Criteria Met	*Fading Procedure*		
				Maintenance	Date NE Introduced	Date Archived
Pre-Built Block Structures						
1. S^D A: Target 1:						
2. S^D A: Target 2:						
3. Targets 1 and 2 random rotation						

4. S^D A: Target 3:						
5. S^D A: Target 4:						
6. S^D A: Targets that met criteria: random rotation						
7. S^D A: Target 5:						
8. S^D A: Target 6:						
9. S^D A: Targets that met criteria: random rotation						
10. Generalize to another environment Environment 1:						
11. Generalize to another environment Environment 2:						
12. Maintenance: Assess in varied environments				2W 1W M		
Pictures of Pre-Built Block Structures						
13. S^D B: Target 1:						
14. S^D B: Target 2:						
15. S^D B:Targets that met criteria: random rotation						
16. S^D B: Target 3:						
17. S^D B: Target 4:						
18. S^D B: Targets that met criteria: random rotation						

19. S^D B: Target 5:						
20. S^D B: Target 6:						
21. S^D B: Targets that met criteria: random rotation						
22. Generalize to another environment. Environment 1:						
23. Generalize to another environment. Environment 2:						
24. Maintenance: Assess in varied environments				2W 1W M		

Specific tips for running this task analysis

- Ensure pre-requisite skills have been taught for this TA. Examples of pre-requisite skills for "Building Block Formations" include mastering "Fine Motor Imitation with Objects" and "Matching Colors" (both TAs found in the first book of Journey of Development ABA Curriculum series).
- If the individual struggles with learning this skill, you may need to first teach "Matching Block Formations to Pictures of Block Formations."
- You can create your own picture cards by building and taking a picture of the structure.

EXTENDING SEQUENCE PATTERNS

LEVEL: □ 1 □ 2 □ 3

S^D: Present individual with a beginning pattern (reading the pattern out loud) and distracter items, and say "Finish the pattern" or "Continue the pattern"	**Response:** Individual will continue the pattern with the appropriate items, while leaving the distracter items
Data Collection: Skill acquisition	**Target Criteria:** 80% or above for 3 consecutive days across 2 people
Materials: Colored items, common objects, pictures or figurines and reinforcement (pictures cards can be found on accompanying CD)	

Fading procedure

Maintenance Criteria: 2W = 4 consecutive scores of 100%; 1W = 4 consecutive scores of 100%; M = 3 consecutive scores of 100%	**Natural Environment (NE) Criterion:** Target has been generalized in NE across 3 novel naturally occurring activities	**Archive Criteria:** Target, maintenance and NE criteria have been met

Target list

Suggestions for targets and probe results

Suggestions for Targets: *Suggestions for extending a 2-sequence pattern:* 1,2,1,2,____; Red car, blue car, red car, ____; Girl, boy, girl, ______; Square, star, square, star,_____; Spoon, fork, spoon, fork, _____; Horse, pig, horse, pig, ______; Sock, shoe, sock, shoe, _____; Pencil, paper, pencil, paper, _____; Apple, orange, apple, orange, ______. *Suggestions for extending a 3-sequence pattern:* 2,4,6,2,4,6,______; Cup, bowl, napkin, cup, bowl, napkin,______; Circle, square, star, circle, square, star,______; Horse, pig, cat, horse, pig, cat_______; Sock, shoe, hat, sock, shoe, hat, ______; Red, yellow, green, red, yellow, green, _____; Pencil, glue, eraser, pencil, glue, eraser, ______; Apple, orange, banana, apple, orange, banana, ______; Car, boat, airplane, car, boat, airplane, ______; Happy face, sad face, angry face, happy face, sad face, angry face_______.

Probe Results (targets in repertoire):

Target	Baseline %	Date Introduced	Date Criteria Met	*Fading Procedure*		
				Maintenance	Date NE Introduced	Date Archived
2-Sequence Pattern (AB pattern)						
1. Target 1 (no distractors):						
2. Target 1 (2 distractors):						

3. Target 2 (no distractors):						
4. Target 2 (2 distractors):						
5. Targets that met criteria: random rotation						
6. Target 3 (no distractors):						
7. Target 3 (2 distractors):						
8. Target 4 (no distractors):						
9. Target 4 (2 distractors):						
10. Targets that met criteria: random rotation						
11. Target 5 (no distractors):						
12. Target 5 (2 distractors):						
13. Target 6 (no distractors):						
14. Target 6 (2 distractors):						
15. Targets that met criteria: random rotation						
16. Target 7 (no distractors):						
17. Target 7 (2 distractors):						
18. Target 8 (no distractors):						

19. Target 8 (2 distractors):						
20. Targets that met criteria: random rotation						
21. Target 9 (no distractors):						
22. Target 9 (2 distractors):						
23. Target 10 (no distractors):						
24. Target 10 (2 distractors):						
25. Targets that met criteria: random rotation						
26. Generalize to another environment Environment 1:						
27. Generalize to another environment Environment 2:						
3-Sequence Pattern (ABC Pattern)						
28. Target 1 (no distractors):						
29. Target 1 (2 distractors):						
30. Target 2 (no distractors):						
31. Target 2 (2 distractors):						
32. Targets that met criteria: random rotation						
33. Target 3 (no distractors):						

34. Target 3 (2 distractors):						
35. Target 4 (no distractors):						
36. Target 4 (2 distractors):						
37. Targets that met criteria: random rotation						
38. Target 5 (no distractors):						
39. Target 5 (2 distractors):						
40. Target 6 (no distractors):						
41. Target 6 (2 distractors):						
42. Targets that met criteria: random rotation						
43. Target 7 (no distractors):						
44. Target 7 (2 distractors):						
45. Target 8 (no distractors):						
46. Target 8 (2 distractors):						
47. Targets that met criteria: random rotation						
48. Target 9 (no distractors):						
49. Target 9 (2 distractors):						

50. Target 10 (no distractors):						
51. Target 10 (2 distractors):						
52. Targets that met criteria: random rotation						
53. Generalize to another environment Environment 1:						
54. Generalize to another environment Environment 2:						
55. Maintenance: Assess in varied environments				2W 1W M		

Specific tips for running this task analysis

- Ensure pre-requisite skills have been taught for this TA. Examples of pre-requisite skills for "Extending Sequence Patterns" are receptive and expressive labels in the first book of the Journey of Development ABA Curriculum series.
- When distractors are present, the individual should finish the next round of the pattern and leave the distractors on the table or put them in a finished container.
- Note that this TA does not follow the typical receptive schedule for the field size (teach in isolation, teach with one distractor and then teach with two distractors). This program is written without distracters (isolation) then with 2 distractors, omitting teaching one distracter. When running this TA with the individuals that we have worked with, once they learn that they don't use all the given objects, it typically does not matter how many distracters are used.
- Other pattern stems can be used to continue this program (ABB, ABCD, AAB, AABB, etc.).

MATCHING BLOCK FORMATIONS TO PICTURES OF BLOCK FORMATIONS

LEVEL: □ 1 □ 2 □ 3

S^D: Present individual with a pre-built block formation and a field of 3 pictures of a block formation and say "Match"	**Response:** Individual will respond by matching the correct picture to the block formation
Data Collection: Skill acquisition	**Target Criteria:** 80% or above for 3 consecutive days across 2 people
Materials: Blocks, pictures of block formations and reinforcement	

Fading procedure

Maintenance Criteria: 2W = 4 consecutive scores of 100%; 1W = 4 consecutive scores of 100%; M = 3 consecutive scores of 100%	**Natural Environment (NE) Criterion:** Target has been generalized in NE across 3 novel naturally occurring activities	**Archive Criteria:** Target, maintenance and NE criteria have been met

Target list

Suggestions for targets and probe results

Suggestions for Targets: Boat, pyramid, house, letters, shapes, car, happy face, flower, tree, and rudimentary animals.

Probe Results (targets in repertoire):

Target	Baseline %	Date Introduced	Date Criteria Met	*Fading Procedure*		
				Maintenance	Date NE Introduced	Date Archived
1. Target 1:						
2. Target 2:						
3. Targets 1 and 2 random rotation						
4. Target 3:						
5. Target 4:						

6. Targets that met criteria: random rotation						
7. Target 5:						
8. Target 6:						
9. Targets that met criteria: random rotation						
10. Target 7:						
11. Target 8:						
12. Targets that met criteria: random rotation						
13. Target 9:						
14. Target 10:						
15. Targets that met criteria: random rotation						
16. Generalize to another environment Environment 1:						
17. Generalize to another environment Environment 2:						
18. Maintenance: Assess in varied environments				2W 1W M		

Specific tips for running this task analysis

- Ensure pre-requisite skills have been taught for this TA. Examples of pre-requisite skills for "Matching Block Formations to Pictures of Block Formations" include mastery of matching objects to pictures (TAs found in the first book of the Journey of Development ABA Curriculum series) and mastery of imitation skills.
- This TA suggests using a field of three (FO3) pictures. If the individual struggles with this skill, you may need to drop back to using a field of one followed by a field of two before introducing field of 3.

- Consider choosing pictures that would exactly match blocks in color and shape for initial targets and then build to targets that are pictures of objects (e.g. a boat and a house with extra graphics).
- Begin by presenting the individual with the number of blocks required to complete the target. As the individual acquires skills for the program, consider adding extra pieces so the individual is matching blocks to pictures and not using the extra pieces.
- Consider using Tangram blocks (blocks of various sizes and colors that when placed together form a specific shape, and can be arranged to match particular designs) and picture cards when generalizing to different materials and pictures.

MATCHING OBJECT ASSOCIATION

LEVEL: □ 1 □ 2 □ 3

S^D: Present individual with an object or picture of an object, and a field of 1, field of 2 or field of 3 associated objects (e.g. socks/shoes and toothbrush/toothpaste). Say "Match things that go together"	**Response:** Individual will match the object or picture of the object to its partner
Data Collection: Skill acquisition	**Target Criteria:** 80% or above for 3 consecutive days across 2 people
Materials: Objects or picture cards of various objects that go together and reinforcement (picture cards can be found on accompanying CD)	

Fading procedure

Maintenance Criteria: 2W = 4 consecutive scores of 100%; 1W = 4 consecutive scores of 100%; M = 3 consecutive scores of 100%	**Natural Environment (NE) Criterion:** Target has been generalized in NE across 3 novel naturally occurring activities	**Archive Criteria:** Target, maintenance and NE criteria have been met

Target list

Suggestions for targets and probe results

Suggestions for Targets: Shoes/socks, toothbrush/toothpaste, crayon/picture, hammer/nails, dog/bone, paint/brush, coat/hat, peanut butter/jelly, paper/pencil, mother/father, lawnmower/grass, snow/snowman, chalk/chalkboard, pillow/bed, train/track, pool/raft, flowers/vase, cloud/sky, shovel/pail and ball/bat.

Probe Results (targets in repertoire):

Target	Baseline %	Date Introduced	Date Criteria Met	*Fading Procedure*		
				Maintenance	Date NE Introduced	Date Archived
1. Target 1 (isolation):						
2. Target 1 (FO2/target and distractor):						
3. Target 1 (FO3/target and 2 distractors):						
4. Target 2 (isolation):						

5. Target 2 (FO2/target and distractor):						
6. Target 2 (FO3/target and 2 distractors):						
7. Targets 1 and 2 random rotation						
8. Target 3 (isolation):						
9. Target 3 (FO2/target and distractor):						
10. Target 3 (FO3/target and 2 distractors):						
11. Target 4 (isolation):						
12. Target 4 (FO2/target and distractor):						
13. Target 4 (FO3/target and 2 distractors):						
14. Targets that met criteria: random rotation						
15. Target 5 (isolation):						
16. Target 5 (FO2/target and distractor):						
17. Target 5 (FO3/target and 2 distractors):						
18. Target 6 (isolation):						
19. Target 6 (FO2/target and distractor):						
20. Target 6 (FO3/target and 2 distractors):						

21. Targets that met criteria: random rotation						
22. Target 7 (isolation):						
23. Target 7 (FO2/target and distractor):						
24. Target 7 (FO3/target and 2 distractors):						
25. Target 8 (isolation):						
26. Target 8 (FO2/target and distractor):						
27. Target 8 (FO3/target and 2 distractors):						
28. Targets that met criteria: random rotation						
29. Target 9 (isolation):						
30. Target 9 (FO2/target and distractor):						
31. Target 9 (FO3/target and 2 distractors):						
32. Target 10 (isolation):						
33. Target 10 (FO2/target and distractor):						
34. Target 10 (FO3/target and 2 distractors):						
35. Targets that met criteria: random rotation						
36. Generalize to another environment Environment 1:						

37. Generalize to another environment Environment 2:						
38. Maintenance: Assess in varied environments				2W 1W M		

Specific tips for running this task analysis

- Ensure pre-requisite skills have been taught for this TA. Examples of pre-requisite skills for "Matching Object Association" include the matching programs offered in the first book of the Journey of Development ABA Curriculum series.
- The concept of this TA is matching, not language comprehension. So always use the same S^D such as "Match." Do NOT change the S^D by adding in the objects to match such as "Match sock to shoe" as these S^Ds require a higher level of language comprehension and they also give the answer to the individual.
- After the individual correctly matches, you can vary and individualize the social praise from "Nice matching" to "Good job matching the sock to the shoe."

MATCHING UPPERCASE TO LOWERCASE LETTERS

LEVEL: □ 1 □ 2 □ 3

S^D: Present individual with a flashcard of an uppercase letter and a FO1, FO2 or FO3 lowercase letters. Say "Match"	**Response:** Individual will match the letter to its appropriate partner
Data Collection: Skill acquisition	**Target Criteria:** 80% or above for 3 consecutive days across 2 people
Materials: Flashcards of all the letters and reinforcement (picture cards can be found on accompanying CD)	

Fading procedure

Maintenance Criteria: 2W = 4 consecutive scores of 100%; 1W = 4 consecutive scores of 100%; M = 3 consecutive scores of 100%	**Natural Environment (NE) Criterion:** Target has been generalized in NE across 3 novel naturally occurring activities	**Archive Criteria:** Target, maintenance and NE criteria have been met

Target list

Suggestions for targets and probe results

Suggestions for Targets: Letters of the alphabet.
Probe Results (targets in repertoire):

Target	**Baseline %**	**Date Introduced**	**Date Criteria Met**	***Fading Procedure***		
				Maintenance	**Date NE Introduced**	**Date Archived**
1. Target 1 (isolation):						
2. Target 1 (FO2/target and distractor):						
3. Target 1 (FO3/target and 2 distractors):						
4. Target 2 (isolation):						
5. Target 2 (FO2/target and distractor):						

6. Target 2 (FO3/target and 2 distractors):						
7. Targets 1 and 2 random rotation						
8. Target 3 (isolation):						
9. Target 3 (FO2/target and distractor):						
10. Target 3 (FO3/target and 2 distractors):						
11. Target 4 (isolation):						
12. Target 4 (FO2/target and distractor):						
13. Target 4 (FO3/target and 2 distractors):						
14. Targets that met criteria: random rotation						
15. Target 5 (isolation):						
16. Target 5 (FO2/target and distractor):						
17. Target 5 (FO3/target and 2 distractors):						
18. Target 6 (isolation):						
19. Target 6 (FO2/target and distractor):						
20. Target 6 (FO3/target and 2 distractors):						
21. Targets that met criteria: random rotation						

22. Target 7 (isolation):						
23. Target 7 (FO2/target and distractor):						
24. Target 7 (FO3/target and 2 distractors):						
25. Target 8 (isolation):						
26. Target 8 (FO2/target and distractor):						
27. Target 8 (FO3/target and 2 distractors):						
28. Targets that met criteria: random rotation						
29. Target 9 (isolation):						
30. Target 9 (FO2/target and distractor):						
31. Target 9 (FO3/target and 2 distractors):						
32. Target 10 (isolation):						
33. Target 10 (FO2/target and distractor):						
34. Target 10 (FO3/target and 2 distractors):						
35. Targets that met criteria: random rotation						
36. Target 11 (isolation):						
37. Target 11 (FO2/target and distractor):						

38. Target 11 (FO3/target and 2 distractors):						
39. Target 12 (isolation):						
40. Target 12 (FO2/target and distractor):						
41. Target 12 (FO3/target and 2 distractors):						
42. Targets that met criteria: random rotation						
43. Target 13 (isolation):						
44. Target 13 (FO2/target and distractor):						
45. Target 13 (FO3/target and 2 distractors):						
46. Target 14 (isolation):						
47. Target 14 (FO2/target and distractor):						
48. Target 14 (FO3/target and 2 distractors):						
49. Targets that met criteria: random rotation						
50. Target 15 (isolation):						
51. Target 15 (FO2/target and distractor):						
52. Target 15 (FO3/target and 2 distractors):						
53. Target 16 (isolation):						

54. Target 16 (FO2/target and distractor):						
55. Target 16 (FO3/target and 2 distractors):						
56. Targets that met criteria: random rotation						
57. Target 17 (isolation):						
58. Target 17 (FO2/target and distractor):						
59. Target 17 (FO3/target and 2 distractors):						
60. Target 18 (isolation):						
61. Target 18 (FO2/target and distractor):						
62. Target 18 (FO3/target and 2 distractors):						
63. Targets that met criteria: random rotation						
64. Target 19 (isolation):						
65. Target 19 (FO2/target and distractor):						
66. Target 19 (FO3/target and 2 distractors):						
67. Target 20 (isolation):						
68. Target 20 (FO2/target and distractor):						
69. Target 20 (FO3/target and 2 distractors):						

70. Targets that met criteria: random rotation						
71. Target 21 (isolation):						
72. Target 21 (FO2/target and distractor):						
73. Target 21 (FO3/target and 2 distractors):						
74. Target 22 (isolation):						
75. Target 22 (FO2/target and distractor):						
76. Target 22 (FO3/target and 2 distractors):						
77. Targets that met criteria: random rotation						
78. Target 23 (isolation):						
79. Target 23 (FO2/target and distractor):						
80. Target 23 (FO3/target and 2 distractors):						
81. Target 24 (isolation):						
82. Target 24 (FO2/target and distractor):						
83. Target 24 (FO3/target and 2 distractors):						
84. Targets that met criteria: random rotation						
85. Target 25 (isolation):						

86. Target 25 (FO2/target and distractor):						
87. Target 25 (FO3/target and 2 distractors):						
88. Target 26 (isolation):						
89. Target 26 (FO2/target and distractor):						
90. Target 26 (FO3/target and 2 distractors):						
91. Targets that met criteria: random rotation						
92. Generalize to another environment Environment 1:						
93. Generalize to another environment Environment 2:						
94. Maintenance: Assess in varied environments				2W 1W M		

Specific tips for running this task analysis

- Ensure pre-requisite skills have been taught for this TA. Examples of pre-requisite skills for "Matching Uppercase to Lowercase Letters" include mastering the matching programs in the first book of the Journey of Development ABA Curriculum series.
- You may not need to run all the targets on this TA. If a target is in repertoire at the probe, then it does not need to be taught and several of the target areas on this TA can be crossed out.

MATCHING LOWERCASE TO UPPERCASE LETTERS

LEVEL: □ 1 □ 2 □ 3

S^D: Present individual with a flashcard of a lowercase letter and a FO1, FO2 or FO3 uppercase letters. Say "Match"	**Response:** Individual will match the letter to its appropriate partner
Data Collection: Skill acquisition	**Target Criteria:** 80% or above for 3 consecutive days across 2 people
Materials: Flashcards of all the letters and reinforcement (picture cards can be found on accompanying CD)	

Fading procedure

Maintenance Criteria: 2W = 4 consecutive scores of 100%; 1W = 4 consecutive scores of 100%; M = 3 consecutive scores of 100%	**Natural Environment (NE) Criterion:** Target has been generalized in NE across 3 novel naturally occurring activities	**Archive Criteria:** Target, maintenance and NE criteria have been met

Target list

Suggestions for targets and probe results

Suggestions for Targets: Letters of the alphabet.
Probe Results (targets in repertoire):

Target	Baseline %	Date Introduced	Date Criteria Met	*Fading Procedure*		
				Maintenance	Date NE Introduced	Date Archived
1. Target 1 (isolation):						
2. Target 1 (FO2/target and distractor):						
3. Target 1 (FO3/target and 2 distractors):						
4. Target 2 (isolation):						
5. Target 2 (FO2/target and distractor):						

6. Target 2 (FO3/target and 2 distractors):						
7. Targets 1 and 2 random rotation						
8. Target 3 (isolation):						
9. Target 3 (FO2/target and distractor):						
10. Target 3 (FO3/target and 2 distractors):						
11. Target 4 (isolation):						
12. Target 4 (FO2/target and distractor):						
13. Target 4 (FO3/target and 2 distractors):						
14. Targets that met criteria: random rotation						
15. Target 5 (isolation):						
16. Target 5 (FO2/target and distractor):						
17. Target 5 (FO3/target and 2 distractors):						
18. Target 6 (isolation):						
19. Target 6 (FO2/target and distractor):						
20. Target 6 (FO3/target and 2 distractors):						
21. Targets that met criteria: random rotation						

22. Target 7 (isolation):						
23. Target 7 (FO2/target and distractor):						
24. Target 7 (FO3/target and 2 distractors):						
25. Target 8 (isolation):						
26. Target 8 (FO2/target and distractor):						
27. Target 8 (FO3/target and 2 distractors):						
28. Targets that met criteria: random rotation						
29. Target 9 (isolation):						
30. Target 9 (FO2/target and distractor):						
31. Target 9 (FO3/target and 2 distractors):						
32. Target 10 (isolation):						
33. Target 10 (FO2/target and distractor):						
34. Target 10 (FO3/target and 2 distractors):						
35. Targets that met criteria: random rotation						
36. Target 11 (isolation):						
37. Target 11 (FO2/target and distractor):						

38. Target 11 (FO3/target and 2 distractors):						
39. Target 12 (isolation):						
40. Target 12 (FO2/target and distractor):						
41. Target 12 (FO3/target and 2 distractors):						
42. Targets that met criteria: random rotation						
43. Target 13 (isolation):						
44. Target 13 (FO2/target and distractor):						
45. Target 13 (FO3/target and 2 distractors):						
46. Target 14 (isolation):						
47. Target 14 (FO2/target and distractor):						
48. Target 14 (FO3/target and 2 distractors):						
49. Targets that met criteria: random rotation						
50. Target 15 (isolation):						
51. Target 15 (FO2/target and distractor):						
52. Target 15 (FO3/target and 2 distractors)						
53. Target 16 (isolation):						

54. Target 16 (FO2/target and distractor):						
55. Target 16 (FO3/target and 2 distractors):						
56. Targets that met criteria: random rotation						
57. Target 17 (isolation):						
58. Target 17 (FO2/target and distractor):						
59. Target 17 (FO3/target and 2 distractors):						
60. Target 18 (isolation):						
61. Target 18 (FO2/target and distractor):						
62. Target 18 (FO3/target and 2 distractors):						
63. Targets that met criteria: random rotation						
64. Target 19 (isolation):						
65. Target 19 (FO2/target and distractor):						
66. Target 19 (FO3/target and 2 distractors):						
67. Target 20 (isolation):						
68. Target 20 (FO2/target and distractor):						
69. Target 20 (FO3/target and 2 distractors):						

70. Targets that met criteria: random rotation						
71. Target 21 (isolation):						
72. Target 21 (FO2/target and distractor):						
73. Target 21 (FO3/target and 2 distractors):						
74. Target 22 (isolation):						
75. Target 22 (FO2/target and distractor):						
76. Target 22 (FO3/target and 2 distractors):						
77. Targets that met criteria: random rotation						
78. Target 23 (isolation):						
79. Target 23 (FO2/target and distractor):						
80. Target 23 (FO3/target and 2 distractors):						
81. Target 24 (isolation):						
82. Target 24 (FO2/target and distractor):						
83. Target 24 (FO3/target and 2 distractors):						
84. Targets that met criteria: random rotation						
85. Target 25 (isolation):						

86. Target 25 (FO2/target and distractor):						
87. Target 25 (FO3/target and 2 distractors):						
88. Target 26 (isolation):						
89. Target 26 (FO2/target and distractor):						
90. Target 26 (FO3/target and 2 distractors):						
91. Targets that met criteria: random rotation						
92. Generalize to another environment Environment 1:						
93. Generalize to another environment Environment 2:						
94. Maintenance: Assess in varied environments				2W 1W M		

Specific tips for running this task analysis

- Ensure pre-requisite skills have been taught for this TA. Examples of pre-requisite skills for "Matching Lowercase to Uppercase Letters" include mastering the matching programs in the first book of the Journey of Development ABA Curriculum series.
- You may not need to run all the targets on this TA. If a target is in repertoire at the probe, then it does not need to be taught and several of the target areas on this TA can be cross out.

MAZES

LEVEL: □ 1 □ 2 □ 3

S^D: Present individual with a maze and say "Complete the maze"	**Response:** Individual will respond by completing the maze
Data Collection: Prompt data (number and type of prompts used)	**Target Criterion:** 0 prompts for 3 consecutive days across 2 people
Materials: Mazes, writing utensil and reinforcement	

Fading procedure

Maintenance Criteria: 2W = 4 consecutive scores of 0 prompts; 1W = 4 consecutive scores of 0 prompts; M = 3 consecutive scores of 0 prompts	**Natural Environment (NE) Criterion:** Target has been generalized in NE across 3 novel naturally occurring activities	**Archive Criteria:** Target, maintenance and NE criteria have been met

Target list

Target	Baseline: Number and Type of Prompts	Date Introduced	Date Criteria Met	*Fading Procedure*		
				Maintenance	Date NE Introduced	Date Archived
1. Completes maze with 1 path choice.						
2. Completes maze with 2 path choices.						
3. Completes maze with 3 path choices.						
4. Generalize to another environment Environment 1:						
5. Generalize to another environment Environment 2:						
6. Maintenance: Assess in varied environments				2W 1W M		

Specific tips for running this task analysis

- Ensure pre-requisite skills have been taught for this TA. Examples of pre-requisite skills for "Mazes" include progress toward mastering one-step instructions and pre-handwriting skills (both TAs found in the first book of the Journey of Development ABA Curriculum series).
- It is not necessary for the individual to stay completely within the lines of the maze, but basically to understand and figure out how to complete the maze. To help the individual become better at staying in lines, one strategy to consider is drawing mazes to be completed that have about a half-inch border. As the individual becomes more proficient at staying in the lines, slowly decrease the width of the border.
- You may want to consider changing the verbal S^D depending on your goals and other programs the individual is involved in. For example, if the individual attends school and the teacher often gives worksheets to complete with a S^D "Do your worksheet," then you may want to change the S^D for this program to be the same as what the teacher says as this will better aid in generalization to other materials.

PUZZLES (SQUARE BORDER AND JIGSAW)

LEVEL: □ 1 □ 2 □ 3

S^D: Present individual with a puzzle and say "Build puzzle"	**Response:** Individual will build the puzzle
Data Collection: Prompt data (number and type of prompts used)	**Target criteria:** 0 prompts for 3 consecutive days across 2 people
Materials: Multiple board puzzles, floor puzzles of varying sizes, jigsaw puzzles and reinforcement	

Fading procedure

Maintenance Criteria: 2W = 4 consecutive scores of 0 prompts; 1W = 4 consecutive scores of 0 prompts; M = 3 consecutive scores of 0 prompts	**Natural Environment (NE) Criterion:** Target has been generalized in NE across 3 novel naturally occurring activities	**Archive Criteria:** Target, maintenance and NE criteria have been met

Target list

Suggestions for targets and probe results

Suggestions for Targets: Puzzles with square border—these are puzzles that have interlocking pieces and fit into a frame. Jigsaw puzzles—these are puzzles with interlocking pieces that do not have a frame (these can include floor puzzles).
Probe Results (targets in repertoire):

Target	Baseline: Number and Type of Prompts	Date Introduced	Date Criteria Met	*Fading Procedure*		
				Maintenance	Date NE Introduced	Date Archived
1. Completes 3–9 piece puzzle with square edged frame.						
2. Completes 10–19 piece puzzle with square edged frame.						
3. Completes 20+ piece puzzle with square edged frame.						
4. Generalize to another environment Environment 1:						

5. Generalize to another environment Environment 2:						
6. Maintenance: Assess in varied environments				2W 1W M		
7. Completes 3–9 piece jigsaw puzzle.						
8. Completes 10–19 piece jigsaw puzzle.						
9. Completes 20+ piece jigsaw puzzle.						
10. Generalize to another environment Environment 1:						
11. Generalize to another environment Environment 2:						
12. Maintenance: Assess in varied environments				2W 1W M		

Specific tips for running this task analysis

- Ensure pre-requisite skills have been taught for this TA. Examples of pre-requisite skills for “Puzzles (Square Border and Jigsaw)” include progress toward mastering one-step instructions, mastering the matching programs, and mastering inset puzzles (all TAs located in the first book of the Journey of Development ABA Curriculum series).
- For individuals who struggle with this program, you may want to consider using a backward chaining teaching procedure whereby you present the first 3–9 piece square edged frame puzzle with all the pieces but one already inserted in the puzzle. Give your S^D and prompt placing the final piece into puzzle. Fade your prompts over time until the individual can independently place the final piece into puzzle. Then you present the same 3–9 piece square edged frame puzzle with all but two pieces already inserted into the puzzle and prompt the individual to place two pieces into the frame. When this is mastered, you continue in this fashion with requiring the individual to put in three pieces, then four, etc. until the individual completes the entire puzzle on their own.
- It is helpful to teach the individual how to empty the puzzle and rebuild it. Thus, once the individual completes the puzzle, give the S^D “Empty” and prompt the individual to turn over the puzzle and empty the pieces. Run the program again where the individual must build the puzzle; remember to fade your prompts each time.
- To increase the individual’s motivation, use puzzles that have pictures of favorite cartoon animals or characters.
- Jigsaw puzzles are the most difficult; use the puzzle box to provide a visual aid to the individual for help in building the puzzle. Utilize their matching skills to match puzzle pieces to those on box and match where it goes on table.

SORTING OBJECTS BY FEATURE

LEVEL: □ 1 □ 2 □ 3

S^D: Present individual with a FO2 objects representing different features; give individual a group of objects to be sorted and say "Sort by [feature]" (e.g. "Sort by weight")	**Response:** Individual will sort the objects into the correct piles
Data Collection: Prompt data (number and type of prompts used)	**Target Criterion:** 0 prompts for 3 consecutive days across 2 people
Materials: Objects to sort, containers and reinforcement	

Fading procedure

Maintenance Criteria: 2W = 4 consecutive scores of 0 prompts; 1W = 4 consecutive scores of 0 prompts; M = 3 consecutive scores of 0 prompts	**Natural Environment (NE) Criterion:** Target has been generalized in NE across 3 novel naturally occurring activities	**Archive Criteria:** Target, maintenance and NE criteria have been met

Target list

Suggestions for targets and probe results

Suggestions for Targets: Different features: color, number (buttons with different number holes, dice, dominoes), shape, texture (objects that are smooth, rough, shiny, dull), size (tall, short, thin, wide, thick), and weight (lightweight such as feathers or cotton balls and heavyweight such as paperweights or batteries).
Probe Results (targets in repertoire):

Target	Baseline: Number and Type of Prompts	Date Introduced	Date Criteria Met	*Fading Procedure*		
				Maintenance	Date NE Introduced	Date Archived
1. Target 1 and 2 (give 3 of each feature to be sorted):						
2. Target 1 and 2 (give 5 of each feature to be sorted):						
3. Target 1 and 2 (give 10 of each feature to be sorted):						

4. Target 3 and 4 (give 3 of each feature to be sorted):						
5. Target 3 and 4 (give 5 of each feature to be sorted):						
6. Target 3 and 4 (give 10 of each feature to be sorted):						
7. Targets that met criteria: random rotation						
8. Target 5 and 6 (give 3 of each feature to be sorted):						
9. Target 5 and 6 (give 5 of each feature to be sorted):						
10. Target 5 and 6 (give 10 of each feature to be sorted):						
11. Targets that met criteria: random rotation						
12. Target 7 and 8 (give 3 of each feature to be sorted):						
13. Target 7 and 8 (give 5 of each feature to be sorted):						
14. Target 7 and 8 (give 10 of each feature to be sorted):						
15. Targets that met criteria: random rotation						
16. Target 9 and 10 (give 3 of each feature to be sorted):						
17. Target 9 and 10 (give 5 of each feature to be sorted):						
18. Target 9 and 10 (give 10 of each feature to be sorted):						
19. Targets that met criteria: random rotation						

20. Targets that met criteria: – FO4, give 10 of each feature to be sorted						
21. Generalize to another environment Environment 1:						
22. Generalize to another environment Environment 2:						
23. Maintenance: Assess in varied environments				2W 1W M		

Specific tips for running this task analysis

- Ensure pre-requisite skills have been taught for this TA. Examples of pre-requisite skills for "Sorting Objects by Feature" include mastering the attending skills program, imitation programs, matching programs, sorting programs, and receptive labels of functions (all TAs found in the first book of the Journey of Development ABA Curriculum series).
- If the individual sorts an object incorrectly, immediately take the incorrect sorted object out of the pile, place it back in the pile and prompt the correct pile for sorting. Do NOT wait until the end of the sorting all the objects to correct and prompt individual.
- When working on any sorting program, it is recommended that you teach the individual to sort objects/pictures in this order: (A) sort identical objects and pictures, (B) sort similar objects and pictures, (C) sort objects/pictures based on attributes or features, (D) sort by groups/categories and (E) sort based on function. When you are sorting objects and pictures, it is less difficult to sort objects (so start with this) and then move on to pictures.

SORTING PICTURES BY FEATURE

LEVEL: □ 1 □ 2 □ 3

S^D: Present individual with a FO2 pictures representing different features; give individual a pile of pictures to be sorted and say "Sort by [feature]" (e.g. "Sort by weight")	**Response:** Individual will sort the pictures into the correct piles
Data Collection: Prompt data (number and type of prompts used)	**Target Criterion:** 0 prompts for 3 consecutive days across 2 people
Materials: Pictures to sort and reinforcement (picture cards can be found on accompanying CD)	

Fading procedure

Maintenance Criteria: 2W = 4 consecutive scores of 0 prompts; 1W = 4 consecutive scores of 0 prompts; M = 3 consecutive scores of 0 prompts	**Natural Environment (NE) Criterion:** Target has been generalized in NE across 3 novel naturally occurring activities	**Archive Criteria:** Target, maintenance and NE criteria have been met

Target list

Suggestions for targets and probe results

Suggestions for Targets: Pictures representing different features: color, number, shape, texture (pictures of objects that are smooth, rough, shiny, dull), size (tall, short, thin, wide, thick), and weight (pictures of lightweight objects such as feathers or cotton balls and heavyweight objects such as paperweights or batteries).
Probe Results (targets in repertoire):

Target	Baseline: Number and Type of Prompts	Date Introduced	Date Criteria Met	*Fading Procedure*		
				Maintenance	Date NE Introduced	Date Archived
1. Target 1 and 2 (give 3 of each feature to be sorted):						
2. Target 1 and 2 (give 5 of each feature to be sorted):						
3. Target 1 and 2 (give 10 of each feature to be sorted):						

4. Target 3 and 4 (give 3 of each feature to be sorted):						
5. Target 3 and 4 (give 5 of each feature to be sorted):						
6. Target 3 and 4 (give 10 of each feature to be sorted):						
7. Targets that met criteria: random rotation						
8. Target 5 and 6 (give 3 of each feature to be sorted):						
9. Target 5 and 6 (give 5 of each feature to be sorted):						
10. Target 5 and 6 (give 10 of each feature to be sorted):						
11. Targets that met criteria: random rotation						
12. Target 7 and 8 (give 3 of each feature to be sorted):						
13. Target 7 and 8 (give 5 of each feature to be sorted):						
14. Target 7 and 8 (give 10 of each feature to be sorted):						
15. Targets that met criteria: random rotation						
16. Target 9 and 10 (give 3 of each feature to be sorted):						
17. Target 9 and 10 (give 5 of each feature to be sorted):						
18. Target 9 and 10 (give 10 of each feature to be sorted):						
19. Targets that met criteria: random rotation						

20. Targets that met criteria: – FO4, give 10 of each feature to be sorted:						
21. Generalize to another environment Environment 1:						
22. Generalize to another environment Environment 2:						
23. Maintenance: Assess in varied environments				2W 1W M		

Specific tips for running this task analysis

- Ensure pre-requisite skills have been taught for this TA. Examples of pre-requisite skills for "Sorting Pictures by Feature" include mastering the attending skills programs, imitation programs, matching programs, sorting programs, and receptive labels of functions (all TAs found in the first book of the Journey of Development ABA Curriculum series) and Sorting Objects by Features (TA can be found in this book).
- If the individual sorts a picture incorrectly, immediately take the incorrect sorted picture out of the pile, place it back in the pile and prompt the correct pile for sorting. Do NOT wait until the end of the sorting all the pictures to correct and prompt individual.
- When working on any sorting program, it is recommended that you teach the individual to sort objects/pictures in this order: (A) sort identical objects and pictures, (B) sort similar objects and pictures, (C) sort objects/pictures based on attributes or features, (D) sort by groups/categories and (E) sort based on function. When you are sorting objects and pictures, it is less difficult to sort objects (so start with this) and then move on to pictures.

SORTING OBJECTS BY FUNCTION

LEVEL: □ 1 □ 2 □ 3

S^D: Present individual with a FO2 objects representing different functions; give individual a group of objects to be sorted and say "Sort [function] and sort [function]" (e.g. "Sort things that fly and sort things you eat")	**Response:** Individual will sort the objects into the correct piles
Data Collection: Prompt data (number and type of prompts used)	**Target Criterion:** 0 prompts for 3 consecutive days across 2 people
Materials: Objects to sort, containers and reinforcement (pictures cards can be found on accompanying CD)	

Fading procedure

Maintenance Criteria: 2W = 4 consecutive scores of 0 prompts; 1W = 4 consecutive scores of 0 prompts; M = 3 consecutive scores of 0 prompts	**Natural Environment (NE) Criterion:** Target has been generalized in NE across 3 novel naturally occurring activities	**Archive Criteria:** Target, maintenance and NE criteria have been met

Target list

Suggestions for targets and probe results

Suggestions for Targets: Things you write with (chalk, pencil, pen, marker, crayon), things you blow (bubbles, candles, horn, noise maker, balloon), things you wear (baby doll clothing items), things you eat (pretend food), things you drink (pretend drinks), things that fly (miniatures objects of birds, airplane, helicopter, kite, hot air balloons), things you ride (miniature horse, bike, motorcycle, scooter, train, roller coaster), things you lick (lollipop, ice cream), things you play with (various toys) and things that make noise (telephone, noisemaker, radio).
Probe Results (targets in repertoire):

Target	Baseline: Number and Type of Prompts	Date Introduced	Date Criteria Met	*Fading Procedure*		
				Maintenance	Date NE Introduced	Date Archived
1. Target 1 and 2 (give 3 of each function to be sorted):						
2. Target 1 and 2 (give 5 of each function to be sorted):						

3. Target 1 and 2 (give 10 of each function to be sorted):						
4. Target 3 and 4 (give 3 of each function to be sorted):						
5. Target 3 and 4 (give 5 of each function to be sorted):						
6. Target 3 and 4 (give 10 of each function to be sorted):						
7. Targets that met criteria: random rotation						
8. Target 5 and 6 (give 3 of each function to be sorted):						
9. Target 5 and 6 (give 5 of each function to be sorted):						
10. Target 5 and 6 (give 10 of each function to be sorted):						
11. Targets that met criteria: random rotation						
12. Target 7 and 8 (give 3 of each function to be sorted):						
13. Target 7 and 8 (give 5 of each function to be sorted):						
14. Target 7 and 8 (give 10 of each function to be sorted):						
15. Targets that met criteria: random rotation						
16. Target 9 and 10 (give 3 of each function to be sorted):						
17. Target 9 and 10 (give 5 of each function to be sorted):						
18. Target 9 and 10 (give 10 of each function to be sorted):						

19. Targets that met criteria: random rotation						
20. Targets that met criteria: – FO4, give 10 of each function to be sorted						
21. Generalize to another environment Environment 1:						
22. Generalize to another environment Environment 2:						
23. Maintenance: Assess in varied environments				2W 1W M		

Specific tips for running this task analysis

- Ensure pre-requisite skills have been taught for this TA. Examples of pre-requisite skills for "Sorting Objects by Function" include mastering the attending skills program, imitation programs, matching programs, sorting programs, and receptive labels of functions (all TAs found in the first book of the Journey of Development ABA Curriculum series).
- If the individual sorts an object incorrectly, immediately take the incorrect sorted object out of the pile, place back in pile and prompt correct pile for sorting. Do NOT wait until the end of the sorting all the objects to correct and prompt individual.
- When working on any sorting program, it is recommended that you teach the individual to sort objects/pictures in this order: (A) sort identical objects and pictures, (B) sort similar objects and pictures, (C) sort objects/pictures based on attributes, (D) sort by groups/categories and (E) sort based on function. When you are sorting objects and pictures, it is less difficult to sort objects (so start with this) and then move onto pictures.

SORTING PICTURES BY FUNCTION

LEVEL: □ 1 □ 2 □ 3

S^D: Present individual with a FO2 pictures representing different functions; give individual a pile of pictures to be sorted and say "Sort [function] and sort [function]" (e.g. "Sort things that fly and sort things you eat")	**Response:** Individual will sort the pictures into the correct piles
Data Collection: Prompt data (number and type of prompts used)	**Target Criterion:** 0 prompts for 3 consecutive days across 2 people
Materials: Pictures to sort and reinforcement (picture cards can be found on accompanying CD)	

Fading procedure

Maintenance Criteria: 2W = 4 consecutive scores of 0 prompts; 1W = 4 consecutive scores of 0 prompts; M = 3 consecutive scores of 0 prompts	**Natural Environment (NE) Criterion:** Target has been generalized in NE across 3 novel naturally occurring activities	**Archive Criteria:** Target, maintenance and NE criteria have been met

Target list

Suggestions for targets and probe results

Suggestions for Targets: Things you write with (chalk, pencil, pen, marker, crayon), things you blow (bubbles, candles, horn, noise maker, balloon), things you wear, things you eat, things you drink, things that fly (birds, airplane, helicopter, kite, hot air balloon), things that live in the zoo, things you ride (horse, bike, motorcycle, scooter, train, roller coaster), things that are in the sky (clouds, sun, moon, stars, birds) and things that are round (ball, pumpkin, tomato, orange, meatball, earth).
Probe Results (targets in repertoire):

Target	Baseline: Number and Type of Prompts	Date Introduced	Date Criteria Met	*Fading Procedure*		
				Maintenance	Date NE Introduced	Date Archived
1. Target 1 and 2 (give 3 of each function to be sorted):						
2. Target 1 and 2 (give 5 of each function to be sorted):						
3. Target 1 and 2 (give 10 of each function to be sorted):						

4. Target 3 and 4 (give 3 of each function to be sorted):						
5. Target 3 and 4 (give 5 of each function to be sorted):						
6. Target 3 and 4 (give 10 of each function to be sorted):						
7. Targets that met criteria: random rotation						
8. Target 5 and 6 (give 3 of each function to be sorted):						
9. Target 5 and 6 (give 5 of each function to be sorted):						
10. Target 5 and 6 (give 10 of each function to be sorted):						
11. Targets that met criteria: random rotation						
12. Target 7 and 8 (give 3 of each function to be sorted):						
13. Target 7 and 8 (give 5 of each function to be sorted):						
14. Target 7 and 8 (give 10 of each function to be sorted):						
15. Targets that met criteria: random rotation						
16. Target 9 and 10 (give 3 of each function to be sorted):						
17. Target 9 and 10 (give 5 of each function to be sorted):						
18. Target 9 and 10 (give 10 of each function to be sorted):						
19. Targets that met criteria: random rotation						

20. Targets that met criteria: – FO4, give 10 of each function to be sorted						
21. Generalize to another environment Environment 1:						
22. Generalize to another environment Environment 2:						
23. Maintenance: Assess in varied environments				2W 1W M		

Specific tips for running this task analysis

- Ensure pre-requisite skills have been taught for this TA. Examples of pre-requisite skills for "Sorting Pictures by Function" include mastering the attending skills program, imitation programs, matching programs, sorting programs, receptive labels of functions (all TAs found in the first book of the Journey of Development ABA Curriculum series) and sorting objects by function.
- If the individual sorts a picture incorrectly, immediately take the incorrect sorted picture out of the pile, place it back in the pile and prompt the correct pile for sorting. Do NOT wait until the end of the sorting all the pictures to correct and prompt individual.
- When working on any sorting program, it is recommended that you teach the individual to sort objects/pictures in this order: (A) sort identical objects and pictures, (B) sort similar objects and pictures, (C) sort objects/pictures based on attributes, (D) sort by groups/categories and (E) sort based on function. When you are sorting objects and pictures, it is less difficult to sort objects (so start with this) and then move on to pictures.

WHAT DOESN'T BELONG?

LEVEL: □ 1 □ 2 □ 3

S^D: Present 2 or 3 pictures that belong together with one picture that doesn't belong and say "What doesn't belong?"	**Response:** Individual will either say or point to the item that doesn't belong
Data Collection: Skill acquisition	**Target Criteria:** 80% or above for 3 consecutive days across 2 people
Materials: Pictures of things that belong and don't belong and reinforcement (picture cards can be found on accompanying CD)	

Fading procedure

Maintenance Criteria: 2W = 4 consecutive scores of 100%; 1W = 4 consecutive scores of 100%; M = 3 consecutive scores of 100%	**Natural Environment (NE) Criterion:** Target has been generalized in NE across 3 novel naturally occurring activities	**Archive Criteria:** Target, maintenance and NE criteria have been met

Target list

Suggestions for targets and probe results

Suggestions for Targets: Animals, clothes, vehicles, furniture, toys, food, drinks, school supplies, things that fly, types of trees, etc.
Probe Results (targets in repertoire):

Target	Baseline %	Date Introduced	Date Criteria Met	*Fading Procedure*		
				Maintenance	Date NE Introduced	Date Archived
1. Target 1 (FO3/target and 2 things that go together):						
2. Target 1 (FO 4/target and 3 things go together):						
3. Target 2 (FO3/ target and 2 things that go together):						
4. Target 2 (FO 4/target and 3 things that go together):						
5. Targets 1 and 2 random rotation						

6. Target 3 (FO3/target and 2 things that go together):						
7. Target 3 (FO 4/target and 3 things go together):						
8. Target 4 (FO3/ target and 2 things that go together):						
9. Target 4 (FO 4/target and 3 things that go together):						
10. Targets that met criteria: random rotation						
11. Target 5 (FO3/target and 2 things that go together):						
12. Target 5 (FO 4/target and 3 things that go together):						
13. Target 6 (FO3/ target and 2 things that go together):						
14. Target 6 (FO 4/target and 3 things that go together):						
15. Targets that met criteria: random rotation						
16. Target 7 (FO3/target and 2 things that go together):						
17. Target 7 (FO 4/target and 3 things go together):						
18. Target 8 (FO3/ target and 2 things that go together):						
19. Target 8 (FO 4/target and 3 things that go together):						
20. Targets that met criteria: random rotation						
21. Target 9 (FO3/target and 2 things that go together):						

22. Target 9 (FO 4/target and 3 things go together):						
23. Target 10 (FO3/target and 2 things that go together):						
24. Target 10 (FO 4/target and 3 things that go together):						
25. Targets that met criteria: random rotation						
26. Generalize to another environment Environment 1:						
27. Generalize to another environment Environment 2:						
28. Maintenance: Assess in varied environments				2W 1W M		

Specific tips for running this task analysis

- Ensure pre-requisite skills have been taught for this TA. Examples of pre-requisite skills for "What Doesn't Belong?" include expressive or receptive identification of items that do not belong.
- Begin teaching what doesn't belong with two similar items and one very different item (e.g. a row boat, a yacht and a cat); as the individual acquires the skills to differentiate between what belongs and what doesn't belong, consider differentiating with function, feature and class (e.g. a car, a truck and scooter; a dog, a cat and a fish; scissors, paper and cake).

Chapter 12

TASK ANALYSES FOR RECEPTIVE LANGUAGE SKILLS

- Discriminating Sounds
- Making a Choice
- Past Tense Verbs
- Irregular Past Tense Verbs
- Plurals
- Irregular Plurals
- Pronouns (He/She)
- Pronouns (His/Her)
- Pronouns (I/You)
- Pronouns (My/Your)
- Pronouns (Their/Our)
- Pronouns (We/They)
- Receptive Instructions Delivered in a Group
- Receptive Instructions (Two-Step)
- Receptive Labels of Attributes
- Receptive Labels of Categories
- Receptive Labels of Community Helpers
- Receptive Labels of Emotions
- Receptive Labels of Function of Body Parts
- Receptive Labels of Function of Objects
- Receptive Labels of Gender
- Receptive Labels of Rooms and Objects in a Room

DISCRIMINATING SOUNDS

LEVEL: □ 1 □ 2 □ 3

S^D: Present individual with a field of 1, 2 or 3 pictures of objects representing different sounds. Say "Touch/Give me/Point to the sound you hear" and then play a sound	**Response:** Individual will touch, give or point to picture representing the sound
Data Collection: Skill acquisition	**Target Criteria:** 80% or above for 3 consecutive days across 2 people
Materials: Picture cards of various objects that make sounds and reinforcement (picture cards can be found on accompanying CD)	

Fading procedure

Maintenance Criteria: 2W = 4 consecutive scores of 100%; 1W = 4 consecutive scores of 100%; M = 3 consecutive scores of 100%	**Natural Environment (NE) Criterion:** Target has been generalized in NE across 3 novel naturally occurring activities	**Archive Criteria:** Target, maintenance and NE criteria have been met

Target list

Suggestions for targets and probe results

Suggestions for Targets: Bell, police car, beach, lightning, hammer, baby crying, person sneezing, ice-cream man, train, phone ringing, morning alarm, bird chirping, fan, running water, waterfall and dog barking.

Probe Results (targets in repertoire):

Target	Baseline %	Date Introduced	Date Criteria Met	*Fading Procedure*		
				Maintenance	**Date NE Introduced**	**Date Archived**
1. Target 1 (isolation):						
2. Target 1 (FO2/target and distractor):						
3. Target 1 (FO3/target and 2 distractors):						
4. Target 2 (isolation):						

5. Target 2 (FO2/target and distractor):						
6. Target 2 (FO3/target and 2 distractors):						
7. Targets 1 and 2 random rotation						
8. Target 3 (isolation):						
9. Target 3 (FO2/target and distractor):						
10. Target 3 (FO3/target and 2 distractors):						
11. Target 4 (isolation):						
12. Target 4 (FO2/target and distractor):						
13. Target 4 (FO3/target and 2 distractors):						
14. Targets that met criteria: random rotation						
15. Target 5 (isolation):						
16. Target 5 (FO2/target and distractor):						
17. Target 5 (FO3/target and 2 distractors):						
18. Target 6 (isolation):						
19. Target 6 (FO2/target and distractor):						
20. Target 6 (FO3/target and 2 distractors):						

21. Targets that met criteria: random rotation						
22. Target 7 (isolation):						
23. Target 7 (FO2/target and distractor):						
24. Target 7 (FO3/target and 2 distractors):						
25. Target 8 (isolation):						
26. Target 8 (FO2/target and distractor):						
27. Target 8 (FO3/target and 2 distractors):						
28. Targets that met criteria: random rotation						
29. Target 9 (isolation):						
30. Target 9 (FO2/target and distractor):						
31. Target 9 (FO3/target and 2 distractors):						
32. Target 10 (isolation):						
33. Target 10 (FO2/target and distractor):						
34. Target 10 (FO3/target and 2 distractors):						
35. Targets that met criteria: random rotation						
36. Generalize to another environment Environment 1:						

37. Generalize to another environment Environment 2:						
38. Maintenance: Assess in varied environments				2W 1W M		

Specific tips for running this task analysis

- Ensure pre-requisite skills have been taught for this TA. Examples of pre-requisite skills for "Discriminating sounds" include appropriate sitting and receptive labels of the objects which you are pairing with a sound.

MAKING A CHOICE

LEVEL: □ 1 □ 2 □ 3

S^D: Present 2 or 3 objects or pictures of objects and say "What do you want?" or "Which one do you want?"	**Response:** Individual will point and/or label the item they want, and engage with that item
Data Collection: Skill acquisition	**Target Criteria:** 80% or above for 3 consecutive days across 2 people
Materials: Preferred and non-preferred objects/pictures of objects and reinforcement	

Fading procedure

Maintenance Criteria: 2W = 4 consecutive scores of 100%; 1W = 4 consecutive scores of 100%; M = 3 consecutive scores of 100%	**Natural Environment (NE) Criterion:** Target has been generalized in NE across 3 novel naturally occurring activities	**Archive Criteria:** Target, maintenance and NE criteria have been met

Target list

Suggestions for targets and probe results

Suggestions for Targets: Chooses reinforcement, chooses which toy to play with, chooses which snack they want, and chooses which drink they want.
Probe Results (targets in repertoire):

Target	Baseline %	Date introduced	Date Criteria Met	*Fading Procedure*		
				Maintenance	**Date NE Introduced**	**Date Archived**
1. Target 1: FO2: Preferred vs. non-preferred object.						
2. Target 2: FO3: Preferred vs. two non-preferred objects.						
3. Target 3: FO3: Any combination of preferred and non-preferred objects.						
4. Targets that met criteria: random rotation						
5. Target 4: FO2: Preferred vs. non-preferred picture.						

6. Target 5: FO3: Preferred vs. two non-preferred pictures.						
7. Target 3: FO3: Any combination of preferred and non-preferred pictures.						
8. Targets that met criteria: random rotation						
9. Generalize to another environment Environment 1:						
10. Generalize to another environment Environment 2:						
11. Maintenance: Assess in varied environments				2W 1W M		

Specific tips for running this task analysis

- Ensure pre-requisite skills have been taught for this TA. Examples of pre-requisite skills for "Making a Choice" include mastering matching identical picture to object, matching non-identical picture to object, following simple directions and receptive or expressive labels of the objects or pictures presented (all TAs found in the first book of the Journey of Development ABA Curriculum series).
- You can generalize the presentation to a reinforcement board that coincides with the individual's token board or "first then" board.
- If the individual is nonverbal, accept the answer to be in the form of augmentative and alternative communication such as sign language, gestural language, written response, PECS (Bondy and Frost 2002) or a communication device.

PAST TENSE VERBS

LEVEL: □ 1 □ 2 □ 3

S^D: Present individual with a field of 1, 2 or 3 picture cards depicting an action. Say "Touch [present tense or past tense]" (e.g. "Touch jump" vs. "Touch jumped")	**Response:** Individual will touch the specified action
Data Collection: Skill acquisition	**Target Criteria:** 80% or above for 3 consecutive days across 2 people
Materials: Picture cards of actions and reinforcement (picture cards can be found on accompanying CD)	

Fading procedure

Maintenance Criteria: 2W = 4 consecutive scores of 100%; 1W = 4 consecutive scores of 100%; M = 3 consecutive scores of 100%	**Natural Environment (NE) Criterion:** Target has been generalized in NE across 3 novel naturally occurring activities	**Archive Criteria:** Target, maintenance and NE criteria have been met

Target list

Suggestions for targets and probe result

Suggestions for Targets: Color/colored, pour/poured, walk/walked, jump/jumped, paint/painted, play/played, help/helped, talk/talked, clap/clapped and brush/brushed.

Probe Results (targets in repertoire):

Target	Baseline %	Date Introduced	Date Criteria Met	*Fading Procedure*		
				Maintenance	Date NE Introduced	Date Archived
1. Target 1 (isolation):						
2. Target 1 (FO2/target and distractor):						
3. Target 1 (FO3/target and 2 distractors):						
4. Target 2 (isolation):						

5. Target 2 (FO2/target and distractor):						
6. Target 2 (FO3/target and 2 distractors):						
7. Targets 1 and 2 random rotation						
8. Target 3 (isolation):						
9. Target 3 (FO2/target and distractor):						
10. Target 3 (FO3/target and 2 distractors):						
11. Target 4 (isolation):						
12. Target 4 (FO2/target and distractor):						
13. Target 4 (FO3/target and 2 distractors):						
14. Targets that met criteria: random rotation						
15. Target 5 (isolation):						
16. Target 5 (FO2/target and distractor):						
17. Target 5 (FO3/target and 2 distractors):						
18. Target 6 (isolation):						
19. Target 6 (FO2/target and distractor):						
20. Target 6 (FO3/target and 2 distractors):						

21. Targets that met criteria: random rotation						
22. Target 7 (isolation):						
23. Target 7 (FO2/target and distractor):						
24. Target 7 (FO3/target and 2 distractors):						
25. Target 8 (isolation):						
26. Target 8 (FO2/target and distractor):						
27. Target 8 (FO3/target and 2 distractors):						
28. Targets that met criteria: random rotation						
29. Target 9 (isolation):						
30. Target 9 (FO2/target and distractor):						
31. Target 9 (FO3/target and 2 distractors):						
32. Target 10 (isolation):						
33. Target 10 (FO2/target and distractor):						
34. Target 10 (FO3/target and 2 distractors):						
35. Targets that met criteria: random rotation						
36. Generalize to another environment Environment 1:						

37. Generalize to another environment Environment 2:						
38. Maintenance: Assess in varied environments				2W 1W M		

Specific tips for running this task analysis

- Ensure pre-requisite skills have been taught for this TA. Examples of pre-requisite skills for "Past Tense Verbs" include receptive and expressive labels found in the first book of the Journey of Development ABA Curriculum series.

IRREGULAR PAST TENSE VERBS

LEVEL: □ 1 □ 2 □ 3

S^D: Present individual with a field of 1, 2 or 3 picture cards depicting an action. Say "Touch [present tense or past tense]" (e.g. "Touch buy" vs. "Touch bought")	**Response:** Individual will touch the specified action
Data Collection: Skill acquisition	**Target Criteria:** 80% or above for 3 consecutive days across 2 people
Materials: Picture cards of actions and reinforcement (picture cards can be found on accompanying CD)	

Fading procedure

Maintenance Criteria: 2W = 4 consecutive scores of 100%; 1W = 4 consecutive scores of 100%; M = 3 consecutive scores of 100%	**Natural Environment (NE) Criterion:** Target has been generalized in NE across 3 novel naturally occurring activities	**Archive Criteria:** Target, maintenance and NE criteria have been met

Target list

Suggestions for targets and probe results

Suggestions for Targets: Catch/caught, build/built, break/broke, blow/blew, buy/bought, choose/chose, go/went, drink/drank, feel/felt, drive/drove, fall/fell, dive/dove, bite/bit, deal/dealt, feed/fed, and draw/drew.
Probe Results (targets in repertoire):

Target	Baseline %	Date Introduced	Date Criteria Met	*Fading Procedure*		
				Maintenance	**Date NE Introduced**	**Date Archived**
1. Target 1 (isolation):						
2. Target 1 (FO2/target and distractor):						
3. Target 1 (FO3/target and 2 distractors):						
4. Target 2 (isolation):						

5. Target 2 (FO2/target and distractor):						
6. Target 2 (FO3/target and 2 distractors):						
7. Targets 1 and 2 random rotation						
8. Target 3 (isolation):						
9. Target 3 (FO2/target and distractor):						
10. Target 3 (FO3/target and 2 distractors):						
11. Target 4 (isolation):						
12. Target 4 (FO2/target and distractor):						
13. Target 4 (FO3/target and 2 distractors):						
14. Targets that met criteria: random rotation						
15. Target 5 (isolation):						
16. Target 5 (FO2/target and distractor):						
17. Target 5 (FO3/target and 2 distractors):						
18. Target 6 (isolation):						
19. Target 6 (FO2/target and distractor):						
20. Target 6 (FO3/target and 2 distractors):						

21. Targets that met criteria: random rotation						
22. Target 7 (isolation):						
23. Target 7 (FO2/target and distractor):						
24. Target 7 (FO3/target and 2 distractors):						
25. Target 8 (isolation):						
26. Target 8 (FO2/target and distractor):						
27. Target 8 (FO3/target and 2 distractors):						
28. Targets that met criteria: random rotation						
29. Target 9 (isolation):						
30. Target 9 (FO2/target and distractor):						
31. Target 9 (FO3/target and 2 distractors):						
32. Target 10 (isolation):						
33. Target 10 (FO2/target and distractor):						
34. Target 10 (FO3/target and 2 distractors):						
35. Targets that met criteria: random rotation						
36. Generalize to another environment Environment 1:						

37. Generalize to another environment Environment 2:						
38. Maintenance: Assess in varied environments				2W 1W M		

Specific tips for running this task analysis

- Ensure pre-requisite skills have been taught for this TA. Examples of pre-requisite skills for "Irregular Past Tense Verbs" include receptive and expressive labels found in the first book of the Journey of Development ABA Curriculum series.

PLURALS

LEVEL: □ 1 □ 2 □ 3

S^D: Present FO2 singular and plural objects/pictures and say "Touch [singular or plural]" (e.g. "Touch car" vs. "Touch cars")	**Response:** Individual will touch singular or plural picture or objects
Data Collection: Skill acquisition	**Target Criteria:** 80% or above for 3 consecutive days across 2 people
Materials: Objects and/or picture cards of objects (pictures need to be in various numbers and groups) and reinforcement (picture cards can be found on accompanying CD)	

Fading procedure

Maintenance Criteria: 2W = 4 consecutive scores of 100%; 1W = 4 consecutive scores of 100%; M = 3 consecutive scores of 100%	**Natural Environment (NE) Criterion:** Target has been generalized in NE across 3 novel naturally occurring activities	**Archive Criteria:** Target, maintenance and NE criteria have been met

Target list

Suggestions for targets and probe results

Suggestions for Targets: Animals/animals, car/cars, dinosaur/dinosaurs, toy/toys, ball/balls, doll/dolls, cup/cups, bed/beds, ball/balls, and crayon/crayons.
Probe Results (targets in repertoire):

Target	Baseline %	Date Introduced	Date Criteria Met	*Fading Procedure*		
				Maintenance	Date NE Introduced	Date Archived
1. Target 1 (isolation):						
2. Target 1 (FO2/target and distractor):						
3. Target 2 (isolation):						
4. Target 2 (FO2/target and distractor):						

5. Targets that met criteria: random rotation						
6. Target 3 (isolation):						
7. Target 3 (FO2/target and distractor):						
8. Target 4 (isolation):						
9. Target 4 (FO2/target and distractor):						
10. Targets that met criteria: random rotation						
11. Target 5 (isolation):						
12. Target 5 (FO2/target and distractor):						
13. Target 6 (isolation):						
14. Target 6 (FO2/target and distractor):						
15. Targets that met criteria: random rotation						
16. Target 7 (isolation):						
17. Target 7 (FO2/target and distractor):						
18. Target 8 (isolation):						
19. Target 8 (FO2/target and distractor):						
20. Targets that met criteria: random rotation						

21. Target 9 (isolation):						
22. Target 9 (FO2/target and distractor):						
23. Target 10 (isolation):						
24. Target 10 (FO2/target and distractor):						
25. Targets that met criteria: random rotation						
26. Generalize to another environment Environment 1:						
27. Generalize to another environment Environment 2:						
28. Maintenance: Assess in varied environments				2W 1W M		

Specific tips for running this task analysis

- Ensure pre-requisite skills have been taught for this TA. Examples of pre-requisite skills for "Plurals" include receptive and expressive labels found in the first book of the Journey of Development ABA Curriculum series.

IRREGULAR PLURALS

LEVEL: □ 1 □ 2 □ 3

S^{D}: Present FO2 singular and plural objects/pictures and say "Touch [singular or plural]" (e.g. "Touch person" vs. "Touch people")	**Response:** Individual will touch singular or plural picture or object
Data Collection: Skill acquisition	**Target Criteria:** 80% or above for 3 consecutive days across 2 people
Materials: Objects and/or picture cards of items representing irregular plurals and reinforcement (picture cards can be found on accompanying CD)	

Fading Procedure

Maintenance Criteria: 2W = 4 consecutive scores of 100%; 1W = 4 consecutive scores of 100%; M = 3 consecutive scores of 100%	**Natural Environment (NE) Criterion:** Target has been generalized in NE across 3 novel naturally occurring activities	**Archive Criteria:** Target, maintenance and NE criteria have been met

Target list

Suggestions for Targets and Probe Results

Suggestions for Targets: Tooth/teeth, foot/feet, person/people, child/children, woman/women, man/men, cactus/cacti, goose/geese, mouse/mice, and words that do not change such as deer, fish and sheep.
Probe Results (targets in repertoire):

Target	Baseline %	Date Introduced	Date Criteria Met	*Fading Procedure* Maintenance	Date NE Introduced	Date Archived
1. Target 1 (isolation):						
2. Target 1 (FO2/target and distractor):						
3. Target 2 (isolation):						
4. Target 2 (FO2/target and distractor):						

5. Targets that met criteria: random rotation						
6. Target 3 (isolation):						
7. Target 3 (FO2/target and distractor):						
8. Target 4 (isolation):						
9. Target 4 (FO2/target and distractor):						
10. Targets that met criteria: random rotation						
11. Target 5 (isolation):						
12. Target 5 (FO2/target and distractor):						
13. Target 6 (isolation):						
14. Target 6 (FO2/target and distractor):						
15. Targets that met criteria: random rotation						
16. Target 7 (isolation):						
17. Target 7 (FO2/target and distractor):						
18. Target 8 (isolation):						
19. Target 8 (FO2/target and distractor):						
20. Targets that met criteria: random rotation						

21. Target 9 (isolation):						
22. Target 9 (FO2/target and distractor):						
23. Target 10 (isolation):						
24. Target 10 (FO2/target and distractor):						
25. Targets that met criteria: random rotation						
26. Generalize to another environment. Environment 1:						
27. Generalize to another environment. Environment 2:						
28. Maintenance: Assess in varied environments				2W 1W M		

Specific tips for running this task analysis

- Ensure pre-requisite skills have been taught for this TA. Examples of pre-requisite skills for "Irregular Plurals" include receptive and expressive labels. TAs can be found in the first book of the Journey of Development ABA Curriculum series.

PRONOUNS (HE/SHE)

LEVEL: □ 1 □ 2 □ 3

S^D: Present individual with a field of 1 or 2 picture cards depicting both genders engaging in the same action or having the same attribute. Say "Touch [x]," "Give me [x]," "Find [x]," or "Point to [x]" (e.g. Point to "He is wearing a red shirt" or "Give me she is digging")	**Response:** Individual will (touch, give, find, point) to the specified gender picture
Data Collection: Skill acquisition	**Target Criteria:** 80% or above for 3 consecutive days across 2 people
Materials: Picture cards of boys/girls engaging in the same actions, with the same characteristic (clothing, holding a particular item etc.) and reinforcement (picture cards can be found on accompanying CD)	

Fading procedure

Maintenance Criteria: 2W = 4 consecutive scores of 100%; 1W = 4 consecutive scores of 100%; M = 3 consecutive scores of 100%	**Natural Environment (NE) Criterion:** Target has been generalized in NE across 3 novel naturally occurring activities	**Archive Criteria:** Target, maintenance and NE criteria have been met

Target list

Suggestions for targets and probe results

Suggestions for Targets: He/she is kicking/swinging/eating/drinking/running/sleeping, etc.; he/she is wearing [x], he/she is holding [x].
Probe Results (targets in repertoire):

Target	Baseline %	Date Introduced	Date Criteria Met	*Fading Procedure*		
				Maintenance	Date NE Introduced	Date Archived
1. Target 1 (isolation):						
2. Target 1 (FO2/target and distractor):						
3. Target 2 (isolation):						

4. Target 2 (FO2/target and distractor):						
5. Targets 1 and 2 random rotation						
6. Target 3 (isolation):						
7. Target 3 (FO2/target and distractor):						
8. Target 4 (isolation):						
9. Target 4 (FO2/target and distractor):						
10. Targets that met criteria: random rotation						
11. Target 5 (isolation):						
12. Target 5 (FO2/target and distractor):						
13. Target 6 (isolation):						
14. Target 6 (FO2/target and distractor):						
15. Targets that met criteria: random rotation						
16. Target 7 (isolation):						
17. Target 7 (FO2/target and distractor):						
18. Target 8 (isolation):						
19. Target 8 (FO2/target and distractor):						

20. Targets that met criteria: random rotation						
21. Target 9 (isolation):						
22. Target 9 (FO2/target and distractor):						
23. Target 10 (isolation):						
24. Target 10 (FO2/target and distractor):						
25. Targets that met criteria: random rotation						
26. Generalize to another environment Environment 1:						
27. Generalize to another environment Environment 2:						
28. Maintenance: Assess in varied environments				2W 1W M		

Specific tips for running this task analysis

- Ensure pre-requisite skills have been taught for this TA. Examples of pre-requisite skills for "Pronouns (He/She)" include receptive and expressive labels (clothing, body parts, functional items, toys, actions, etc.) found in the first book of the Journey of Development ABA Curriculum series, and mastery of receptive/expressive labels of gender (TA found in this curriculum book).
- When using pictures or figures, make sure that the pictures are identical in all aspects except gender (e.g. picture of a girl jumping vs. a picture of a boy jumping etc.)
- When using pictures or figurines, be sure to generalize the skill to men/women/boys/girls.

PRONOUNS (HIS/HER)

LEVEL: □ 1 □ 2 □ 3

S^D: Present individual with a field of 1 or 2 picture cards depicting both genders with a similar attribute. Say "Touch [x]," "Give me [x]," "Find [x]," or "Point to [x]" (e.g. "Touch his/her [body part/clothing item/object]"	**Response:** Individual will (touch, give, find, point to) the specified gender picture
Data Collection: Skill acquisition	**Target Criteria:** 80% or above for 3 consecutive days across 2 people
Materials: Pictures of boys/men, girls/women and figurines, and reinforcement (picture cards can be found on accompanying CD)	

Fading procedure

Maintenance Criteria: 2W = 4 consecutive scores of 100%; 1W = 4 consecutive scores of 100%; M = 3 consecutive scores of 100%	**Natural Environment (NE) Criterion:** Target has been generalized in NE across 3 novel naturally occurring activities	**Archive Criteria:** Target, maintenance and NE criteria have been met

Target list

Suggestions for targets and probe results

Suggestions for Targets: His/her arm/leg/head/hair/fingers; his/her shirt/pants/shoes/coat/socks; his/her ball/toy/blanket/bag/drink.

Probe Results (targets in repertoire):

Target	Baseline %	Date Introduced	Date Criteria Met	*Fading Procedure*		
				Maintenance	Date NE Introduced	Date Archived
1. Target 1 (isolation):						
2. Target 1 (FO2/target and distractor):						
3. Target 2 (isolation):						
4. Target 2 (FO2/target and distractor):						

5. Targets 1 and 2 random rotation						
6. Target 3 (isolation):						
7. Target 3 (FO2/target and distractor):						
8. Target 4 (isolation):						
9. Target 4 (FO2/target and distractor):						
10. Targets that met criteria: random rotation						
11. Target 5 (isolation):						
12. Target 5 (FO2/target and distractor):						
13. Target 6 (isolation):						
14. Target 6 (FO2/target and distractor):						
15. Targets that met criteria: random rotation						
16. Target 7 (isolation):						
17. Target 7 (FO2/target and distractor):						
18. Target 8 (isolation):						
19. Target 8 (FO2/target and distractor):						
20. Targets that met criteria: random rotation						

21. Target 9 (isolation):						
22. Target 9 (FO2/target and distractor):						
23. Target 10 (isolation):						
24. Target 10 (FO2/target and distractor):						
25. Targets that met criteria: random rotation						
26. Generalize to another environment Environment 1:						
27. Generalize to another environment Environment 2:						
28. Maintenance: Assess in varied environments				2W 1W M		

Specific tips for running this task analysis

- Ensure pre-requisite skills have been taught for this TA. Examples of pre-requisite skills for "Pronouns (His/Her)" include receptive and expressive labels of clothing, body parts, functional objects, etc. (all TAs can be found in the first book of the Journey of Development ABA Curriculum series).
- When using pictures or figurines, be sure to generalize the skill to men/women/boys/girls.

PRONOUNS (I/YOU)

LEVEL: □ 1 □ 2 □ 3

S^D: Present a field of 1 or 2 pictures of instructor or individual engaging in same action. Say "Touch I am/you are [action]" (e.g. "Touch I am clapping" or "Touch you are clapping")	**Response:** Individual will touch the specified picture card ("you are" = instructor, "I am" = individual)
Data Collection: Skill acquisition	**Target Criteria:** 80% or above for 3 consecutive days across 2 people
Materials: Pictures of instructor and individual engaging in same actions, and reinforcement	

Fading procedure

Maintenance Criteria: 2W = 4 consecutive scores of 100%; 1W = 4 consecutive scores of 100%; M = 3 consecutive scores of 100%	**Natural Environment (NE) Criterion:** Target has been generalized in NE across 3 novel naturally occurring activities	**Archive Criteria:** Target, maintenance and NE criteria have been met

Target list

Suggestions for targets and probe results

Suggestions for Targets: Pictures of the instructor and individual engaging in various actions: clapping, sleeping, jumping, eating, drinking, brushing teeth, brushing hair, watching TV, reading and writing.
Probe Results (targets in repertoire):

Target	Baseline %	Date Introduced	Date Criteria Met	*Fading Procedure*		
				Maintenance	Date NE Introduced	Date Archived
1. Target 1 (isolation):						
2. Target 1 (FO2/target and distractor):						
3. Target 2 (isolation):						
4. Target 2 (FO2/target and distractor):						

5. Targets 1 and 2 random rotation						
6. Target 3 (isolation):						
7. Target 3 (FO2/target and distractor):						
8. Target 4 (isolation):						
9. Target 4 (FO2/target and distractor):						
10. Targets that met criteria: random rotation						
11. Target 5 (isolation):						
12. Target 5 (FO2/target and distractor):						
13. Target 6 (isolation):						
14. Target 6 (FO2/target and distractor):						
15. Targets that met criteria: random rotation						
16. Target 7 (isolation):						
17. Target 7 (FO2/target and distractor):						
18. Target 8 (isolation):						
19. Target 8 (FO2/target and distractor):						
20. Targets that met criteria: random rotation						

21. Target 9 (isolation):						
22. Target 9 (FO2/target and distractor):						
23. Target 10 (isolation):						
24. Target 10 (FO2/target and distractor):						
25. Targets that met criteria: random rotation						
26. Generalize to another environment Environment 1:						
27. Generalize to another environment Environment 2:						
28. Maintenance: Assess in varied environments				2W 1W M		

Specific tips for running this task analysis

- Ensure pre-requisite skills have been taught for this TA. Examples of pre-requisite skills for "Pronouns (I/You)" include "Receptive Labels of Actions" and "Receptive Labels of Familiar People" (both TAs found in the first book of the Journey of Development ABA Curriculum series).
- When presenting the pictures of actions, be sure to have two pictures of the same action (e.g. individual clapping and instructor clapping) so the individual must differentiate between the pronouns (not the action).

PRONOUNS (MY/YOUR)

LEVEL: □ 1 □ 2 □ 3

S^D: "Touch my/your [body part/clothing/item]" (e.g. "Touch my shirt" or "Touch your drink")	**Response:** Individual will touch specified body part/clothing/item ("my" = individual, "your" = instructor)
Data Collection: Skill acquisition	**Target Criteria:** 80% or above for 3 consecutive days across 2 people
Materials: Personal items and clothing, and reinforcement	

Fading procedure

Maintenance Criteria: 2W = 4 consecutive scores of 100%; 1W = 4 consecutive scores of 100%; M = 3 consecutive scores of 100%	**Natural Environment (NE) Criterion:** Target has been generalized in NE across 3 novel naturally occurring activities	**Archive Criteria:** Target, maintenance and NE criteria have been met

Target list

Suggestions for targets and probe results

Suggestions for Targets: My/your arm/leg/head/hair/fingers; my/your shirt/pants/shoes/coat/socks; my/your ball/toy/bag/drink.
Probe Results (targets in repertoire):

Target	Baseline %	Date Introduced	Date Criteria Met	*Fading Procedure*		
				Maintenance	Date NE Introduced	Date Archived
1. Target 1 (isolation):						
2. Target 1 (FO2/target and distractor):						
3. Target 2 (isolation):						
4. Target 2 (FO2/target and distractor):						
5. Targets 1 and 2 random rotation						

6. Target 3 (isolation):						
7. Target 3 (FO2/target and distractor):						
8. Target 4 (isolation):						
9. Target 4 (FO2/target and distractor):						
10. Targets that met criteria: random rotation						
11. Target 5 (isolation):						
12. Target 5 (FO2/target and distractor):						
13. Target 6 (isolation):						
14. Target 6 (FO2/target and distractor):						
15. Targets that met criteria: random rotation						
16. Target 7 (isolation):						
17. Target 7 (FO2/target and distractor):						
18. Target 8 (isolation):						
19. Target 8 (FO2/target and distractor):						
20. Targets that met criteria: random rotation						
21. Target 9 (isolation):						

22. Target 9 (FO2/target and distractor):						
23. Target 10 (isolation):						
24. Target 10 (FO2/target and distractor):						
25. Targets that met criteria: random rotation						
26. Generalize to another environment Environment 1:						
27. Generalize to another environment Environment 2:						
28. Maintenance: Assess in varied environments				2W 1W M		

Specific tips for running this task analysis

- Ensure pre-requisite skills have been taught for this TA. Examples of pre-requisite skills for "Pronouns (My/Your)" include receptive and expressive labels of clothing, body parts, functional objects (TAs found in the first book of the Journey of Development ABA Curriculum series).

PRONOUNS (THEIR/OUR)

LEVEL: □ 1 □ 2 □ 3

S^D: Present a field of 1 or 2 pictures of instructor and individual holding same object or peers/strangers holding same object. Say "Point to our/their [x]" (e.g. "Point to our pencils" or "Point to their pencils")	**Response:** Individual will point to specified picture depicting the pronoun
Data Collection: Skill acquisition	**Target Criteria:** 80% or above for 3 consecutive days across 2 people
Materials: Picture cards of instructor and individual holding objects and peers/strangers holding same objects, and reinforcement	

Fading procedure

Maintenance Criteria: 2W = 4 consecutive scores of 100%; 1W = 4 consecutive scores of 100%; M = 3 consecutive scores of 100%	**Natural Environment (NE) Criterion:** Target has been generalized in NE across 3 novel naturally occurring activities	**Archive Criteria:** Target, maintenance and NE criteria have been met

Target list

Suggestions for targets and probe result

Suggestions for Targets: Their/our pencils/toys/drinks/snacks/balls/bikes/books/bags/dolls/phones.
Probe Results (targets in repertoire):

Target	Baseline %	Date Introduced	Date Criteria Met	*Fading Procedure*		
				Maintenance	**Date NE Introduced**	**Date Archived**
1. Target 1 (isolation):						
2. Target 1 (FO2/target and distractor):						
3. Target 2 (isolation):						
4. Target 2 (FO2/target and distractor):						

5. Targets 1 and 2 random rotation						
6. Target 3 (isolation):						
7. Target 3 (FO2/target and distractor):						
8. Target 4 (isolation):						
9. Target 4 (FO2/target and distractor):						
10. Targets that met criteria: random rotation						
11. Target 5 (isolation):						
12. Target 5 (FO2/target and distractor):						
13. Target 6 (isolation):						
14. Target 6 (FO2/target and distractor):						
15. Targets that met criteria: random rotation						
16. Target 7 (isolation):						
17. Target 7 (FO2/target and distractor):						
18. Target 8 (isolation):						
19. Target 8 (FO2/target and distractor):						
20. Targets that met criteria: random rotation						

21. Target 9 (isolation):						
22. Target 9 (FO2/target and distractor):						
23. Target 10 (isolation):						
24. Target 10 (FO2/target and distractor):						
25. Targets that met criteria: random rotation						
26. Generalize to another environment Environment 1:						
27. Generalize to another environment Environment 2:						
28. Maintenance: Assess in varied environments				2W 1W M		

Specific tips for running this task analysis

- Ensure pre-requisite skills have been taught for this TA. Examples of pre-requisite skills for "Pronouns (Their/Our)" include receptive and expressive labels of functional objects, leisure items, food and drink (all TAs found in the first book of the Journey of Development ABA Curriculum series) and mastery of receptive/expressive labels of gender (TA found in this curriculum book).
- When the targeted pronoun is "their" the individual should touch each of their peers' objects for a correct response.
- When the targeted pronoun is "our" they should touch the individual's and instructor's objects.

PRONOUNS (WE/THEY)

LEVEL: □ 1 □ 2 □ 3

S^D: Present a field of 1 or 2 pictures of instructor and individual engaging in various activities or peers/strangers engaging in those same activities. Say "Point to We are eating" or "Point to They are digging")	**Response:** Individual will point to the specified picture (we = instructor and individual; they = others/peers/strangers)
Data Collection: Skill acquisition	**Target Criteria:** 80% or above for 3 consecutive days across 2 people
Materials: Picture cards of instructor and individual engaging in various activities and peers/strangers engaging in those same activities, and reinforcement	

Fading procedure

Maintenance Criteria: 2W = 4 consecutive scores of 100%; 1W = 4 consecutive scores of 100%; M = 3 consecutive scores of 100%	**Natural Environment (NE) Criterion:** Target has been generalized in NE across 3 novel naturally occurring activities	**Archive Criteria:** Target, maintenance and NE criteria have been met

Target list

Suggestions for targets and probe results

Suggestions for Targets: We/they picture cards (i.e. we/they are digging, we/they are clapping, we/they are jumping, we/they are drinking, we/they are blowing bubbles, we/they are painting, we/they are sleeping, we/they are playing a game, we/they are coloring, and we/they are swinging).

Probe Results (targets in repertoire):

Target	Baseline %	Date Introduced	Date Criteria Met	*Fading Procedure*		
				Maintenance	Date NE Introduced	Date Archived
1. Target 1 (isolation):						
2. Target 1 (FO2/target and distractor):						
3. Target 2 (isolation):						
4. Target 2 (FO2/target and distractor):						

5. Targets 1 and 2 random rotation						
6. Target 3 (isolation):						
7. Target 3 (FO2/target and distractor):						
8. Target 4 (isolation):						
9. Target 4 (FO2/target and distractor):						
10. Targets that met criteria: random rotation						
11. Target 5 (isolation):						
12. Target 5 (FO2/target and distractor):						
13. Target 6 (isolation):						
14. Target 6 (FO2/target and distractor):						
15. Targets that met criteria: random rotation						
16. Target 7 (isolation):						
17. Target 7 (FO2/target and distractor):						
18. Target 8 (isolation):						
19. Target 8 (FO2/target and distractor):						
20. Targets that met criteria: random rotation						

21. Target 9 (isolation):						
22. Target 9 (FO2/target and distractor):						
23. Target 10 (isolation):						
24. Target 10 (FO2/target and distractor):						
25. Targets that met criteria: random rotation						
26. Generalize to another environment Environment 1:						
27. Generalize to another environment Environment 2:						
28. Maintenance: Assess in varied environments				2W 1W M		

Specific tips for running this task analysis

- Ensure pre-requisite skills have been taught for this TA. Examples of pre-requisite skills for "Pronouns (We/They)" include receptive and expressive labels of actions (TA found in the first book of the Journey of Development ABA Curriculum series) and mastery of receptive/expressive labels of gender (TA found in this curriculum book).
- When presenting pictures of groups, present identical action pictures, so the individual is discriminating between the pronouns not the actions.

RECEPTIVE INSTRUCTIONS DELIVERED IN A GROUP

LEVEL: □ 1 □ 2 □ 3

S^D: When in a group of peers, the instructor gives an instruction to the group	**Response:** Individual will respond by following the directive
Data Collection: Skill acquisition	**Target Criteria:** 80% or above for 3 consecutive days across 2 people
Materials: Reinforcement	

Fading procedure

Maintenance Criteria: 2W = 4 consecutive scores of 100%; 1W = 4 consecutive scores of 100%; M = 3 consecutive scores of 100%	**Natural Environment (NE) Criterion:** Target has been generalized in NE across 3 novel naturally occurring activities	**Archive Criteria:** Target, maintenance and NE criteria have been met

Target list

Suggestions for targets and probe results

Suggestions for Targets: Stand up, line up, sit down, give me [x], everyone jump, clap your hands, everyone follow me, put your paper/project on the shelf, pick it up, get out your [x], and throw away [x].
Probe Results (targets in repertoire):

Target	Baseline %	Date Introduced	Date Criteria Met	*Fading Procedure*		
				Maintenance	**Date NE Introduced**	**Date Archived**
1. Target 1:						
2. Target 2:						
3. Targets 1 and 2 random rotation						
4. Target 3:						
5. Target 4:						

6. Targets that met criteria: random rotation						
7. Target 5:						
8. Target 6:						
9. Targets that met criteria: random rotation						
10. Target 7:						
11. Target 8:						
12. Targets that met criteria: random rotation						
13. Target 9:						
14. Target 10:						
15. Targets that met criteria: random rotation						
16. Generalize to another environment Environment 1:						
17. Generalize to another environment Environment 2:						
18. Maintenance: Assess in varied environments				2W 1W M		

RECEPTIVE INSTRUCTIONS (TWO-STEP)

LEVEL: □ 1 □ 2 □ 3

S^D: Give a 2-step verbal directive (e.g. clap hands and then touch head, stand up and turn around, etc.)	**Response:** Individual will respond by following the directives in the order they are presented
Data Collection: Skill acquisition	**Target Criteria:** 80% or above for 3 consecutive days across 2 people
Materials: Reinforcement	

Fading procedure

Maintenance Criteria: 2W = 4 consecutive scores of 100%; 1W = 4 consecutive scores of 100%; M = 3 consecutive scores of 100%	**Natural Environment (NE) Criterion:** Target has been generalized in NE across 3 novel naturally occurring activities	**Archive Criteria:** Target, maintenance and NE criteria have been met

Target list

Suggestions for targets and probe results

Suggestions for Targets: Get [x] and give to [person], stand up and get [x], clap hands and touch head, stand up and stomp feet, stand up and turn around, pick up [x] and put on shelf, give me the blue [x] and the red [x], walk across room and get [x], sit down and put hands on table, and pick up crayon and color.
Probe Results (targets in repertoire):

Target	Baseline %	Date Introduced	Date Criteria Met	*Fading Procedure*		
				Maintenance	Date NE Introduced	Date Archived
1. Target 1:						
2. Target 2:						
3. Targets 1 and 2 random rotation						
4. Target 3:						
5. Target 4:						

6. Targets that met criteria: random rotation						
7. Target 5:						
8. Target 6:						
9. Targets that met criteria: random rotation						
10. Target 7:						
11. Target 8:						
12. Targets that met criteria: random rotation						
13. Target 9:						
14. Target 10:						
15. Targets that met criteria: random rotation						
16. Generalize to another environment Environment 1:						
17. Generalize to another environment Environment 2:						
18. Maintenance: Assess in varied environments				2W 1W M		

Specific tips for running this task analysis

- Ensure pre-requisite skills have been taught for this TA. Examples of pre-requisite skills for "Receptive Instructions (Two-Step)" include mastering "Receptive Instructions (One-Step)" from the first book in the Journey of Development ABA Curriculum series.

RECEPTIVE LABELS OF ATTRIBUTES

LEVEL: □ 1 □ 2 □ 3

S^D: Present individual with a field of 1 or 2 picture cards and say "Touch [x], Give me [x] or Point to [x]" (e.g. "Touch dirty" or "Touch short)"	**Response:** Individual will touch, give or point to the item
Data Collection: Skill acquisition	**Target Criteria:** 80% or above for 3 consecutive days across 2 people
Materials: Picture cards of attributes and reinforcement (picture cards can be found on accompanying CD)	

Fading procedure

Maintenance Criteria: 2W = 4 consecutive scores of 100%; 1W = 4 consecutive scores of 100%; M = 3 consecutive scores of 100%	**Natural Environment (NE) Criterion:** Target has been generalized in NE across 3 novel naturally occurring activities	**Archive Criteria:** Target, maintenance and NE criteria have been met

Target list

Suggestions for targets and probe results

Suggestions for Targets: Broken, empty, full, dirty, clean, round, tall, short, big, little, wet, dry, hot, cold, hard, soft, dark, light, old, new, and young.
Probe Results (targets in repertoire):

Target	Baseline %	Date Introduced	Date Criteria Met	*Fading Procedure*		
				Maintenance	Date NE Introduced	Date Archived
1. Target 1 (isolation):						
2. Target 1 (FO2/target and distractor):						
3. Target 2 (isolation):						
4. Target 2 (FO2/target and distractor):						
5. Targets 1 and 2 random rotation						

6. Target 3 (isolation):						
7. Target 3 (FO2/target and distractor):						
8. Target 4 (isolation):						
9. Target 4 (FO2/target and distractor):						
10. Targets that met criteria: random rotation						
11. Target 5 (isolation):						
12. Target 5 (FO2/target and distractor):						
13. Target 6 (isolation):						
14. Target 6 (FO2/target and distractor):						
15. Targets that met criteria: random rotation						
16. Target 7 (isolation):						
17. Target 7 (FO2/target and distractor):						
18. Target 8 (isolation):						
19. Target 8 (FO2/target and distractor):						
20. Targets that met criteria: random rotation						
21. Target 9 (isolation):						

22. Target 9 (FO2/target and distractor):						
23. Target 10 (isolation):						
24. Target 10 (FO2/target and distractor):						
25. Targets that met criteria: random rotation						
26. Generalize to another environment Environment 1:						
27. Generalize to another environment Environment 2:						
28. Maintenance: Assess in varied environments				2W 1W M		

Specific tips for running this task analysis

- Ensure pre-requisite skills have been taught for this TA. Examples of pre-requisite skills for "Receptive Labels of Attributes" include mastering the receptive labels programs in the first book of the Journey of Development ABA Curriculum series.
- Be alert to not giving inadvertent prompts or clues to the answer. For example, if you are teaching the attribute "wet," do not show two different animals (1 dry and 1 wet) and say "Touch wet dog." The individual may be touching dog, not learning and touching the attribute wet. Thus, be sure to use picture cards are of the same object or, in this example, the same type of animal (two dogs, one dry and one wet).
- When teaching an attribute pair, make sure to teach with multiple examples (e.g. dirty/clean sock, dirty/clean pictures of hands, dirty/clean shirt etc.).

RECEPTIVE LABELS OF CATEGORIES

LEVEL: □ 1 □ 2 □ 3

S^D: Present individual with a field of 1, 2 or 3 objects or pictures from different categories and say "Touch [x]," "Give me [x]" or "Point to [x]," (e.g. a cat, a glass of milk and a spoon and say "Touch the animal")	**Response:** Individual will (touch, give, point to) the item within the named category
Data Collection: Skill acquisition	**Target Criteria:** 80% or above for 3 consecutive days across 2 people
Materials: Objects/pictures of items within various categories and reinforcement (picture cards can be found on accompanying CD)	

Fading procedure

Maintenance Criteria: 2W = 4 consecutive scores of 100%; 1W = 4 consecutive scores of 100%; M = 3 consecutive scores of 100%	**Natural Environment (NE) Criterion:** Target has been generalized in NE across 3 novel naturally occurring activities	**Archive Criteria:** Target, maintenance and NE criteria have been met

Target list

Suggestions for targets and probe results

Suggestions for Targets: Food, clothing, animals, drinks, toys, vehicles, people, colors, letters and instruments.
Probe Results (targets in repertoire):

Target	Baseline %	Date Introduced	Date Criteria Met	*Fading Procedure*		
				Maintenance	Date NE Introduced	Date Archived
1. Target 1 (isolation):						
2. Target 1 (FO2/target and distractor):						
3. Target 1 (FO3/target and 2 distractors):						
4. Target 2 (isolation):						

5. Target 2 (FO2/target and distractor):						
6. Target 2 (FO3/target and 2 distractors):						
7. Targets 1 and 2 random rotation						
8. Target 3 (isolation):						
9. Target 3 (FO2/target and distractor):						
10. Target 3 (FO3/target and 2 distractors):						
11. Target 4 (isolation):						
12. Target 4 (FO2/target and distractor):						
13. Target 4 (FO3/target and 2 distractors):						
14. Targets that met criteria: random rotation						
15. Target 5 (isolation):						
16. Target 5 (FO2/target and distractor):						
17. Target 5 (FO3/target and 2 distractors):						
18. Target 6 (isolation):						
19. Target 6 (FO2/target and distractor):						
20. Target 6 (FO3/target and 2 distractors):						

21. Targets that met criteria: random rotation						
22. Target 7 (isolation):						
23. Target 7 (FO2/target and distractor):						
24. Target 7 (FO3/target and 2 distractors):						
25. Target 8 (isolation):						
26. Target 8 (FO2/target and distractor):						
27. Target 8 (FO3/target and 2 distractors):						
28. Targets that met criteria: random rotation						
29. Target 9 (isolation):						
30. Target 9 (FO2/target and distractor):						
31. Target 9 (FO3/target and 2 distractors):						
32. Target 10 (isolation):						
33. Target 10 (FO2/target and distractor):						
34. Target 10 (FO3/target and 2 distractors):						
35. Targets that met criteria: random rotation						
36. Generalize to another environment Environment 1:						

37. Generalize to another environment Environment 2:						
38. Maintenance: Assess in varied environments				2W 1W M		

Specific tips for running this task analysis

- Ensure pre-requisite skills have been taught for this TA. Examples of pre-requisite skills for "Receptive Labels of Categories" include mastering receptive and expressive labels for the items within each category used; such as receptive/expressive labels of food, clothing, animals, drinks, toys, vehicles, familiar people, etc. (TAs in the first book of the Journey of Development ABA Curriculum series).

RECEPTIVE LABELS OF COMMUNITY HELPERS

LEVEL: □ 1 □ 2 □ 3

S^D: Present individual with a field of 1, 2 or 3 picture cards of community helpers and say "Touch [x]", "Give me [x]" or "Point to [x]" (e.g. "Point to doctor")	**Response:** Individual will touch, give or point to the specific community helper
Data Collection: Skill acquisition	**Target Criteria:** 80% or above for 3 consecutive days across 2 people
Materials: Picture cards of community helpers and reinforcement (picture cards can be found on accompanying CD)	

Fading procedure

Maintenance Criteria: 2W = 4 consecutive scores of 100%; 1W = 4 consecutive scores of 100%; M = 3 consecutive scores of 100%	**Natural Environment (NE) Criterion:** Target has been generalized in NE across 3 novel naturally occurring activities	**Archive Criteria:** Target, maintenance and NE criteria have been met

Target list

Suggestions for targets and probe results

Suggestions for Targets: Doctor, teacher, pilot, fireman, dentist, policeman, mailman, nurse, librarian, astronaut and farmer.
Probe Results (targets in repertoire):

Target	Baseline %	Date Introduced	Date Criteria Met	*Fading Procedure*		
				Maintenance	Date NE Introduced	Date Archived
1. Target 1 (isolation):						
2. Target 1 (FO2/target and distractor):						
3. Target 1 (FO3/target and 2 distractors):						
4. Target 2 (isolation):						
5. Target 2 (FO2/target and distractor):						

6. Target 2 (FO3/target and 2 distractors):						
7. Targets that met criteria: random rotation						
8. Target 3 (isolation):						
9. Target 3 (FO2/target and distractor):						
10. Target 3 (FO3/target and 2 distractors):						
11. Target 4 (isolation):						
12. Target 4 (FO2/target and distractor):						
13. Target 4 (FO3/target and 2 distractors):						
14. Targets that met criteria: random rotation						
15. Target 5 (isolation):						
16. Target 5 (FO2/target and distractor):						
17. Target 5 (FO3/target and 2 distractors):						
18. Target 6 (isolation):						
19. Target 6 (FO2/target and distractor):						
20. Target 6 (FO3/target and 2 distractors):						
21. Targets that met criteria: random rotation						
22. Target 7 (isolation):						

23. Target 7 (FO2/target and distractor):						
24. Target 7 (FO3/target and 2 distractors):						
25. Target 8 (isolation):						
26. Target 8 (FO2/target and distractor):						
27. Target 8 (FO3/target and 2 distractors):						
28. Targets that met criteria: random rotation						
29. Target 9 (isolation):						
30. Target 9 (FO2/target and distractor):						
31. Target 9 (FO3/target and 2 distractors):						
32. Target 10 (isolation):						
33. Target 10 (FO2/target and distractor):						
34. Target 10 (FO3/target and 2 distractors):						
35. Targets that met criteria: random rotation						
36. Generalize to another environment Environment 1:						
37. Generalize to another environment Environment 2:						
38. Maintenance: Assess in varied environments				2W 1W M		

Specific tips for running this task analysis

- Ensure pre-requisite skills have been taught for this TA. Examples of pre-requisite skills for "Receptive Labels of Community Helpers" include receptive and expressive labels in the first book of the Journey of Development ABA Curriculum series.

RECEPTIVE LABELS OF EMOTIONS

LEVEL: □ 1 □ 2 □ 3

S^D: Present individual with a field of 1,2 or 3 picture cards of emotions and say "Touch [x]", "Give me [x]", "Find [x]", or "Point to [x]" (e.g. "Find scared")	**Response:** Individual will touch, give, find or point to the specified emotion
Data Collection: Skill acquisition	**Target Criteria:** 80% or above for 3 consecutive days across 2 people
Materials: Picture cards of various faces showing different emotions and reinforcement (picture cards can be found on accompanying CD)	

Fading procedure

Maintenance Criteria: 2W = 4 consecutive scores of 100%; 1W = 4 consecutive scores of 100%; M = 3 consecutive scores of 100%	**Natural Environment (NE) Criterion:** Target has been generalized in NE across 3 novel naturally occurring activities	**Archive Criteria:** Target, maintenance and NE criteria have been met

Target list

Suggestions for targets and probe results

Suggestions for Targets: Happy, sad, mad, scared, tired, silly, surprised, sick, relaxed and shy.
Probe Results (targets in repertoire):

Target	Baseline %	Date Introduced	Date Criteria Met	*Fading Procedure*		
				Maintenance	Date NE Introduced	Date Archived
1. Target 1 (isolation):						
2. Target 1 (FO2/target and distractor):						
3. Target 1 (FO3/target and 2 distractors):						
4. Target 2 (isolation):						
5. Target 2 (FO2/target and distractor):						

6. Target 2 (FO3/target and 2 distractors):						
7. Targets 1 and 2 random rotation						
8. Target 3 (isolation):						
9. Target 3 (FO2/target and distractor):						
10. Target 3 (FO3/target and 2 distractors):						
11. Target 4 (isolation):						
12. Target 4 (FO2/target and distractor):						
13. Target 4 (FO3/target and 2 distractors):						
14. Targets that met criteria: random rotation						
15. Target 5 (isolation):						
16. Target 5 (FO2/target and distractor):						
17. Target 5 (FO3/target and 2 distractors):						
18. Target 6 (isolation):						
19. Target 6 (FO2/target and distractor):						
20. Target 6 (FO3/target and 2 distractors):						
21. Targets that met criteria: random rotation						
22. Target 7 (isolation):						

23. Target 7 (FO2/target and distractor):						
24. Target 7 (FO3/target and 2 distractors):						
25. Target 8 (isolation):						
26. Target 8 (FO2/target and distractor):						
27. Target 8 (FO3/target and 2 distractors):						
28. Targets that met criteria: random rotation						
29. Target 9 (isolation):						
30. Target 9 (FO2/target and distractor):						
31. Target 9 (FO3/target and 2 distractors):						
32. Target 10 (isolation):						
33. Target 10 (FO2/target and distractor):						
34. Target 10 (FO3/target and 2 distractors):						
35. Targets that met criteria: random rotation						
36. Generalize to another environment Environment 1:						
37. Generalize to another environment Environment 2:						
38. Maintenance: Assess in varied environments				2W 1W M		

Specific tips for running this task analysis

- Ensure pre-requisite skills have been taught for this TA. Examples of pre-requisite skills for "Receptive Labels of Emotions" include receptive and expressive labels in the first book of the Journey of Development ABA Curriculum series.
- Emotions chosen to teach should be the more basic emotions. In the third book of the Journey of Development ABA Curriculum series, emotions which are more difficult to recognize are taught (e.g. confused).

RECEPTIVE LABELS OF FUNCTION OF BODY PARTS

LEVEL: □ 1 □ 2 □ 3

S^D: Present individual with a field of 1, 2 or 3 picture cards of body parts and say "Give me what you [x] with," "Find what you [x] with," or "Point to what you [x] with" (e.g. "Point to what you hear with")	**Response:** Individual will give, find or point to the specified body part based on the function
Data Collection: Skill acquisition	**Target Criteria:** 80% or above for 3 consecutive days across 2 people
Materials: Picture cards of body parts and reinforcement (picture cards can be found on accompanying CD)	

Fading procedure

Maintenance Criteria: 2W = 4 consecutive scores of 100%; 1W = 4 consecutive scores of 100%; M = 3 consecutive scores of 100%	**Natural Environment (NE) Criterion:** Target has been generalized in NE across 3 novel naturally occurring activities	**Archive Criteria:** Target, maintenance and NE criteria have been met

Target list

Suggestions for targets and probe results

Suggestions for Targets: See/eyes, hear/ears, smell/nose, eat/mouth, touch/hands, walk/legs, talk/mouth, kiss/lips, write/hand and scratch/fingers.
Probe Results (targets in repertoire):

Target	Baseline %	Date Introduced	Date Criteria Met	*Fading Procedure*		
				Maintenance	Date NE Introduced	Date Archived
1. Target 1 (isolation):						
2. Target 1 (FO2/target and distractor):						
3. Target 1 (FO3/target and 2 distractors):						
4. Target 2 (isolation):						

5. Target 2 (FO2/target and distractor):						
6. Target 2 (FO3/target and 2 distractors):						
7. Targets 1 and 2 random rotation						
8. Target 3 (isolation):						
9. Target 3 (FO2/target and distractor):						
10. Target 3 (FO3/target and 2 distractors):						
11. Target 4 (isolation):						
12. Target 4 (FO2/target and distractor):						
13. Target 4 (FO3/target and 2 distractors):						
14. Targets that met criteria: random rotation						
15. Target 5 (isolation):						
16. Target 5 (FO2/target and distractor):						
17. Target 5 (FO3/target and 2 distractors):						
18. Target 6 (isolation):						
19. Target 6 (FO2/target and distractor):						
20. Target 6 (FO3/target and 2 distractors):						

21. Targets that met criteria: random rotation						
22. Target 7 (isolation):						
23. Target 7 (FO2/target and distractor):						
24. Target 7 (FO3/target and 2 distractors):						
25. Target 8 (isolation):						
26. Target 8 (FO2/target and distractor):						
27. Target 8 (FO3/target and 2 distractors):						
28. Targets that met criteria: random rotation						
29. Target 9 (isolation):						
30. Target 9 (FO2/target and distractor):						
31. Target 9 (FO3/target and 2 distractors):						
32. Target 10 (isolation):						
33. Target 10 (FO2/target and distractor):						
34. Target 10 (FO3/target and 2 distractors):						
35. Targets that met criteria: random rotation						
36. Generalize to another environment Environment 1:						

37. Generalize to another environment Environment 2:						
38. Maintenance: Assess in varied environments				2W 1W M		

Specific tips for running this task analysis

- Ensure pre-requisite skills have been taught for this TA. Examples of pre-requisite skills for "Receptive Labels of Function of Body Parts" include receptive and expressive labels in the first book of the Journey of Development ABA Curriculum series.

RECEPTIVE LABELS OF FUNCTION OF OBJECTS

LEVEL: □ 1 □ 2 □ 3

S^D: Present individual with a field of 1, 2 or 3 picture cards of objects and say "Touch what you [function] with," "Give me what you [function] with," or "Point to what you [function] with" [e.g. "Point to what you drink with"]	**Response:** Individual will touch, give or point to specified objects based on the function
Data Collection: Skill acquisition	**Target Criteria:** 80% or above for 3 consecutive days across 2 people
Materials: Picture cards of various objects and reinforcement (picture cards can be found on accompanying CD)	

Fading procedure

Maintenance Criteria: 2W = 4 consecutive scores of 100%; 1W = 4 consecutive scores of 100%; M = 3 consecutive scores of 100%	**Natural Environment (NE) Criterion:** Target has been generalized in NE across 3 novel naturally occurring activities	**Archive Criteria:** Target, maintenance and NE criteria have been met

Target list

Suggestions for targets and probe results

Suggestions for Targets: Drink (cup), eat (fork), cut (knife or scissors), color (crayon), play (toys), sit (chair), ride (bike), dry hands (towel), watch cartoons (TV), write (pencil), sleep (bed), sweep (broom), blow nose (tissue), throw (ball), brush teeth (toothbrush), brush hair (hairbrush), wash face (wash cloth), tell time (clock), take picture (camera), and drive (car).
Probe Results (targets in repertoire):

Target	Baseline %	Date Introduced	Date Criteria Met	*Fading Procedure*		
				Maintenance	**Date NE Introduced**	**Date Archived**
1. Target 1 (isolation):						
2. Target 1 (FO2/target and distractor):						
3. Target 1 (FO3/target and 2 distractors):						

4. Target 2 (isolation):						
5. Target 2 (FO2/target and distractor):						
6. Target 2 (FO3/target and 2 distractors):						
7. Targets 1 and 2 random rotation						
8. Target 3 (isolation):						
9. Target 3 (FO2/target and distractor):						
10. Target 3 (FO3/target and 2 distractors):						
11. Target 4 (isolation):						
12. Target 4 (FO2/target and distractor):						
13. Target 4 (FO3/target and 2 distractors):						
14. Targets that met criteria: random rotation						
15. Target 5 (isolation):						
16. Target 5 (FO2/target and distractor):						
17. Target 5 (FO3/target and 2 distractors):						
18. Target 6 (isolation):						
19. Target 6 (FO2/target and distractor):						

20. Target 6 (FO3/target and 2 distractors):						
21. Targets that met criteria: random rotation						
22. Target 7 (isolation):						
23. Target 7 (FO2/target and distractor):						
24. Target 7 (FO3/target and 2 distractors):						
25. Target 8 (isolation):						
26. Target 8 (FO2/target and distractor):						
27. Target 8 (FO3/target and 2 distractors):						
28. Targets that met criteria: random rotation						
29. Target 9 (isolation):						
30. Target 9 (FO2/target and distractor):						
31. Target 9 (FO3/target and 2 distractors):						
32. Target 10 (isolation):						
33. Target 10 (FO2/target and distractor):						
34. Target 10 (FO3/target and 2 distractors):						
35. Targets that met criteria: random rotation						

36. Generalize to another environment Environment 1:						
37. Generalize to another environment Environment 2:						
38. Maintenance: Assess in varied environments				2W 1W M		

Specific tips for running this task analysis

- Ensure pre-requisite skills have been taught for this TA. Examples of pre-requisite skills for "Receptive Labels of Function of Objects" include receptive and expressive labels in the first book of the Journey of Development ABA Curriculum series.
- Be sure to use a variety of objects from different categories, such as play materials (ride a bike) and materials representing daily living skills (blow nose with a tissue).

RECEPTIVE LABELS OF GENDER

LEVEL: □ 1 □ 2 □ 3

S^D: Present individual with a field of 1 or 2 picture cards of gender and say "Touch [gender]" or "Give me [gender]" or "Point to [gender]" (e.g. "Touch boy")	**Response:** Individual will touch, give or point to the specified gender
Data Collection: Skill acquisition	**Target Criteria:** 80% or above for 3 consecutive days across 2 people
Materials: Picture cards/figurines depicting gender and reinforcement (picture cards can be found on accompanying CD)	

Fading procedure

Maintenance Criteria: 2W = 4 consecutive scores of 100%; 1W = 4 consecutive scores of 100%; M = 3 consecutive scores of 100%	**Natural Environment (NE) Criterion:** Target has been generalized in NE across 3 novel naturally occurring activities	**Archive Criteria:** Target, maintenance and NE criteria have been met

Target list

Suggestions for targets and probe results

Suggestions for Targets: Boy, girl, man and woman (i.e. Barbie, little people, doll house figurines, flashcards, felt people)

Probe Results (targets in repertoire):

Target	Baseline %	Date Introduced	Date Criteria Met	*Fading Procedure*		
				Maintenance	Date NE Introduced	Date Archived
1. Target 1 (isolation):						
2. Target 1 (FO2/target and distractor):						
3. Target 2 (isolation):						
4. Target 2 (FO2/target and distractor):						
5. Targets 1 and 2 random rotation						

6. Target 3 (isolation):						
7. Target 3 (FO2/target and distractor):						
8. Target 4 (isolation):						
9. Target 4 (FO2/target and distractor):						
10. Targets that met criteria: random rotation						
11. Generalize to another environment Environment 1:						
12. Generalize to another environment Environment 2:						
13. Maintenance: Assess in varied environments				2W 1W M		

Specific tips for running this task analysis

- Ensure pre-requisite skills have been taught for this TA. Examples of pre-requisite skills for "Receptive Labels of Gender" include receptive and expressive labels in the first book of the Journey of Development ABA Curriculum series.
- Make sure when targeting the specific category (boy or girl) that you use sufficient examples that vary in look (i.e. hair color, clothing), to ensure that the individual learns that a boy can have brown or blond hair and wears various clothes (shorts, jeans, sweatpants). When using sufficient examples, you can use a different picture of a boy (or girl) for each trial. Make sure you note if there is a particular picture the individual repeatedly gets incorrect as you can specifically target this one picture if necessary.

RECEPTIVE LABELS OF ROOMS AND OBJECTS IN A ROOM

LEVEL: □ 1 □ 2 □ 3

S^D: A. Present individual with a field of 1, 2 or 3 picture cards of rooms and say "Touch [x]" or "Point to [x]" (e.g. "Touch kitchen") B. Present individual with a field of 1, 2 or 3 picture cards of objects in a room and say "Touch the room that has a [x]" or "Point to the room that has a [x]" (e.g. "Touch the room that has a bed")	**Response:** Individual will touch or point to the specified room
Data Collection: Skill acquisition	**Target Criteria:** 80% or above for 3 consecutive days across 2 people
Materials: Picture cards of rooms, objects in rooms and reinforcement (picture cards can be found on accompanying CD)	

Fading procedure

Maintenance Criteria: 2W = 4 consecutive scores of 100%; 1W = 4 consecutive scores of 100%; M = 3 consecutive scores of 100%	**Natural Environment (NE) Criterion:** Target has been generalized in NE across 3 novel naturally occurring activities	**Archive Criteria:** Target, maintenance and NE criteria have been met

Target list

Suggestions for targets and probe results

Suggestions for Targets: *Rooms:* kitchen, living room, dining room, bedroom, bathroom, playroom, classroom, library, basement and gym. *Objects in Rooms:* couch, refrigerator, bed, toilet, TV, microwave, dresser, shower/tub, chair and table.
Probe Results (targets in repertoire):

Target	Baseline %	Date Introduced	Date Criteria Met	*Fading Procedure*		
				Maintenance	**Date NE Introduced**	**Date Archived**
Labels of Rooms						
1. Target 1 (isolation):						
2. Target 1 (FO2/target and distractor):						
3. Target 1 (FO3/target and 2 distractors):						

4. Target 2 (isolation):						
5. Target 2 (FO2/target and distractor):						
6. Target 2 (FO3/target and 2 distractors):						
7. Targets that met criteria: random rotation						
8. Target 3 (isolation):						
9. Target 3 (FO2/target and distractor):						
10. Target 3 (FO3/target and 2 distractors):						
11. Target 4 (isolation):						
12. Target 4 (FO2/target and distractor):						
13. Target 4 (FO3/target and 2 distractors):						
14. Targets that met criteria: random rotation						
15. Target 5 (isolation):						
16. Target 5 (FO2/target and distractor):						
17. Target 5 (FO3/target and 2 distractors):						
18. Target 6 (isolation):						
19. Target 6 (FO2/target and distractor):						

20. Target 6 (FO3/target and 2 distractors):						
21. Targets that met criteria: random rotation						
22. Target 7 (isolation):						
23. Target 7 (FO2/target and distractor):						
24. Target 7 (FO3/target and 2 distractors):						
25. Target 8 (isolation):						
26. Target 8 (FO2/target and distractor):						
27. Target 8 (FO3/target and 2 distractors):						
28. Targets that met criteria: random rotation						
29. Target 9 (isolation):						
30. Target 9 (FO2/target and distractor):						
31. Target 9 (FO3/target and 2 distractors):						
32. Target 10 (isolation):						
33. Target 10 (FO2/target and distractor):						
34. Target 10 (FO3/target and 2 distractors)						
35. Targets that met criteria: random rotation						

36. Generalize to another environment Environment 1:						
37. Generalize to another environment Environment 2:						
38. Maintenance: Assess in varied environments				2W 1W M		
Labels of Room based on their Objects						
1. Target 1 (isolation):						
2. Target 1 (FO2/target and distractor):						
3. Target 1 (FO3/target and 2 distractors):						
4. Target 2 (isolation):						
5. Target 2 (FO2/target and distractor):						
6. Target 2 (FO3/target and 2 distractors):						
7. Targets that met criteria: random rotation						
8. Target 3 (isolation):						
9. Target 3 (FO2/target and distractor):						
10. Target 3 (FO3/target and 2 distractors):						
11. Target 4 (isolation):						
12. Target 4 (FO2/target and distractor):						

13. Target 4 (FO3/target and 2 distractors):						
14. Targets that met criteria: random rotation						
15. Target 5 (isolation):						
16. Target 5 (FO2/target and distractor):						
17. Target 5 (FO3/target and 2 distractors):						
18. Target 6 (isolation):						
19. Target 6 (FO2/target and distractor):						
20. Target 6 (FO3/target and 2 distractors):						
21. Targets that met criteria: random rotation						
22. Target 7 (isolation):						
23. Target 7 (FO2/target and distractor):						
24. Target 7 (FO3/target and 2 distractors):						
25. Target 8 (isolation):						
26. Target 8 (FO2/target and distractor):						
27. Target 8 (FO3/target and 2 distractors):						
28. Targets that met criteria: random rotation						

29. Target 9 (isolation):						
30. Target 9 (FO2/target and distractor):						
31. Target 9 (FO3/target and 2 distractors):						
32. Target 10 (isolation):						
33. Target 10 (FO2/target and distractor):						
34. Target 10 (FO3/target and 2 distractors):						
35. Targets that met criteria: random rotation						
36. Generalize to another environment Environment 1:						
37. Generalize to another environment Environment 2:						
38. Maintenance: Assess in varied environments				2W 1W M		

Specific tips for running this task analysis

- Ensure pre-requisite skills have been taught for this TA. Examples of pre-requisite skills for "Receptive Labels of Rooms and Objects in a Room" include receptive and expressive labels in the first book of the Journey of Development ABA Curriculum series.
- Individualize this program for the individual by walking around the family's home and taking note of the rooms in the home and the objects in each room. Teach the objects in the rooms of the individual's home, along with popular room objects in any home. Picture cards can be individualized by taking actual pictures of the rooms and objects in the rooms of the individual's home.

Chapter 13

TASK ANALYSES FOR EXPRESSIVE LANGUAGE SKILLS

- Answering Simple "What" Questions
- Answering Simple "When" Questions
- Answering Simple "Where" Questions
- Answering Simple "Where" Questions about a Classroom
- Answering Simple "Which" Questions
- Answering Simple "Who" Questions
- Answering Simple Yes/No Questions
- Answering Social Questions
- Describing Pictures
- Discriminating Sounds
- Expanding Sentence Length (Action–Object)
- Expanding Sentence Length (Subject–Action)
- Expanding Sentence Length (Subject–Action–Object)
- Expanding Sentence Length (Subject–Object)
- Expanding Sentence Starters
- Expressing Displeasure
- Expressive Labels of Attributes
- Expressive Labels of Categories
- Expressive Labels of Community Helpers
- Expressive Labels of Emotions
- Expressive Labels of Function of Body Parts
- Expressive Labels of Function of Objects
- Expressive Labels of Gender
- Expressive Labels of Rooms and Objects in a Room
- Intraverbal Fill-Ins of Predictable Routines
- Manners
- Past Tense Verbs
- Irregular Past Tense Verbs

- Plurals
- Irregular Plurals
- Pronouns (He/She)
- Pronouns (His/Him/Her)
- Pronouns (I/You)
- Pronouns (My/Your)
- Pronouns (Theirs/Ours)
- Pronouns (We/They)
- Providing Simple Directions to Another
- Reciprocating Information
- Requesting Needed or Missing Materials
- Simple Requests Using Questions
- Simple Requests Using Sentences
- Verbal Imitation of Phrases

ANSWERING SIMPLE "WHAT" QUESTIONS

LEVEL: □ 1 □ 2 □ 3

S^D: A. Present a picture card and ask a simple "what" question about the picture B. Ask a simple "what" question (no picture cues)	**Response:** Individual will correctly answer (i.e. verbally, by PECS (Bondy and Frost 2002) or by sign) the question
Data Collection: Skill acquisition	**Target Criteria:** 80% or above for 3 consecutive days across 2 people
Materials: Picture cards and reinforcement (picture cards can be found on accompanying CD)	

Fading procedure

Maintenance Criteria: 2W = 4 consecutive scores of 100%; 1W = 4 consecutive scores of 100%; M = 3 consecutive scores of 100%	**Natural Environment (NE) Criterion:** Target has been generalized in NE across 3 novel naturally occurring activities	**Archive Criteria:** Target, maintenance and NE criteria have been met

Target list

Suggestions for targets and probe results

Suggestions for Targets: *Using Picture Cues*: What does [x] have? What is [x] eating? What is [x] drinking? What is [x] writing with? What is (x) brushing? What is [x] washing? What is [x] doing? What is [x] using? What is [x] smelling? What is [x] driving? *Without Picture Cues:* What do we sit on? (chair), What do monkeys eat? (bananas), What do we color with? (crayons), What do we use to tell time? (clock), What do we use when it rains? (umbrella), What do you sleep on? (bed), What do you watch cartoons on? (TV), What do you sweep with? (broom), What do you blow your nose with? (tissue), What do we wear on our feet when it snows? (boots).

Probe Results (targets in repertoire):

Target	Baseline %	Date Introduced	Date Criteria Met	*Fading Procedure*		
				Maintenance	Date NE Introduced	Date Archived
1. S^D A: Target 1:						
2. S^D A: Target 2:						
3. Targets 1 and 2 random rotation						

4. S^D A: Target 3:						
5. S^D A: Target 4:						
6. Targets that met criteria: random rotation						
7. S^D A: Target 5:						
8. S^D A: Target 6:						
9. Targets that met criteria: random rotation						
10. S^D A: Target 7:						
11. S^D A: Target 8:						
12. Targets that met criteria: random rotation						
13. S^D A: Target 9:						
14. S^D A: Target 10:						
15. Targets that met criteria: random rotation						
16. Generalize to another environment Target 1:						
17. Generalize to another environment Target 2:						
18. Maintenance: Assess in varied environments				2W 1W M		
19. S^D B: Target 1:						
20. S^D B: Target 2:						

21. Targets 1 and 2 random rotation						
22. S^D B: Target 3:						
23. S^D B: Target 4:						
24. Targets that met criteria: random rotation						
25. S^D B: Target 5:						
26. S^D B: Target 6:						
27. Targets that met criteria: random rotation						
28. S^D B: Target 7:						
29. S^D B: Target 8:						
30. Targets that met criteria: random rotation						
31. S^D B: Target 9:						
32. S^D B: Target 10:						
33. Targets that met criteria: random rotation						
34. Generalize to another environment Environment 1:						
35. Generalize to another environment Environment 2:						
36. Maintenance: Assess in varied environments				2W 1W M		

Specific tips for running this task analysis

- Ensure pre-requisite skills have been taught for this TA. Examples of pre-requisite skills for "Answering Simple 'What' Questions" include mastering expressive labels in the first book of the Journey of Development ABA Curriculum series and progress made toward expressive labels in this curriculum book.
- If the individual is nonverbal, accept the answer in the form of a sign, written response, PECS (Bondy and Frost 2002) or augmentative device.
- If the individual presents with echolalia where you prompt the response and the individual echoes the question and response, one strategy to consider using is to present the S^D (question) in a lower voice followed by immediately giving the prompted response (within 1 second of the question) in a louder voice. By changing tone in voice, it helps the individual discriminate the S^D from the desired response. It is then important to fade the change in tone by stating the S^D more loudly and prompted response lower until both have same variation in tone. If the individual imitates you and changes their tone in voice while providing response, it is important to determine what tone will be expected for a correct response. This helps the individual to learn that the correct label is reinforced and not the particular tone in voice.

ANSWERING SIMPLE "WHEN" QUESTIONS

LEVEL: □ 1 □ 2 □ 3

S^D: Ask a simple "when" question (e.g. "When do we eat?")	**Response:** Individual will correctly answer (i.e. verbally, by PECS (Bondy and Frost 2002) or by sign) the question
Data Collection: Skill acquisition	**Target Criteria:** 80% or above for 3 consecutive days across 2 people
Materials: Reinforcement	

Fading procedure

Maintenance Criteria: 2W = 4 consecutive scores of 100%; 1W = 4 consecutive scores of 100%; M = 3 consecutive scores of 100%	**Natural Environment (NE) Criterion:** Target has been generalized in NE across 3 novel naturally occurring activities	**Archive Criteria:** Target, maintenance and NE criteria have been met

Target list

Suggestions for targets and probe results

Suggestions for Targets: When do we go to bed? (night), When do we eat? (hungry), When do we wake up? (morning), When do you go to doctor? (sick), When do you take a bath? (dirty), When does the sun come up? (morning), When do we turn on lights? (dark), When do we drink? (thirsty), When do we laugh? (funny), When do we rest? (tired).
Probe Results (targets in repertoire):

Target	Baseline %	Date Introduced	Date Criteria Met	*Fading Procedure*		
				Maintenance	Date NE Introduced	Date Archived
1. Target 1:						
2. Target 2:						
3. Targets 1 and 2 random rotation						
4. Target 3:						

5. Target 4:						
6. Targets that met criteria: random rotation						
7. Target 5:						
8. Target 6:						
9. Targets that met criteria: random rotation						
10. Target 7:						
11. Target 8:						
12. Targets that met criteria: random rotation						
13. Target 9:						
14. Target 10:						
15. Targets that met criteria: random rotation						
16. Generalize to another environment Environment 1:						
17. Generalize to another environment Environment 2:						
18. Maintenance: Assess in varied environments				2W 1W M		

Specific tips for running this task analysis

- Ensure pre-requisite skills have been taught for this TA. Examples of pre-requisite skills for "Answering Simple 'When' Questions" include mastering expressive labels in the first book of the Journey of Development ABA Curriculum series and progress made toward expressive labels in this curriculum book. The individual should also have made progress toward answering simple "what" questions.
- If the individual is nonverbal, accept the answer in the form of an alternative or augmentative communication such as sign, written response, PECS (Bondy and Frost 2002) or a communication device.

ANSWERING SIMPLE "WHERE" QUESTIONS

LEVEL: □ 1 □ 2 □ 3

S^D: Ask a simple "where" question (e.g. "Where do we go to sleep?")	**Response:** Individual will correctly answer (i.e. verbally, by PECS (Bondy and Frost 2002) or by sign) the question
Data Collection: Skill acquisition	**Target Criteria:** 80% or above for 3 consecutive days across 2 people
Materials: Reinforcement	

Fading procedure

Maintenance Criteria: 2W = 4 consecutive scores of 100%; 1W = 4 consecutive scores of 100%; M = 3 consecutive scores of 100%	**Natural Environment (NE) Criterion:** Target has been generalized in NE across 3 novel naturally occurring activities	**Archive Criteria:** Target, maintenance and NE criteria have been met

Target list

Suggestions for Targets and Probe Results

Suggestions for Targets: Where do we sleep? (bed/bedroom), Where do we eat? (table/kitchen), Where do we wash our hands? (sink), Where do we throw things away? (garbage can), Where do we take a bath? (bathtub/bathroom), Where do we swim? (pool), Where do we buy groceries? (grocery store), Where do you go when you are sick? (hospital), Where do you get books from? (library/bookstore), Where do we see stars? (sky).
Probe Results (targets in repertoire):

Target	Baseline %	Date Introduced	Date Criteria Met	*Fading Procedure*		
				Maintenance	Date NE Introduced	Date Archived
1. Target 1:						
2. Target 2:						
3. Targets 1 and 2 random rotation						
4. Target 3:						

5. Target 4:						
6. Targets that met criteria: random rotation						
7. Target 5:						
8. Target 6:						
9. Targets that met criteria: random rotation						
10. Target 7:						
11. Target 8:						
12. Targets that met criteria: random rotation						
13. Target 9:						
14. Target 10:						
15. Targets that met criteria: random rotation						
16. Generalize to another environment Environment 1:						
17. Generalize to another environment Environment 2:						
18. Maintenance: Assess in varied environments				2W 1W M		

Specific tips for running this task analysis

- Ensure pre-requisite skills have been taught for this TA. Examples of pre-requisite skills for "Answering Simple 'Where' Questions" include mastering expressive labels in the first book of the Journey of Development ABA Curriculum series and progress made toward expressive labels in this curriculum book. The individual should also have made progress toward answering simple "what" questions.

ANSWERING SIMPLE "WHERE" QUESTIONS ABOUT A CLASSROOM

LEVEL: □ 1 □ 2 □ 3

S^D: Ask a simple "where" question about items and activities in the classroom (e.g. "Where do we put our pencil when we are not using it?")	**Response:** Individual will correctly answer (i.e. verbally, by PECS (Bondy and Frost 2002) or by sign) the question
Data Collection: Skill acquisition	**Target Criteria:** 80% or above for 3 consecutive days across 2 people
Materials: Reinforcement	

Fading procedure

Maintenance Criteria: 2W = 4 consecutive scores of 100%; 1W = 4 consecutive scores of 100%; M = 3 consecutive scores of 100%	**Natural Environment (NE) Criterion:** Target has been generalized in NE across 3 novel naturally occurring activities	**Archive Criteria:** Target, maintenance and NE criteria have been met

Target list

Suggestions for targets and probe results

Suggestions for Targets: Where do we wash our hands? (sink), Where do we throw things away? (garbage can), Where do you get books from? (library), Where does the teacher sit? (her desk/in front), Where do we go to eat our lunch? (cafeteria), Where do we put our pencil when we are not using it? (desk), Where do you learn about the weather? (circle/circle time/floor), Where do you find [x]?
Probe Results (targets in repertoire):

Target	Baseline %	Date Introduced	Date Criteria Met	*Fading Procedure*		
				Maintenance	**Date NE Introduced**	**Date Archived**
1. Target 1:						
2. Target 2:						
3. Targets 1 and 2 random rotation						
4. Target 3:						

5. Target 4:						
6. Targets that met criteria: random rotation						
7. Target 5:						
8. Target 6:						
9. Targets that met criteria: random rotation						
10. Target 7:						
11. Target 8:						
12. Targets that met criteria: random rotation						
13. Target 9:						
14. Target 10:						
15. Targets that met criteria: random rotation						
16. Generalize to another environment Environment 1:						
17. Generalize to another environment Environment 2:						
18. Maintenance: Assess in varied environments				2W 1W M		

Specific tips for running this task analysis

- Ensure pre-requisite skills have been taught for this TA. Examples of pre-requisite skills for "Answering Simple 'Where' Questions about a Classroom" include mastering expressive labels in the first book of the Journey of Development ABA Curriculum series and progress made toward expressive labels in this curriculum book. The individual should also have made progress toward answering simple "what" and "where" questions.

ANSWERING SIMPLE "WHICH" QUESTIONS

LEVEL: □ 1 □ 2 □ 3

S^D: Present a field of 3 pictures or objects and ask a simple "which" question (e.g. "Which toy is yours?" or "Which one is an animal?")	**Response:** Individual will correctly answer (i.e. verbally, by PECS (Bondy and Frost 2002) or by sign) the question
Data Collection: Skill acquisition	**Target Criteria:** 80% or above for 3 consecutive days across 2 people
Materials: Objects, pictures of objects and emotions, and reinforcement (picture cards can be found on accompanying CD)	

Fading procedure

Maintenance Criteria: 2W = 4 consecutive scores of 100%; 1W = 4 consecutive scores of 100%; M = 3 consecutive scores of 100%	**Natural Environment (NE) Criterion:** Target has been generalized in NE across 3 novel naturally occurring activities	**Archive Criteria:** Target, maintenance and NE criteria have been met

Target list

Suggestions for targets and probe results

Suggestions for Targets: Which [x] is [attribute]? Which [item] is yours? Which one do you want (preference)? Which person is [feeling]? Which one is a [category]? Which one do you [action]? Which one do you use to [function]?
Probe Results (targets in repertoire):

Target	Baseline %	Date Introduced	Date Criteria Met	*Fading Procedure*		
				Maintenance	Date NE Introduced	Date Archived
1. Target 1:						
2. Target 2:						
3. Targets 1 and 2 random rotation						
4. Target 3:						

5. Target 4:						
6. Targets that met criteria: random rotation						
7. Target 5:						
8. Target 6:						
9. Targets that met criteria: random rotation						
10. Target 7:						
11. Target 8:						
12. Targets that met criteria: random rotation						
13. Target 9:						
14. Target 10:						
15. Targets that met criteria: random rotation						
16. Generalize to another environment Environment 1:						
17. Generalize to another environment Environment 2:						
18. Maintenance: Assess in varied environments				2W 1W M		

Specific tips for running this task analysis

- Ensure pre-requisite skills have been taught for this TA. Examples of pre-requisite skills for "Answering Simple 'Which' Questions" include mastering answering simple "what" and "where" questions, and expressive labels of emotions and attributes (TAs found in the first book of the Journey of Development ABA Curriculum series).
- When choosing targets, a minimum of 2 examples for each question/target should be taught (i.e. 2 different attributes, 2 different categories, etc.).

ANSWERING SIMPLE "WHO" QUESTIONS

LEVEL: □ 1 □ 2 □ 3

S^D: A. Present a picture of a person or community helper and ask "Who is this?" B. Ask a simple "Who" question (e.g. "Who do you like to play with?")	**Response:** Individual will correctly answer (i.e. verbally, by PECS (Bondy and Frost 2002) or by sign) the question
Data Collection: Skill acquisition	**Target Criteria:** 80% or above for 3 consecutive days across 2 people
Materials: Pictures of people in individual's life, community helper pictures (picture cards can be found on accompanying CD) and reinforcement	

Fading procedure

Maintenance Criteria: 2W = 4 consecutive scores of 100%; 1W = 4 consecutive scores of 100%; M = 3 consecutive scores of 100%	**Natural Environment (NE) Criterion:** Target has been generalized in NE across 3 novel naturally occurring activities	**Archive Criteria:** Target, maintenance and NE criteria have been met

Target list

Suggestions for targets and probe results

Suggestions for Targets: *S^D A*: Show pictures of people in the individual's life such as Mommy/Daddy/brother/sister/peer/neighbor/pet or a picture of a community helper such as policeman/fireman/teacher. *S^D B*: Who do you like to play with? Who goes to school with you? Who do you share a bedroom with? Who lives next door? Who made you breakfast today? Who takes you to karate class? Who do you live with? Who do you go to summer camp with?

Probe Results (targets in repertoire):

Target	Baseline %	Date Introduced	Date Criteria Met	*Fading Procedure*		
				Maintenance	**Date NE Introduced**	**Date Archived**
1. S^D A: Target 1:						
2. S^D A: Target 2:						
3. Targets 1 and 2 random rotation						
4. S^D A: Target 3:						

5. S^D A: Target 4:						
6. Targets that met criteria: random rotation						
7. S^D A: Target 5:						
8. S^D A: Target 6:						
9. Targets that met criteria: random rotation						
10. S^D A: Target 7:						
11. S^D A: Target 8:						
12. Targets that met criteria: random rotation						
13. S^D A: Target 9:						
14. S^D A: Target 10:						
15. Targets that met criteria: random rotation						
16. Generalize to another environment Environment 1:						
17. Generalize to another environment Environment 2:						
18. Maintenance: Assess in varied environments				2W 1W M		
19. S^D B: Target 1:						
20. S^D B: Target 2:						

21. Targets 1 and 2 random rotation						
22. S^D B: Target 3:						
23. S^D B: Target 4:						
24. Targets that met criteria: random rotation						
25. S^D B: Target 5:						
26. S^D B: Target 6:						
27. Targets that met criteria: random rotation						
28. S^D B: Target 7:						
29. S^D B: Target 8:						
30. Targets that met criteria: random rotation						
31. S^D B: Target 9:						
32. S^D B: Target 10:						
33. Targets that met criteria: random rotation						
34. Generalize to another environment Environment 1:						
35. Generalize to another environment Environment 2:						
36. Maintenance: Assess in varied environments				2W 1W M		

Specific tips for running this task analysis

- Ensure pre-requisite skills have been taught for this TA. Examples of pre-requisite skills for “Answering Simple ‘Who’ Questions” include expressive labels in the first book of the Journey of Development ABA Curriculum series and progress made toward expressive labels in this curriculum book. The individual should also have made progress toward answering simple “what” and “where” questions.
- If the individual is nonverbal, accept the answer in the form of augmentative and alternative communication such as sign language, written response, PECS (Bondy and Frost 2002) or a communication device.

ANSWERING SIMPLE YES/NO QUESTIONS

LEVEL: □ 1 □ 2 □ 3

S^D: A. Present a picture of an action and ask "Is this [action]?" (e.g. "Is this swimming?") B. "Do you [x] with [object]?" (e.g. "Do you sleep on a bed?")	**Response:** Individual will correctly answer yes or no (i.e. verbally, by PECS (Bondy and Frost 2002) or by sign) to the question
Data Collection: Skill acquisition	**Target Criteria:** 80% or above for 3 consecutive days across 2 people
Materials: Pictures of actions and reinforcement (picture cards can be found on accompanying CD)	

Fading procedure

Maintenance Criteria: 2W = 4 consecutive scores of 100%; 1W = 4 consecutive scores of 100%; M = 3 consecutive scores of 100%	**Natural Environment (NE) Criterion:** Target has been generalized in NE across 3 novel naturally occurring activities	**Archive Criteria:** Target, maintenance and NE criteria have been met

Target list

Suggestions for targets and probe results

Suggestions for Targets: *S^D A*: Is this swimming/jumping/sleeping/eating/singing/writing/playing/etc. *S^D B*: Do you [x] with object? Drink/cup, eat/fork, cut food/knife, color/crayon, cut/scissors, play/toys, sit on/chair, ride/bike, dry hands/towel, write/pencil, sleep/bed, sweep/broom and blow nose/tissue, throw/ball, brush teeth/toothbrush, brush hair/hairbrush, wash face/wash cloth, tell time/clock, take pictures/camera.
Probe Results (targets in repertoire):

Target	Baseline %	Date Introduced	Date Criteria Met	*Fading Procedure*		
				Maintenance	Date NE Introduced	Date Archived
1. S^D A: Target 1 (requiring positive response for a minimum of 5 actions):						
2. S^D A: Target 2 (requiring negative response for a minimum of 5 actions):						
3. S^D A: Targets that met criteria: random rotation						

4. Generalize to another environment Environment 1:						
5. Generalize to another environment Environment 2:						
6. Maintenance: Assess in varied environments				2W 1W M		
7. S^D B: Target 1 (requiring positive response for a minimum of 5 functions):						
8. S^D B: Target 2 (requiring negative response for a minimum of 5 functions):						
9. S^D B: Targets that met criteria: random rotation						
10. Generalize to another environment Environment 1:						
11. Generalize to another environment Environment 2:						
12. Maintenance: Assess in varied environments				2W 1W M		

Specific tips for running this task analysis

- Ensure pre-requisite skills have been taught for this TA. Examples of pre-requisite skills for "Answering Simple Yes/No Questions" are receptive and expressive labels of actions and functions of objects (TAs found in the first book of the Journey of Development ABA Curriculum series).
- If individual is nonverbal, accept correct answer in the form of gesture (nodding or shaking head) or a written response/alternative communication.
- The purpose of this TA is ability to answer yes or no (not identify actions or functions); thus you should use only those picture cards in which the individual has already mastered and maintained the ability to receptively label these things.
- When running Targets 1 and 2 for the S^Ds, be sure to rotate desirable and undesirable objects so no pattern is created. For example, ask questions requiring the following responses: yes, no, no, yes, yes, no, etc.

ANSWERING SOCIAL QUESTIONS

LEVEL: □ 1 □ 2 □ 3

S^D: Ask a social question (e.g. "What is your favorite color?")	**Response:** Individual will correctly answer (i.e. verbally, by PECS (Bondy and Frost 2002) or by sign) the question
Data Collection: Skill acquisition	**Target Criteria:** 80% or above for 3 consecutive days across 2 people
Materials: Reinforcement	

Fading procedure

Maintenance Criteria: 2W = 4 consecutive scores of 100%; 1W = 4 consecutive scores of 100%; M = 3 consecutive scores of 100%	**Natural Environment (NE) Criterion:** Target has been generalized in NE across 3 novel naturally occurring activities	**Archive Criteria:** Target, maintenance and NE criteria have been met

Target list

Suggestions for targets and probe results

Suggestions for Targets: What is your favorite color? Who is your teacher? What is your [pet's] name? Who is in your class? What's your favorite TV show? Where do you like to go on the weekends? What was your favorite vacation? What do you want to be when you grow up? What grade are you in? What do you want to play next?
Probe Results (targets in repertoire):

Target	Baseline %	Date Introduced	Date Criteria Met	*Fading Procedure*		
				Maintenance	**Date NE Introduced**	**Date Archived**
1. Target 1:						
2. Target 2:						
3. Targets that met criteria: random rotation						
4. Target 3:						

5. Target 4:						
6. Targets that met criteria: random rotation						
7. Target 5:						
8. Target 6:						
9. Targets that met criteria: random rotation						
10. Target 7:						
11. Target 8:						
12. Targets that met criteria: random rotation						
13. Target 9:						
14. Target 10:						
15. Targets that met criteria: random rotation						
16. Generalize to another environment Environment 1:						
17. Generalize to another environment Environment 2:						
18. Maintenance: Assess in varied environments				2W 1W M		

Specific tips for running this task analysis

- Ensure pre-requisite skills have been taught for this TA. Examples of pre-requisite skills for "Answering Social Questions" include mastering "Verbal Imitation" and "Answering Simple Social Questions" (TAs found in the first books of the Journey of Development ABA Curriculum series). Pre-requisite skills for nonverbal individuals include motor skills for signing the answer or touching icons on an alternative communication device.

DESCRIBING PICTURES

LEVEL: □ 1 □ 2 □ 3

S^D: Present a picture of a person engaging in an action and say "Tell me about this picture"	**Response:** Individual will provide a minimum of 2 sentences describing the picture with any of the following characteristics: who is in the picture (e.g. boy), attribute of person (e.g. the person is tall), feeling of the person (e.g. they are excited), where they are (e.g. park), or description of the scene (e.g. sunny day)
Data Collection: Skill acquisition	**Target Criteria:** 80% or above for 3 consecutive days across 2 people
Materials: Pictures of people in a scene and reinforcement (picture cards can be found on accompanying CD)	

Fading procedure

Maintenance Criteria: 2W = 4 consecutive scores of 100%; 1W = 4 consecutive scores of 100%; M = 3 consecutive scores of 100%	**Natural Environment (NE) Criterion:** Target has been generalized in NE across 3 novel naturally occurring activities	**Archive Criteria:** Target, maintenance and NE criteria have been met

Target list

Suggestions for targets and probe results

Suggestions for Targets: Kids playing at a playground, boy graduating from high school, basketball player during a game, people riding in a canoe, kids at an amusement park, girl playing soccer, kids in a classroom, two people shaking hands, someone crying, and people at a birthday party.
Probe Results (targets in repertoire):

Target	Baseline %	Date Introduced	Date Criteria Met	*Fading Procedure*		
				Maintenance	Date NE Introduced	Date Archived
1. Target 1:						
2. Target 2:						
3. Targets 1 and 2 random rotation						
4. Target 3:						

5. Target 4:						
6. Targets that met criteria: random rotation						
7. Target 5:						
8. Target 6:						
9. Targets that met criteria: random rotation						
10. Target 7:						
11. Target 8:						
12. Targets that met criteria: random rotation						
13. Target 9:						
14. Target 10:						
15. Targets that met criteria: random rotation						
16. Generalize to another environment Environment 1:						
17. Generalize to another environment Environment 2:						
18. Maintenance: Assess in varied environments				2W 1W M		

Specific tips for running this task analysis

- Ensure pre-requisite skills have been taught for this TA. Examples of pre-requisite skills for "Describing Pictures" include expressive labels of actions (TA found in the first book of the Journey of Development ABA Curriculum series), and expanding sentence length, receptive/expressive labels of gender, and receptive and expressive labels attributes (TAs found in this curriculum book).

DISCRIMINATING SOUNDS

LEVEL: □ 1 □ 2 □ 3

S^D: Play an environmental sound and ask "What do you hear?"	**Response:** Individual will correctly label the sound
Data Collection: Skill acquisition	**Target Criteria:** 80% or above for 3 consecutive days across 2 people
Materials: Recordings of various sounds and reinforcement	

Fading procedure

Maintenance Criteria: 2W = 4 consecutive scores of 100%; 1W = 4 consecutive scores of 100%; M = 3 consecutive scores of 100%	**Natural Environment (NE) Criterion:** Target has been generalized in NE across 3 novel naturally occurring activities	**Archive Criteria:** Target, maintenance and NE criteria have been met

Target list

Suggestions for targets and probe results

Suggestions for Targets: Bell, police car, beach, lightning, hammer, baby crying, sneeze, ice-cream man, train, phone ringing, morning alarm, bird chirping, fan, running water, waterfall and dog barking.
Probe Results (targets in repertoire):

Target	Baseline %	Date Introduced	Date Criteria Met	*Fading Procedure*		
				Maintenance	Date NE Introduced	Date Archived
1. Target 1:						
2. Target 2:						
3. Targets 1 and 2 random rotation						
4. Target 3:						
5. Target 4:						

6. Targets that met criteria: random rotation						
7. Target 5:						
8. Target 6:						
9. Targets that met criteria: random rotation						
10. Target 7:						
11. Target 8:						
12. Targets that met criteria: random rotation						
13. Target 9:						
14. Target 10:						
15. Targets that met criteria: random rotation						
16. Generalize to another environment Environment 1:						
17. Generalize to another environment Environment 2:						
18. Maintenance: Assess in varied environments				2W 1W M		

Specific tips for running this task analysis

- Ensure pre-requisite skills have been taught for this TA. Examples of pre-requisite skills for "Discriminating Sounds" include mastering expressive labels in the first book of the Journey of Development ABA Curriculum series and receptively discriminating sounds (TA found in this curriculum).
- You can create your own recordings by downloading sounds from the internet. Alternatively, you could use the actual objects that make sounds (just hide them from view), for example, an alarm clock or a bell. In addition, there are CDs and apps that you could purchase that contain various sounds.

EXPANDING SENTENCE LENGTH (ACTION–OBJECT)

LEVEL: □ 1 □ 2 □ 3

S^D: Present a picture depicting an action and ask "What is the boy/girl doing?" or "What is the man/woman doing?"	**Response:** Individual will answer (i.e. verbally, by PECS (Bondy and Frost 2002) or by sign) the question; answer will be an action and an object (e.g. brushing teeth)
Data Collection: Skill acquisition	**Target Criteria:** 80% or above for 3 consecutive days across 2 people
Materials: Action pictures and reinforcement (picture cards can be found on accompanying CD)	

Fading procedure

Maintenance Criteria: 2W = 4 consecutive scores of 100%; 1W = 4 consecutive scores of 100%; M = 3 consecutive scores of 100%	**Natural Environment (NE) Criterion:** Target has been generalized in NE across 3 novel naturally occurring activities	**Archive Criteria:** Target, maintenance and NE criteria have been met

Target list

Suggestions for targets and probe results

Suggestions for Targets: Kicking ball, eating [x], drinking [x], riding bike, blowing bubbles, brushing teeth, brushing hair, washing hands, reading book, watching TV, throwing ball, driving car, playing puzzle, cutting with scissors, catching ball, cooking [x], pouring [x], holding [x], feeding baby and raising hand.
Probe Results (targets in repertoire):

Target	Baseline %	Date Introduced	Date Criteria Met	*Fading Procedure*		
				Maintenance	**Date NE Introduced**	**Date Archived**
1. Target 1:						
2. Target 2:						
3. Targets 1 and 2 random rotation						
4. Target 3:						

5. Target 4:						
6. Targets that met criteria: random rotation						
7. Target 5:						
8. Target 6:						
9. Targets that met criteria: random rotation						
10. Target 7:						
11. Target 8:						
12. Targets that met criteria: random rotation						
13. Target 9:						
14. Target 10:						
15. Targets that met criteria: random rotation						
16. Generalize to another environment Environment 1:						
17. Generalize to another environment Environment 2:						
18. Maintenance: Assess in varied environments				2W 1W M		

Specific tips for running this task analysis

- Ensure pre-requisite skills have been taught for this TA. Examples of pre-requisite skills for "Expanding Sentence Length (Action–Object)" include mastering expressive labels of objects and expressive labels of actions (both TAs found in the first book of the Journey of Development ABA Curriculum series).
- If individual is nonverbal, accept the answer in the form of a sign, written response, PECS (Bondy and Frost 2002) or augmentative device.

EXPANDING SENTENCE LENGTH (SUBJECT–ACTION)

LEVEL: □ 1 □ 2 □ 3

S^D: Present a picture of a familiar person engaging in an action and say "Tell me about the picture"	**Response:** Individual will label the picture (i.e. verbally, by PECS (Bondy and Frost 2002) or by sign); answer will be a subject and action (e.g. Mommy is eating)
Data Collection: Skill acquisition	**Target Criteria:** 80% or above for 3 consecutive days across 2 people
Materials: Pictures of familiar people engaging in actions and reinforcement	

Fading procedure

Maintenance Criteria: 2W = 4 consecutive scores of 100%; 1W = 4 consecutive scores of 100%; M = 3 consecutive scores of 100%	**Natural Environment (NE) Criterion:** Target has been generalized in NE across 3 novel naturally occurring activities	**Archive Criteria:** Target, maintenance and NE criteria have been met

Target list

Suggestions for targets and probe results

Suggestions for Targets: Mommy/Daddy/baby/sibling/grandparent/girl/boy/cartoon character is sleeping/eating/clapping/jumping/drinking/hugging/washing/pouring/brushing/laughing.
Probe Results (targets in repertoire):

Target	Baseline %	Date Introduced	Date Criteria Met	*Fading Procedure*		
				Maintenance	Date NE Introduced	Date Archived
1. Target 1:						
2. Target 2:						
3. Targets 1 and 2 random rotation						
4. Target 3:						
5. Target 4:						

6. Targets that met criteria: random rotation						
7. Target 5:						
8. Target 6:						
9. Targets that met criteria: random rotation						
10. Target 7:						
11. Target 8:						
12. Targets that met criteria: random rotation						
13. Target 9:						
14. Target 10:						
15. Targets that met criteria: random rotation						
16. Generalize to another environment Environment 1:						
17. Generalize to another environment Environment 2:						
18. Maintenance: Assess in varied environments				2W 1W M		

Specific tips for running this task analysis

- Ensure pre-requisite skills have been taught for this TA. Examples of pre-requisite skills for "Expanding Sentence Length (Subject–Action)" include mastering expressive labels of familiar people and expressive labels of actions (both TAs found in the first book of the Journey of Development ABA Curriculum series).

EXPANDING SENTENCE LENGTH (SUBJECT–ACTION–OBJECT)

LEVEL: □ 1 □ 2 □ 3

S^D: Present a picture of a familiar person engaging in an action and ask "What's happening?" Alternatively, present a picture of an unfamiliar person and ask "What's happening?"	**Response:** Individual will answer (i.e. verbally, by PECS (Bondy and Frost 2002) or by sign) the question using a subject, action and object (e.g. "Tommy is kicking the ball"). Alternatively, individual will respond "Boy is kicking the ball"
Data Collection: Skill acquisition	**Target Criteria:** 80% or above for 3 consecutive days across 2 people
Materials: People–action–object pictures and reinforcement (picture cards can be found on accompanying CD)	

Fading procedure

Maintenance Criteria: 2W = 4 consecutive scores of 100%; 1W = 4 consecutive scores of 100%; M = 3 consecutive scores of 100%	**Natural Environment (NE) Criterion:** Target has been generalized in NE across 3 novel naturally occurring activities	**Archive Criteria:** Target, maintenance and NE criteria have been met

Target list

Suggestions for targets and probe results

Suggestions for Targets: Familiar person/boy/girl/man/woman is kicking ball/eating [x]/drinking [x]/riding bike/blowing bubbles/brushing teeth/brushing hair/washing hands/reading book/cutting paper/throwing ball/watching TV/playing puzzle/playing a game/catching ball/cooking [x]/pouring [x]/holding [x]/feeding baby/raising hand.

Probe Results (targets in repertoire):

Target	Baseline %	Date Introduced	Date Criteria Met	*Fading Procedure*		
				Maintenance	Date NE Introduced	Date Archived
1. Target 1:						
2. Target 2:						

3. Targets 1 and 2 random rotation						
4. Target 3:						
5. Target 4:						
6. Targets that met criteria: random rotation						
7. Target 5:						
8. Target 6:						
9. Targets that met criteria: random rotation						
10. Target 7:						
11. Target 8:						
12. Targets that met criteria: random rotation						
13. Target 9:						
14. Target 10:						
15. Targets that met criteria: random rotation						
16. Generalize to another environment Environment 1:						

17. Generalize to another environment Environment 2:						
18. Maintenance: Assess in varied environments				2W 1W M		

Specific tips for running this task analysis

- Ensure pre-requisite skills have been taught for this TA. Examples of pre-requisite skills for "Expanding Sentence Length (Subject–Action–Object)" include "Mastering Expressive Labels of Familiar People," "Expressive Labels of Functional Objects" (and leisure objects), and "Expressive Labels of Actions" (TAs found in the first book of the Journey of Development ABA Curriculum series).

EXPANDING SENTENCE LENGTH (SUBJECT–OBJECT)

LEVEL: □ 1 □ 2 □ 3

S^D: Present an item that belongs to a familiar person and ask "Whose is this?"	**Response:** Individual will answer (i.e. verbally, by PECS (Bondy and Frost 2002) or by sign) the question; answer will be subject and object (e.g. Mommy's purse)
Data Collection: Skill acquisition	**Target Criteria:** 80% or above for 3 consecutive days across 2 people
Materials: Items that belong to familiar people and reinforcement	

Fading procedure

Maintenance Criteria: 2W = 4 consecutive scores of 100%; 1W = 4 consecutive scores of 100%; M = 3 consecutive scores of 100%	**Natural Environment (NE) Criterion:** Target has been generalized in NE across 3 novel naturally occurring activities	**Archive Criteria:** Target, maintenance and NE criteria have been met

Target list

Suggestions for targets and probe results

Suggestions for Targets: Mommy's/Daddy's/sibling's/teacher's hat/purse/lunch box/toy/book/coat/book bag/cup/car.
Probe Results (targets in repertoire):

Target	Baseline %	Date Introduced	Date Criteria Met	*Fading Procedure*		
				Maintenance	Date NE Introduced	Date Archived
1. Target 1:						
2. Target 2:						
3. Targets 1 and 2 random rotation						
4. Target 3:						
5. Target 4:						

6. Targets that met criteria: random rotation						
7. Target 5:						
8. Target 6:						
9. Targets that met criteria: random rotation						
10. Target 7:						
11. Target 8:						
12. Targets that met criteria: random rotation						
13. Target 9:						
14. Target 10:						
15. Targets that met criteria: random rotation						
16. Generalize to another environment Environment 1:						
17. Generalize to another environment Environment 2:						
18. Maintenance: Assess in varied environments				2W 1W M		

Specific tips for running this task analysis

- Ensure pre-requisite skills have been taught for this TA. Examples of pre-requisite skills for “Expanding Sentence Length (Subject–Object)” include mastering “Expressive Labels of Familiar People” and “Expressive Labels of Functional Objects” (both TAs found in the first book of the Journey of Development ABA Curriculum series).
- If the individual is nonverbal, accept the answer in the form of a sign, written response, PECS (Bondy and Frost 2002) or augmentative device.
- When choosing objects, be sure that the individual will easily know who the item belongs to.

EXPANDING SENTENCE STARTERS

LEVEL: □ 1 □ 2 □ 3

S^D: Ask a question evoking a new sentence starter e.g. "What do you see?" "What do you have?" "What is it?" "What are these?" "Can you…?")	**Response:** Individual will answer (i.e. verbally, by PECS (Bondy and Frost 2002) or by sign) the question with the sentence starter (i.e. I see…, I have…, It is a …, They are…, etc.)
Data Collection: Skill acquisition	**Target Criteria:** 80% or above for 3 consecutive days across 2 people
Materials: Reinforcement	

Fading procedure

Maintenance Criteria: 2W = 4 consecutive scores of 100%; 1W = 4 consecutive scores of 100%; M = 3 consecutive scores of 100%	**Natural Environment (NE) Criterion:** Target has been generalized in NE across 3 novel naturally occurring activities	**Archive Criteria:** Target, maintenance and NE criteria have been met

Target list

Suggestions for targets and probe results

Suggestions for Targets: I see [x], There's [x], That's a [x], I have [x], It is a [x], I can [x], They are [x], I hear [x], I want [x], I need [x], and Look at the [x].
Probe Results (targets in repertoire):

Target	Baseline %	Date Introduced	Date Criteria Met	*Fading Procedure*		
				Maintenance	Date NE Introduced	Date Archived
1. Target 1:						
2. Target 2:						
3. Targets 1 and 2 random rotation						
4. Target 3:						

5. Target 4:						
6. Targets that met criteria: random rotation						
7. Target 5:						
8. Target 6:						
9. Targets that met criteria: random rotation						
10. Target 7:						
11. Target 8:						
12. Targets that met criteria: random rotation						
13. Target 9:						
14. Target 10:						
15. Targets that met criteria: random rotation						
16. Generalize to another environment Environment 1:						
17. Generalize to another environment Environment 2:						
18. Maintenance: Assess in varied environments				2W 1W M		

Specific tips for running this task analysis

- Ensure pre-requisite skills have been taught for this TA. Examples of pre-requisite skills for "Expanding Sentence Starters" include mastering "Expressive Labels of Objects" and "Expressive Labels of Actions" (both TAs found in the first book of the Journey of Development ABA Curriculum series) and "Expanding Sentence Length (Subject–Action–Object)" (TA found in this curriculum book).
- If individual is nonverbal, accept the answer in the form of a sign, written response, PECS (Bondy and Frost 2002) or augmentative device.

EXPRESSING DISPLEASURE

LEVEL: □ 1 □ 2 □ 3

S^D: Contrive a situation in which the individual will be required to express displeasure (e.g. individual will say "It's mine" when instructor takes away toy)	**Response:** Individual will make an appropriate comment expressing displeasure pertaining to the situation
Data Collection: Prompt data (number and type of prompts used)	**Target criteria:** 0 prompts for 3 consecutive days across 2 people
Materials: Reinforcement	

Fading procedure

Maintenance Criteria: 2W = 4 consecutive scores of 0 prompts; 1W = 4 consecutive scores of 0 prompts; M = 3 consecutive scores of 0 prompts	**Natural Environment (NE) Criterion:** Target has been generalized in NE across 3 novel naturally occurring activities	**Archive Criteria:** Target, maintenance and NE criteria have been met

Target list

Suggestions for targets and probe results

Suggestions for Targets: Take a preferred object from individual to teach "It's mine" or "I had that first." Offer a non-preferred item to the individual to teach "No" or "I don't want that." Tease the individual to teach "Stop it" or "Leave me alone." Offer a non-preferred activity to teach "I don't want to" or "I don't like that." Make a hurtful comment to teach "That hurt my feelings" or "That's not nice." Turn off a toy the individual is playing with or the television show they were watching to teach "I was watching/playing with that."

Probe Results (targets in repertoire):

Target	Baseline: Number and Type of Prompts	Date Introduced	Date Criteria Met	*Fading Procedure*		
				Maintenance	Date NE Introduced	Date Archived
1. Target 1:						
2. Target 2:						

3. Targets that met criteria: random rotation						
4. Target 3:						
5. Target 4:						
6. Targets that met criteria: random rotation						
7. Target 5:						
8. Target 6:						
9. Targets that met criteria: random rotation						
10. Target 7:						
11. Target 8:						
12. Targets that met criteria: random rotation						
13. Target 9:						
14. Target 10:						
15. Targets that met criteria: random rotation						
16. Generalize to another environment Environment 1:						
17. Generalize to another environment Environment 2:						
18. Maintenance: Assess in varied environments				2W 1W M		

EXPRESSIVE LABELS OF ATTRIBUTES

LEVEL: □ 1 □ 2 □ 3

S^D: Present a picture or object and say "Tell me one thing about the [x]," for example, "Tell me one thing about the car"	**Response:** Individual will label at least one attribute of the object or picture
Data Collection: Skill acquisition	**Target Criteria:** 80% or above for 3 consecutive days across 2 people
Materials: Pictures/objects depicting various attributes and reinforcement (picture cards can be found on accompanying CD)	

Fading procedure

Maintenance Criteria: 2W = 4 consecutive scores of 100%; 1W = 4 consecutive scores of 100%; M = 3 consecutive scores of 100%	**Natural Environment (NE) Criterion:** Target has been generalized in NE across 3 novel naturally occurring activities	**Archive Criteria:** Target, maintenance and NE criteria have been met

Target list

Suggestions for targets and probe results

Suggestions for Targets: Broken, empty, full, dirty, clean, round, tall, short, big, little, wet, dry, hot, cold, hard, soft, dark, light, old, new, and young.

Probe Results (targets in repertoire):

Target	Baseline %	Date Introduced	Date Criteria Met	*Fading Procedure*		
				Maintenance	**Date NE Introduced**	**Date Archived**
1. Target 1:						
2. Target 2:						
3. Targets 1 and 2 random rotation						
4. Target 3:						
5. Target 4:						

6. Targets that met criteria: random rotation						
7. Target 5:						
8. Target 6:						
9. Targets that met criteria: random rotation						
10. Target 7:						
11. Target 8:						
12. Targets that met criteria: random rotation						
13. Target 9:						
14. Target 10:						
15. Targets that met criteria: random rotation						
16. Generalize to another environment Environment 1:						
17. Generalize to another environment Environment 2:						
18. Maintenance: Assess in varied environments				2W 1W M		

Specific tips for running this task analysis

- Ensure pre-requisite skills have been taught for this TA. Examples of pre-requisite skills for "Expressive Labels of Attributes" include mastering expressive labels in the first book of the Journey of Development ABA Curriculum series and "Receptive Labels of Attributes" (TA found in this curriculum book).
- Initially, the individual is likely to just name the object on the picture card. Simply present with S^D again with a verbal prompt of using the attribute with the object. For example, if individual says "It's a building," you present S^D again and quickly provide verbal prompt "It's a tall building."
- An alternative teaching strategy is to present two objects or pictures of an item varying in one attribute and give the S^D (e.g. present a big spoon and a little spoon then give the S^D.)

EXPRESSIVE LABELS OF CATEGORIES

LEVEL: □ 1 □ 2 □ 3

S^D: "Name 5 [category]" (e.g. "Name 5 animals")	**Response:** Individual will name 5 items that belong in the specified category
Data Collection: Skill acquisition	**Target Criteria:** 80% or above for 3 consecutive days across 2 people
Materials: Reinforcement	

Fading procedure

Maintenance Criteria: 2W = 4 consecutive scores of 100%; 1W = 4 consecutive scores of 100%; M = 3 consecutive scores of 100%	**Natural Environment (NE) Criterion:** Target has been generalized in NE across 3 novel naturally occurring activities	**Archive Criteria:** Target, maintenance and NE criteria have been met

Target list

Suggestions for targets and probe results

Suggestions for Targets: Food, clothing, animals, drinks, toys, vehicles, people, colors, letters, and instruments.
Probe Results (targets in repertoire):

Target	Baseline %	Date Introduced	Date Criteria Met	*Fading Procedure*		
				Maintenance	**Date NE Introduced**	**Date Archived**
1. Target 1:						
2. Target 2:						
3. Targets 1 and 2 random rotation						
4. Target 3:						
5. Target 4:						

6. Targets that met criteria: random rotation						
7. Target 5:						
8. Target 6:						
9. Targets that met criteria: random rotation						
10. Target 7:						
11. Target 8:						
12. Targets that met criteria: random rotation						
13. Target 9:						
14. Target 10:						
15. Targets that met criteria: random rotation						
16. Generalize to another environment Environment 1:						
17. Generalize to another environment Environment 2:						
18. Maintenance: Assess in varied environments				2W 1W M		

Specific tips for running this task analysis

- Ensure pre-requisite skills have been taught for this TA. Examples of pre-requisite skills for "Expressive Labels of Categories" include mastering "Sorting by Groups and Categories" (TA found in the first book of the Journey of Development ABA Curriculum series).
- If the individual has difficulty labeling what belongs within the specified category, first have the individual sort into categories and then use the pictures as visual prompts to label within the category. Use different pictures for the sorting trials to avoid rote responding.

EXPRESSIVE LABELS OF COMMUNITY HELPERS

LEVEL: □ 1 □ 2 □ 3

S^D: Present individual with an object or picture of a community helper and say "What is this?"	**Response:** Individual will label the object or picture
Data Collection: Skill acquisition	**Target Criteria:** 80% or above for 3 consecutive days across 2 people
Materials: Objects or pictures of community helpers and reinforcement (picture cards can be found on accompanying CD)	

Fading procedure

Maintenance Criteria: 2W = 4 consecutive scores of 100%; 1W = 4 consecutive scores of 100%; M = 3 consecutive scores of 100%	**Natural Environment (NE) Criterion:** Target has been generalized in NE across 3 novel naturally occurring activities	**Archive Criteria:** Target, maintenance and NE criteria have been met

Target list

Suggestions for targets and probe results

Suggestions for Targets: Doctor, teacher, pilot, fireman, dentist, policeman, mailman, nurse, librarian, astronaut and farmer.
Probe Results (targets in repertoire):

Target	Baseline %	Date Introduced	Date Criteria Met	*Fading Procedure*		
				Maintenance	Date NE Introduced	Date Archived
1. Target 1:						
2. Target 2:						
3. Targets 1 and 2 random rotation						
4. Target 3:						
5. Target 4:						

6. Targets that met criteria: random rotation						
7. Target 5:						
8. Target 6:						
9. Targets that met criteria: random rotation						
10. Target 7:						
11. Target 8:						
12. Targets that met criteria: random rotation						
13. Target 9:						
14. Target 10:						
15. Targets that met criteria: random rotation						
16. Generalize to another environment Environment 1:						
17. Generalize to another environment Environment 2:						
18. Maintenance: Assess in varied environments				2W 1W M		

Specific tips for running this task analysis

- Ensure pre-requisite skills have been taught for this TA. Examples of pre-requisite skills for "Expressive Labels of Community Helpers" include mastering expressive labels in the first book of the Journey of Development ABA Curriculum series and "Receptive Labels of Community Helpers" (TA found in this curriculum book).
- If individual is nonverbal, accept the answer in the form of a sign, written response, PECS (Bondy and Frost 2002) or augmentative device.

EXPRESSIVE LABELS OF EMOTIONS

LEVEL: □ 1 □ 2 □ 3

S^D: Present individual with a picture of a person's face depicting an emotion and ask "What is he/she feeling?" or "How does he/she feel?"	**Response:** Individual will label the emotion depicted in the picture
Data Collection: Skill acquisition	**Target Criteria:** 80% or above for 3 consecutive days across 2 people
Materials: Pictures of individuals depicting various emotions and reinforcement (picture cards can be found on accompanying CD)	

Fading procedure

Maintenance Criteria: 2W = 4 consecutive scores of 100%; 1W = 4 consecutive scores of 100%; M = 3 consecutive scores of 100%	**Natural Environment (NE) Criterion:** Target has been generalized in NE across 3 novel naturally occurring activities	**Archive Criteria:** Target, maintenance and NE criteria have been met

Target list

Suggestions for targets and probe results

Suggestions for Targets: Happy, sad, mad, scared, tired, silly, surprised, sick, relaxed, and shy.

Probe Results (targets in repertoire):

Target	Baseline %	Date Introduced	Date Criteria Met	*Fading Procedure*		
				Maintenance	Date NE Introduced	Date Archived
1. Target 1:						
2. Target 2:						
3. Targets 1 and 2 random rotation						
4. Target 3:						
5. Target 4:						

6. Targets that met criteria: random rotation						
7. Target 5:						
8. Target 6:						
9. Targets that met criteria: random rotation						
10. Target 7:						
11. Target 8:						
12. Targets that met criteria: random rotation						
13. Target 9:						
14. Target 10:						
15. Targets that met criteria: random rotation						
16. Generalize to another environment Environment 1:						
17. Generalize to another environment Environment 2:						
18. Maintenance: Assess in varied environments				2W 1W M		

Specific tips for running this task analysis

- Ensure pre-requisite skills have been taught for this TA. Examples of pre-requisite skills for "Expressive Labels of Emotions" include mastering expressive labels in the first book of the Journey of Development ABA Curriculum series and "Receptive Labels of Emotions" (TA found in this curriculum book).
- Emotions chosen to teach should be the more basic emotions. In the third book of the Journey of Development ABA Curriculum series, emotions which are more difficult to recognize will be taught (e.g. confused).

EXPRESSIVE LABELS OF FUNCTION OF BODY PARTS

LEVEL: □ 1 □ 2 □ 3

S^D: A. "What do you [x] with?" (e.g. "What do you see with?") B. "What do you do with your [x]?" (e.g. "What do you do with your eyes?")	**Response:** Individual will answer the question with verbalization, written word, sign, PECS (Bondy and Frost 2002) or augmentative device
Data Collection: Skill acquisition	**Target Criteria:** 80% or above for 3 consecutive days across 2 people
Materials: Reinforcement	

Fading procedure

Maintenance Criteria: 2W = 4 consecutive scores of 100%; 1W = 4 consecutive scores of 100%; M = 3 consecutive scores of 100%	**Natural Environment (NE) Criterion:** Target has been generalized in NE across 3 novel naturally occurring activities	**Archive Criteria:** Target, maintenance and NE criteria have been met

Target list

Suggestions for targets and probe results

Suggestions for Targets: *S^D A*: What do you see with? (eyes), What do you hear with? (ears), What do you smell with? (nose), What do you eat with? (mouth), What do you touch with? (hands/fingers), What do you walk with? (legs), What do you talk with? (mouth), What do you kiss with? (lips), What do you write with? (hand) and What do you jump with? (legs). *S^D B*: What do you do with your eyes? (see), What do you do with your nose? (smell), What do you do with your mouth? (taste/talk), What do you do with your legs? (walk/jump), What do you do with your hands? (touch), What do you do with ears? (hear), What do you do with your teeth? (chew), What do you do with your tongue? (lick).
Probe Results (targets in repertoire):

Target	Baseline %	Date Introduced	Date Criteria Met	*Fading Procedure* Maintenance	Date NE Introduced	Date Archived
1. S^D A: Target 1:						
2. S^D A: Target 2:						
3. Targets 1 and 2 random rotation						

4. S^D A: Target 3:						
5. S^D A: Target 4:						
6. Targets that met criteria: random rotation						
7. S^D A: Target 5:						
8. S^D A: Target 6:						
9. Targets that met criteria: random rotation						
10. S^D A: Target 7:						
11. S^D A: Target 8:						
12. Targets that met criteria: random rotation						
13. S^D A: Target 9:						
14. S^D A: Target 10:						
15. Targets that met criteria: random rotation						
16. Generalize to another environment Environment 1:						
17. Generalize to another environment Environment 2:						
18. Maintenance: Assess in varied environments.				2W 1W M		
19. S^D B: Target 1:						
20. S^D B: Target 2:						

21. Targets 1 and 2 random rotation						
22. S^D B: Target 3:						
23. S^D B: Target 4:						
24. Targets that met criteria: random rotation						
25. S^D B: Target 5:						
26. S^D B: Target 6:						
27. Targets that met criteria: random rotation						
28. S^D B: Target 7:						
29. S^D B: Target 8:						
30. Targets that met criteria: random rotation						
31. S^D B: Target 9:						
32. S^D B: Target 10:						
33. Targets that met criteria: random rotation						
34. Generalize to another environment Environment 1:						
35. Generalize to another environment Environment 2:						
36. Maintenance: Assess in varied environments				2W 1W M		

Specific tips for running this task analysis

- Ensure pre-requisite skills have been taught for this TA. Examples of pre-requisite skills for "Expressive Labels of Function of Body Parts" include mastering expressive labels in the first book of the Journey of Development ABA Curriculum series, especially "Expressive Labels of Body Parts."
- If individual is nonverbal, accept the answer in the form of a sign, written response, PECS (Bondy and Frost 2002) or augmentative device.

EXPRESSIVE LABELS OF FUNCTION OF OBJECTS

LEVEL: □ 1 □ 2 □ 3

S^D: A. "What do you [function] with?" (e.g. "What do you drink with?") B. "What do you do with a [x]?" (e.g. "What do you do with a cup?")	**Response:** Individual will correctly answer the question with verbalization, written word, sign, PECS (Bondy and Frost 2002) or augmentative device
Data Collection: Skill acquisition	**Target Criteria:** 80% or above for 3 consecutive days across 2 people
Materials: Reinforcement	

Fading procedure

Maintenance Criteria: 2W = 4 consecutive scores of 100%; 1W = 4 consecutive scores of 100%; M = 3 consecutive scores of 100%	**Natural Environment (NE) Criterion:** Target has been generalized in NE across 3 novel naturally occurring activities	**Archive Criteria:** Target, maintenance and NE criteria have been met

Target list

Suggestions for targets and probe results

Suggestions for Targets: *S^D A*: Drink (cup), eat (fork), cut food (knife), color (crayon), cut (scissors), play (toys), dry hands (towel), write (pencil), sweep (broom), blow nose (tissue), brush teeth (toothbrush), brush hair (hairbrush), wash face (wash cloth), tell time (clock), take picture (camera) and drive (car). *S^D B*: Cup (drink), fork (eat), knife (cut food), crayon (color), scissors (cut), book (read), toys (play), bike (ride), towel (dry hands), pencil (write), bed (sleep), broom (sweep), tissue (blow nose), toothbrush (brush teeth), hairbrush (brush hair), wash cloth (wash face), clock (tells time), and camera (take pictures).
Probe Results (targets in repertoire):

Target	Baseline %	Date Introduced	Date Criteria Met	*Fading Procedure* Maintenance	Date NE Introduced	Date Archived
1. S^D A: Target 1:						
2. S^D A: Target 2:						
3. Targets 1 and 2 random rotation						

4. S^D A: Target 3:						
5. S^D A: Target 4:						
6. Targets that met criteria: random rotation						
7. S^D A: Target 5:						
8. S^D A: Target 6:						
9. Targets that met criteria: random rotation						
10. S^D A: Target 7:						
11. S^D A: Target 8:						
12. Targets that met criteria: random rotation						
13. S^D A: Target 9:						
14. S^D A: Target 10:						
15. Targets that met criteria: random rotation						
16. Generalize to another environment Environment 1:						
17. Generalize to another environment Environment 2:						
18. Maintenance: Assess in varied environments				2W 1W M		
19. S^D B: Target 1:						
20. S^D B: Target 2:						

21. Targets 1 and 2 random rotation						
22. S^D B: Target 3:						
23. S^D B: Target 4:						
24. Targets that met criteria: random rotation						
25. S^D B: Target 5:						
26. S^D B: Target 6:						
27. Targets that met criteria: random rotation						
28. S^D B: Target 7:						
29. S^D B: Target 8:						
30. Targets that met criteria: random rotation						
31. S^D B: Target 9:						
32. S^D B: Target 10:						
33. Targets that met criteria: random rotation						
34. Generalize to another environment Environment 1:						
35. Generalize to another environment Environment 2:						
36. Maintenance: Assess in varied environments				2W 1W M		

Specific tips for running this task analysis

- Ensure pre-requisite skills have been taught for this TA. Examples of pre-requisite skills for "Expressive Labels of Function of Objects" include mastering expressive labels in the first book of the Journey of Development ABA Curriculum series.
- If individual is nonverbal, accept the answer in the form of a sign, written response, PECS (Bondy and Frost 2002) or augmentative device.
- One prompt to consider using during this TA is a visual prompt. For example, when asking what we drink out of, you could show a picture of a cup.

EXPRESSIVE LABELS OF GENDER

LEVEL: □ 1 □ 2 □ 3

S^D: Present individual with a picture or figurine of a male or female and ask "What is it?"	**Response:** Individual will label the gender of the picture or figurine
Data Collection: Skill acquisition	**Target Criteria:** 80% or above for 3 consecutive days across 2 people
Materials: Picture cards/figurines depicting gender and reinforcement (picture cards can be found on accompanying CD)	

Fading procedure

Maintenance Criteria: 2W = 4 consecutive scores of 100%; 1W = 4 consecutive scores of 100%; M = 3 consecutive scores of 100%	**Natural Environment (NE) Criterion:** Target has been generalized in NE across 3 novel naturally occurring activities	**Archive Criteria:** Target, maintenance and NE criteria have been met

Target list

Suggestions for targets and probe results

Suggestions for Targets: Boy, girl, man, woman (i.e. Barbies, little people, doll house figurines, flashcards, felt people).

Probe Results (targets in repertoire):

Target	Baseline %	Date Introduced	Date Criteria Met	*Fading Procedure* Maintenance	Date NE Introduced	Date Archived
1. Target 1:						
2. Target 2:						
3. Targets 1 and 2 random rotation						
4. Target 3:						
5. Target 4:						

6. Targets that met criteria: random rotation						
7. Generalize to another environment Environment 1:						
8. Generalize to another environment Environment 2:						
9. Maintenance: Assess in varied environments				2W 1W M		

Specific tips for running this task analysis

- Ensure pre-requisite skills have been taught for this TA. Examples of pre-requisite skills for "Expressive Labels of Gender" include expressive labels in the first book of the Journey of Development ABA Curriculum series and "Receptive Labels of Gender" (TA found in this curriculum book).

EXPRESSIVE LABELS OF ROOMS AND OBJECTS IN A ROOM

LEVEL: □ 1 □ 2 □ 3

S^D: A. "What room does a [x] go in?" (e.g. "What room does a couch go in?") B. "What things go in the [x]?" (e.g. "What things go in the living room?")	**Response:** Individual will correctly answer the question with verbalization, written word, sign, PECS (Bondy and Frost 2002) or augmentative device
Data Collection: Skill acquisition	**Target Criteria:** 80% or above for 3 consecutive days across 2 people
Materials: Reinforcement	

Fading procedure

Maintenance Criteria: 2W = 4 consecutive scores of 100%; 1W = 4 consecutive scores of 100%; M = 3 consecutive scores of 100%	**Natural Environment (NE) Criterion:** Target has been generalized in NE across 3 novel naturally occurring activities	**Archive Criteria:** Target, maintenance and NE criteria have been met

Target list

Suggestions for targets and probe results

Suggestions for Targets: S^D *A*: Couch (living room), refrigerator (kitchen), bed (bedroom), toilet (bathroom), TV (living room), microwave (kitchen), dresser (bedroom), shower/tub (bathroom), stove (kitchen), table (dining room). S^D *B*: Kitchen (sink, refrigerator, stove), living room (couch, TV, chair), dining room (table, chairs, china cabinet), bedroom (bed, dresser, end table), bathroom (toilet, bathtub, shower), playroom (toys, games, books), classroom (desks, chairs, chalk board), library (books, maps, computers), basement (use objects individual has in his/her basement since this varies significantly) and laundry room (washer, dryer, clothes).

Probe Results (targets in repertoire):

Target	Baseline %	Date Introduced	Date Criteria Met	*Fading Procedure*		
				Maintenance	Date NE Introduced	Date Archived
1. S^D A: Target 1:						
2. S^D A: Target 2:						
3. Targets 1 and 2 random rotation						

4. S^D A: Target 3:						
5. S^D A: Target 4:						
6. Targets that met criteria: random rotation						
7. S^D A: Target 5:						
8. S^D A: Target 6:						
9. Targets that met criteria: random rotation						
10. S^D A: Target 7:						
11. S^D A: Target 8:						
12. Targets that met criteria: random rotation						
13. S^D A: Target 9:						
14. S^D A: Target 10:						
15. Targets that met criteria: random rotation						
16. Generalize to another environment Environment 1:						
17. Generalize to another environment Environment 2:						
18. Maintenance: Assess in varied environments				2W 1W M		
19. S^D B: Target 1:						
20. S^D B: Target 2:						

21. Targets 1 and 2 random rotation						
22. S^D B: Target 3:						
23. S^D B: Target 4:						
24. Targets that met criteria: random rotation						
25. S^D B: Target 5:						
26. S^D B: Target 6:						
27. Targets that met criteria: random rotation						
28. S^D B: Target 7:						
29. S^D B: Target 8:						
30. Targets that met criteria: random rotation						
31. S^D B: Target 9:						
32. S^D B: Target 10:						
33. Targets that met criteria: random rotation						
34. Generalize to another environment Environment 1:						
35. Generalize to another environment Environment 2:						
36. Maintenance: Assess in varied environments				2W 1W M		

Specific tips for running this task analysis

- Ensure pre-requisite skills have been taught for this TA. Examples of pre-requisite skills for "Expressive Labels of Rooms and Objects in a Room" include mastering expressive labels in the first book of the Journey of Development ABA Curriculum series and "Receptive Labels of Rooms and Objects in a Room" (TA found in this curriculum book).
- If individual is nonverbal, accept the answer in the form of a sign, written response, PECS (Bondy and Frost 2002) or augmentative device.
- Instructor should determine in advance how many items need to be listed for the response to S^D B (we recommend at least 2 items).

INTRAVERBAL FILL-INS OF PREDICTABLE ROUTINES

LEVEL: □ 1 □ 2 □ 3

S^D: While engaging in a predictable routine, say the beginning of the statement that would require the individual to complete the statement (e.g., While racing cars say "Ready, Set, _____")	**Response:** Individual will complete the statement with the correct intraverbal fill-in
Data Collection: Skill acquisition	**Target Criteria:** 80% or above for 3 consecutive days across 2 people
Materials: Variety of predictable routines that would occasion a statement about the routine, and reinforcement	

Fading procedure

Maintenance Criteria: 2W = 4 consecutive scores of 100%; 1W = 4 consecutive scores of 100%; M = 3 consecutive scores of 100%	**Natural Environment (NE) Criterion:** Target has been generalized in NE across 3 novel naturally occurring activities	**Archive Criteria:** Target, maintenance and NE criteria have been met

Target list

Suggestions for targets and probe results

Suggestions for Targets: "Ready set (go)"—running a race, turning toy on and off, pushing a toy, blowing up balloon and letting it go; "1,2,3 (up)" or "Up up and (away)—ball in air, airplane taking off, swinging individual in the air; "Put on your socks and (shoes)"—before going outside, when getting dressed inside; "Turn it (on)"—TV, radio, toy; "Peek-a-(boo)"—with instructor, with items hiding under a blanket; and "I'm going to get (you)"—playing chase, tickling.

Probe Results (targets in repertoire):

Target	Baseline %	Date Introduced	Date Criteria Met	*Fading Procedure*		
				Maintenance	Date NE Introduced	Date Archived
1. Target 1:						
2. Target 2:						
3. Targets that met criteria: random rotation						

4. Target 3:						
5. Target 4:						
6. Targets that met criteria: random rotation						
7. Target 5:						
8. Target 6:						
9. Targets that met criteria: random rotation						
10. Generalize to another environment Environment 1:						
11. Generalize to another environment Environment 2:						
12. Maintenance: Assess in varied environments				2W 1W M		

Specific tips for running this task analysis

- Ensure pre-requisite skills have been taught for this TA. Examples of pre-requisite skills for "Intraverbal Fill-Ins of Predictable Routines" include joint attention and having some form of communication to request basic wants and needs.
- This program should be taught in a fun environment to reduce the challenges of producing a verbal response. If the individual does not demonstrate a verbal response, it is suggested to have the individual demonstrate an accompanying gesture. For example, if the instructor waits 5–10 seconds for the individual to say "go" and it is difficult for the individual to readily imitate, the instructor should prompt the individual to gesture a functional motion with their hand, and then move on with the action and play routine.
- It is critical that the activity does not begin until the fill-in to the phrase is completed.

MANNERS

LEVEL: □ 1 □ 2 □ 3

S^D: Contrive (role play or in vivo) a situation where the individual should use manners	**Response:** Individual will use manners, appropriate to the context
Data Collection: Skill acquisition	**Target Criteria:** 80% or above for 3 consecutive days across 2 people
Materials: Other adults/peers and reinforcement	

Fading procedure

Maintenance Criteria: 2W = 4 consecutive scores of 100%; 1W = 4 consecutive scores of 100%; M = 3 consecutive scores of 100%	**Natural Environment (NE) Criterion:** Target has been generalized in NE across 3 novel naturally occurring activities	**Archive Criteria:** Target, maintenance and NE criteria have been met

Target list

Suggestions for targets and probe results

Suggestions for Targets: "Thank you" (receiving something), "Excuse me" (interrupting), "Please" (requesting something), "Excuse me" (to have another person move), "Bless you" (someone sneezing), "You're welcome" (after someone says thank you), "Excuse me" (after a passing gas/burp), "No, thank you" (declining an item), "Nice to meet you" (meeting someone new), covering mouth when coughing or sneezing, and holding the door for someone behind them.
Probe Results (targets in repertoire):

Target	Baseline %	Date Introduced	Date Criteria Met	*Fading Procedure* Maintenance	Date NE Introduced	Date Archived
1. Target 1:						
2. Target 2:						
3. Targets 1 and 2 random rotation						
4. Target 3:						

5. Target 4:						
6. Targets that met criteria: random rotation						
7. Target 5:						
8. Target 6:						
9. Targets that met criteria: random rotation						
10. Target 7:						
11. Target 8:						
12. Targets that met criteria: random rotation						
13. Target 9:						
14. Target 10:						
15. Targets that met criteria: random rotation						
16. Generalize to another environment Environment 1:						
17. Generalize to another environment Environment 2:						
18. Maintenance: Assess in varied environments				2W 1W M		

Specific tips for running this task analysis

- Ensure pre-requisite skills have been taught for this TA. Examples of pre-requisite skills for "Manners" include verbal imitation, simple requests and receptive/expressive label programs (TAs found in the first book of the Journey of Development ABA Curriculum series).
- This TA uses skill acquisition data collection. It is possible to run 4 out of 5 trials (80%), if the instructor finds it difficult to contrive all situations.
- For Level 3 individuals, you can also run this program as role playing or stating a situation and having them answer what the individual would do.

PAST TENSE VERBS

LEVEL: □ 1 □ 2 □ 3

S^D: Present individual with a picture card depicting an action and ask "What is he/she doing?" Alternatively, engage in an action with the individual and ask, "What are you doing? Then remove the picture or stop the activity and ask, "What did you/he/she do?"	**Response:** Individual will answer the question with the correct verb tense (e.g. "He clapped," "I jumped," etc.)
Data Collection: Skill acquisition	**Target Criteria:** 80% or above for 3 consecutive days across 2 people
Materials: Pictures of actions and reinforcement (picture cards can be found on accompanying CD)	

Fading procedure

Maintenance Criteria: 2W = 4 consecutive scores of 100%; 1W = 4 consecutive scores of 100%; M = 3 consecutive scores of 100%	**Natural Environment (NE) Criterion:** Target has been generalized in NE across 3 novel naturally occurring activities	**Archive Criteria:** Target, maintenance and NE criteria have been met

Target list

Suggestions for targets and probe results

Suggestions for Targets: Color/colored, pour/poured, walk/walked, jump/jumped, hop/hopped, play/played, help/helped, talk/talked, clap/clapped and brush/brushed.
Probe Results (targets in repertoire):

Target	Baseline %	Date Introduced	Date Criteria Met	*Fading Procedure*		
				Maintenance	Date NE Introduced	Date Archived
1. Target 1:						
2. Target 2:						
3. Targets 1 and 2 random rotation						

4. Target 3:						
5. Target 4:						
6. Targets that met criteria: random rotation						
7. Target 5:						
8. Target 6:						
9. Targets that met criteria: random rotation						
10. Target 7:						
11. Target 8:						
12. Targets that met criteria: random rotation						
13. Target 9:						
14. Target 10:						
15. Targets that met criteria: random rotation						
16. Generalize to another environment Environment 1:						
17. Generalize to another environment Environment 2:						
18. Maintenance: Assess in varied environments				2W 1W M		

Specific tips for running this task analysis

- Ensure pre-requisite skills have been taught for this TA. Examples of pre-requisite skills for "Past Tense Verbs" include "Receptive Instructions (One-Step)," receptive labels and "Expressive Labels of Actions" (TAs found in the first book of the Journey of Development ABA Curriculum series).

IRREGULAR PAST TENSE VERBS

LEVEL: ☐ 1 ☐ 2 ☐ 3

S^D: Present individual with a picture card depicting an action and ask "What is he/she doing?" Alternatively, engage in an action with the individual and ask, "What are you doing? Then remove the picture or stop the activity and ask "What did you/he/she do?"	**Response:** Individual will answer the question with the correct verb tense (e.g. "He built," "I drew," etc.)
Data Collection: Skill acquisition	**Target Criteria:** 80% or above for 3 consecutive days across 2 people
Materials: Pictures of actions and reinforcement (picture cards can be found on accompanying CD)	

Fading procedure

Maintenance Criteria: 2W = 4 consecutive scores of 100%; 1W = 4 consecutive scores of 100%; M = 3 consecutive scores of 100%	**Natural Environment (NE) Criterion:** Target has been generalized in NE across 3 novel naturally occurring activities	**Archive Criteria:** Target, maintenance and NE criteria have been met

Target list

Suggestions for targets and probe results

Suggestions for Targets: Catch/caught, build/built, break/broke, blow/blew, buy/bought, choose/chose, go/went, drink/drank, feel/felt, drive/drove, fall/fell, dive/dove, bite/bit, deal/dealt, feed/fed, and draw/drew.

Probe Results (targets in repertoire):

Target	Baseline %	Date Introduced	Date Criteria Met	*Fading Procedure*		
				Maintenance	Date NE Introduced	Date Archived
1. Target 1:						
2. Target 2:						
3. Targets 1 and 2 random rotation						

4. Target 3:						
5. Target 4:						
6. Targets that met criteria: random rotation						
7. Target 5:						
8. Target 6:						
9. Targets that met criteria: random rotation						
10. Target 7:						
11. Target 8:						
12. Targets that met criteria: random rotation						
13. Target 9:						
14. Target 10:						
15. Targets that met criteria: random rotation						
16. Generalize to another environment Environment 1:						
17. Generalize to another environment Environment 2:						
18. Maintenance: Assess in varied environments				2W 1W M		

Specific tips for running this task analysis

- Ensure pre-requisite skills have been taught for this TA. Examples of pre-requisite skills for "Irregular Past Tense Verbs" include "Receptive Instructions (One-Step)," receptive labels and "Expressive Labels of Actions" (TAs found in the first book of the Journey of Development ABA Curriculum series).

PLURALS

LEVEL: □ 1 □ 2 □ 3

S^D: Present singular or plural objects or pictures of singular or plurals objects, and ask "What is it?"	**Response:** Individual will label picture or objects using singular or plural correctly (i.e. "car" vs. "cars")
Data Collection: Skill acquisition	**Target Criteria:** 80% or above for 3 consecutive days across 2 people
Materials: Objects and/or picture cards of various numbers of items, and reinforcement (picture cards can be found on accompanying CD)	

Fading procedure

Maintenance Criteria: 2W = 4 consecutive scores of 100%; 1W = 4 consecutive scores of 100%; M = 3 consecutive scores of 100%	**Natural Environment (NE) Criterion:** Target has been generalized in NE across 3 novel naturally occurring activities	**Archive Criteria:** Target, maintenance and NE criteria have been met

Target list

Suggestions for targets and probe results

Suggestions for Targets: Animal/animals, car/cars, dinosaur/dinosaurs, toy/toys, ball/balls, doll/dolls, chair/chairs, computer/computers, etc.

Probe Results (targets in repertoire):

Target	Baseline %	Date Introduced	Date Criteria Met	*Fading Procedure*		
				Maintenance	**Date NE Introduced**	**Date Archived**
1. Target 1: Singular						
2. Target 2: Plural						
3. Targets that met criteria: random rotation						
4. Target 3: Singular						
5. Target 4: Plural						

6. Targets that met criteria: random rotation						
7. Target 5: Singular						
8. Target 6: Plural						
9. Targets that met criteria: random rotation						
10. Target 7: Singular						
11. Target 8: Plural						
12. Targets that met criteria: random rotation						
13. Target 9: Singular						
14. Target 10: Plural						
15. Targets that met criteria: random rotation						
16. Generalize to another environment Environment 1:						
17. Generalize to another environment Environment 2:						
18. Maintenance: Assess in varied environments				2W 1W M		

Specific tips for running this task analysis

- Ensure pre-requisite skills have been taught for this TA. Examples of pre-requisite skills for "Plurals" include receptive and expressive labels in the first book of the Journey of Development ABA Curriculum series and receptive labels (TA found in this curriculum book).
- In teaching this program, the individual is likely to baseline out of the singular targets since they should have learned this skill in expressive labels programs.
- Targets 1 and 2 should be of the same object. This is also true for Targets 3 and 4, Targets 5 and 6, Targets 7 and 8, and Targets 9 and 10.

IRREGULAR PLURALS

LEVEL: □ 1 □ 2 □ 3

S^D: Present singular or plural objects/pictures and say, "What is it?"	**Response:** Individual will label picture/objects (i.e. "person" vs. "people")
Data Collection: Skill acquisition	**Target Criteria:** 80% or above for 3 consecutive days across 2 people
Materials: Objects and/or picture cards of items representing irregular plurals and reinforcement (picture cards can be found on accompanying CD)	

Fading procedure

Maintenance Criteria: 2W = 4 consecutive scores of 100%; 1W = 4 consecutive scores of 100%; M = 3 consecutive scores of 100%	**Natural Environment (NE) Criterion:** Target has been generalized in NE across 3 novel naturally occurring activities	**Archive Criteria:** Target, maintenance and NE criteria have been met

Target list

Suggestions for targets and probe results

Suggestions for Targets: Tooth/teeth, foot/feet, person/people, child/children, woman/women, man/men, cactus/cacti, goose/geese, mouse/mice, and words that do not change—deer, fish and sheep.

Probe Results (targets in repertoire):

Target	Baseline %	Date Introduced	Date Criteria Met	*Fading Procedure*		
				Maintenance	**Date NE Introduced**	**Date Archived**
1. Target 1: Singular						
2. Target 2: Plural						
3. Targets that met criteria: random rotation						
4. Target 3: Singular						
5. Target 4: Plural						

6. Targets that met criteria: random rotation						
7. Target 5: Singular						
8. Target 6: Plural						
9. Targets that met criteria: random rotation						
10. Target 7: Singular						
11. Target 8: Plural						
12. Targets that met criteria: random rotation						
13. Target 9: Singular						
14. Target 10: Plural						
15. Targets that met criteria: random rotation						
16. Generalize to another environment Environment 1:						
17. Generalize to another environment Environment 2:						
18. Maintenance: Assess in varied environments				2W 1W M		

Specific tips for running this task analysis

- Ensure pre-requisite skills have been taught for this TA. Examples of pre-requisite skills for "Irregular Plurals" include receptive and expressive labels in the first book of the Journey of Development ABA Curriculum series, receptive and expressive plurals, and receptive irregular plurals (TAs found in this curriculum book).
- In teaching this program, the individual is likely to baseline out of the singular targets since they should have learned this skill in expressive labels programs.
- Targets 1 and 2 should be of the same object. This is also true for Targets 3 and 4, Targets 5 and 6, Targets 7 and 8, and Targets 9 and 10.

PRONOUNS (HE/SHE)

LEVEL: □ 1 □ 2 □ 3

S^D: Present a picture of a person engaging in an action or a picture of a person with a specific feature and ask "Who is [x]" or "Who has [x]?" (e.g. "Who is eating pizza?" or "Who has blond hair?")	**Response:** Individual will answer using the pronoun "He/she" (e.g. "He is," "She does," or "She has blond hair")
Data Collection: Skill acquisition	**Target Criteria:** 80% or above for 3 consecutive days across 2 people
Materials: Pictures of males/females engaging in various actions or with different features, and reinforcement (picture cards can be found on accompanying CD)	

Fading procedure

Maintenance Criteria: 2W = 4 consecutive scores of 100%; 1W = 4 consecutive scores of 100%; M = 3 consecutive scores of 100%	**Natural Environment (NE) Criterion:** Target has been generalized in NE across 3 novel naturally occurring activities	**Archive Criteria:** Target, maintenance and NE criteria have been met

Target list

Suggestions for targets and probe results

Suggestions for Targets: *Actions*: Kicking ball, eating, drinking, riding bike, blowing bubbles, brushing teeth, brushing hair, washing hands, reading book, cutting paper, throwing ball, watching TV, playing with the puzzle, catching the ball, cooking, wearing [x] and raising hand. *Features*: Hair color, eye color, clothing item, item held in the hands (e.g. Who has a book?) and emotion (e.g. Who is smiling?).
Probe Results (targets in repertoire):

Target	Baseline %	Date Introduced	Date Criteria Met	*Fading Procedure* Maintenance	Date NE Introduced	Date Archived
Pronouns with Actions						
1. Target 1: "He is [action]."						
2. Target 2: "She is [action]."						
3. Targets 1 and 2 random rotation						

4. Generalize to another environment Environment 1:						
5. Generalize to another environment Environment 2						
Pronouns with Features						
6. Target 3: "He has [feature]."						
7. Target 4: "She has [feature]."						
8. Targets that met criteria: random rotation						
9. Generalize to another environment Environment 1:						
10. Generalize to another environment Environment 2:						
11. Maintenance: Assess in varied environments				2W 1W M		

Specific tips for running this task analysis

- Ensure pre-requisite skills have been taught for this TA. Examples of pre-requisite skills for "Pronouns (He/She)" include receptive and expressive labels of clothing, body parts, functional items, toys and actions (TAs found in the first book of the Journey of Development ABA Curriculum series) and mastery of receptive/expressive labels of gender and receptive "Pronouns (He/She)" (TAs found in this curriculum book).
- When using pictures or figurines, be sure to generalize the skill to men/women/boys/girls.

PRONOUNS (HIS/HIM/HER)

LEVEL: □ 1 □ 2 □ 3

S^D: Show a picture of a boy/man and girl/woman with same item, say "This is his [item] and this is…" or "This [item] belongs to her and this [item] belong to …"	**Response:** Individual will respond using the correct pronoun: "His," "Him" or "Hers"
Data Collection: Skill acquisition	**Target Criteria:** 80% or above for 3 consecutive days across 2 people
Materials: Pictures of boys/girls or men/women with various items, and reinforcement (picture cards can be found on accompanying CD)	

Fading procedure

Maintenance Criteria: 2W = 4 consecutive scores of 100%; 1W = 4 consecutive scores of 100%; M = 3 consecutive scores of 100%	**Natural Environment (NE) Criterion:** Target has been generalized in NE across 3 novel naturally occurring activities	**Archive Criteria:** Target, maintenance and NE criteria have been met

Target list

Suggestions for targets and probe results

Suggestions for Targets: His/her ice-cream/ball/arm/book/toy/jacket/shoe/hair/truck/drink.
Probe Results (targets in repertoire):

Target	Baseline %	Date Introduced	Date Criteria Met	*Fading Procedure*		
				Maintenance	Date NE Introduced	Date Archived
1. Target 1: His						
2. Target 2: Her						
3. Target 3: Him						
4. Targets that met criteria: random rotation						
5. Generalize to another environment Environment 1:						

6. Generalize to another environment Environment 2:						
7. Maintenance: Assess in varied environments				2W 1W M		

Specific tips for running this task analysis

- Ensure pre-requisite skills have been taught for this TA. Examples of pre-requisite skills for "Pronouns (His/Him/Her)" include receptive and expressive labels of clothing, body parts, functional items and toys (TAs found in the first book of the Journey of Development ABA Curriculum series) and mastery of receptive/expressive labels of gender and receptive pronouns (TAs found in this curriculum book).

PRONOUNS (I/YOU)

LEVEL: □ 1 □ 2 □ 3

S^D: A. Instructor or individual engages in an action, or shows a picture of the instructor or individual engaging in an action and says "Who is [action]?" B. Instructor or individual holds an object and says "Who has the [object]?" C. Instructor asks a question based on feature "Who has/is [feature]?" (e.g. "Who has curly hair?" "Who is wearing jeans?" "Who has a brother?")	**Response:** A. Individual will use the appropriate pronoun (I or you) in a simple sentence (e.g. "I am jumping") B. Individual will use the appropriate pronoun (I or you) in a simple sentence (e.g. "I have the ball") C. Individual will use the appropriate pronoun (I or you) in a simple sentence (e.g. "You are wearing jeans")
Data Collection: Skill acquisition	**Target Criteria:** 80% or above for 3 consecutive days across 2 people
Materials: Pictures of instructor and individual engaging in various actions, objects and reinforcement	

Fading procedure

Maintenance Criteria: 2W = 4 consecutive scores of 100%; 1W = 4 consecutive scores of 100%; M = 3 consecutive scores of 100%	**Natural Environment (NE) Criterion:** Target has been generalized in NE across 3 novel naturally occurring activities	**Archive Criteria:** Target, maintenance and NE criteria have been met

Target list

Suggestions for targets and probe results

Suggestions for Targets: *Actions*: Clapping, sleeping, jumping, eating, drinking, brushing teeth, brushing hair, watching TV, reading and writing. *Holding various objects*: Ball, car, airplane etc. *Feature*: Colored shirt, blond/brown/black hair, wearing [x], etc.

Probe Results (targets in repertoire):

Target	Baseline %	Date Introduced	Date Criteria Met	*Fading Procedure*		
				Maintenance	**Date NE Introduced**	**Date Archived**
Pronouns with Actions						
1. Target 1: "I am [action]"						
2. Target 2: "You are [action]"						

3. Targets that met criteria: random rotation						
4. Generalize to another environment Environment 1:						
5. Generalize to another environment Environment 2:						
Pronouns with Objects						
6. Target 3: "I have [object]"						
7. Target 4: "You have [object]"						
8. Targets that met criteria: random rotation						
9. Generalize to another environment Environment 1:						
10. Generalize to another environment Environment 2:						
Pronouns with Feature						
11. Target 5: "you have/are [feature]"						
12. Target 6: "I have/am [feature]"						
13. Targets that met criteria: random rotation						
14. Generalize to another environment Environment 1:						
15. Generalize to another environment Environment 2:						
16. Maintenance: Assess in varied environments				2W 1W M		

Specific tips for running this task analysis

- Ensure pre-requisite skills have been taught for this TA. Examples of pre-requisite skills for "Pronouns (I/You)" include receptive and expressive labels of actions, familiar people, functional objects, functional items and toys (TAs found in the first book of the Journey of Development ABA Curriculum series) and mastery of receptive "Pronouns (I/You)" (TA found in this curriculum book).
- When presenting the pictures of actions, be sure to have two pictures of the same action (e.g. individual clapping and instructor clapping) so the individual is differentiating between the pronoun and not the action.

PRONOUNS (MY/YOUR)

LEVEL: □ 1 □ 2 □ 3

S^D: Present an object belonging to the individual or instructor and ask "Whose [item]?" or point to a clothing item or body part on the individual or instructor and ask "Whose [clothing item]?" or "Whose [body part]?"	**Response:** Individual will answer using the pronoun "My" or "Your"
Data Collection: Skill acquisition	**Target Criteria:** 80% or above for 3 consecutive days across 2 people
Materials: Objects and reinforcement	

Fading procedure

Maintenance Criteria: 2W = 4 consecutive scores of 100%; 1W = 4 consecutive scores of 100%; M = 3 consecutive scores of 100%	**Natural Environment (NE) Criterion:** Target has been generalized in NE across 3 novel naturally occurring activities	**Archive Criteria:** Target, maintenance and NE criteria have been met

Target list

Suggestions for targets and probe results

Suggestions for Targets: *Items*: Objects belonging to individual or instructor. *Clothing items*: Shirt, pants, hat, coat, belt, etc. *Body Parts*: Head, nose, hand, arm, leg, foot, etc.
Probe Results (targets in repertoire):

Target	Baseline %	Date Introduced	Date Criteria Met	*Fading Procedure*		
				Maintenance	Date NE Introduced	Date Archived
Pronouns with Objects						
1. Target 1: "My [object]"						
2. Target 2: "Your [object]"						
3. Targets that met criteria: random rotation						

4. Generalize to another environment Environment 1:						
5. Generalize to another environment Environment 2:						
Pronouns with Clothing Items						
6. Target 3: “My [clothing item]”						
7. Target 4: “Your [clothing item]”						
8. Targets that met criteria: random rotation						
9. Generalize to another environment Environment 1:						
10. Generalize to another environment Environment 2:						
Pronouns with Body Part						
11. Target 5: “You have/are [feature]”						
12. Target 6: “I have/am [feature]”						
13. Targets that met criteria: random rotation						
14. Generalize to another environment Environment 1:						
15. Generalize to another environment Environment 2:						
16. Maintenance: Assess in varied environments				2W 1W M		

Specific tips for running this task analysis

- Ensure pre-requisite skills have been taught for this TA. Examples of pre-requisite skills for “Pronouns (My/Your)” include receptive and expressive labels of functional objects, clothing items, body parts and toys (TAs found in the first book of the Journey of Development ABA Curriculum series) and mastery of receptive “Pronouns (My/Your)” (TA found in this curriculum book).

PRONOUNS (THEIRS/OURS)

LEVEL: □ 1 □ 2 □ 3

S^D: Present objects or pictures of objects belonging to the instructor and individual or another group (i.e. peers, parents), and ask “Whose [x] are these?” or “Whose is this?” (e.g. “Whose pencils are these?)	**Response:** Individual will answer using the pronoun “Theirs” or “Ours”
Data Collection: Skill acquisition	**Target Criteria:** 80% or above for 3 consecutive days across 2 people
Materials: Objects or pictures of objects that belong to the instructor and individual or belong to peers/another group, and reinforcement	

Fading procedure

Maintenance Criteria: 2W = 4 consecutive scores of 100%; 1W = 4 consecutive scores of 100%; M = 3 consecutive scores of 100%	**Natural Environment (NE) Criterion:** Target has been generalized in NE across 3 novel naturally occurring activities	**Archive Criteria:** Target, maintenance and NE criteria have been met

Target list

Suggestions for targets and probe results

Suggestions for Targets: Ours and Theirs. *Use Objects*: Pencils, tablet, books, stickers, art work, snack food, reinforcer, program materials, timer and markers.
Probe Results (targets in repertoire):

Target	Baseline %	Date Introduced	Date Criteria Met	*Fading Procedure*		
				Maintenance	Date NE Introduced	Date Archived
1. Target 1: Ours						
2. Target 2: Theirs						
3. Targets 1 and 2 random rotation						
4. Generalize to another environment Environment 1:						

5. Generalize to another environment Environment 2:						
6. Maintenance: Assess in varied environments				2W 1W M		

Specific tips for running this task analysis

- Ensure pre-requisite skills have been taught for this TA. Examples of pre-requisite skills for “Pronouns (Theirs/Ours)” include receptive and expressive labels of functional objects, school supplies, food, drink and toys (TAs found in the first book of the Journey of Development ABA Curriculum series) and mastery of receptive “Pronouns (Theirs/Ours)” (TA found in this curriculum book).

PRONOUNS (WE/THEY)

LEVEL: □ 1 □ 2 □ 3

S^D: Present a picture of instructor and individual or of people engaging in an action and ask "Who is [action]?" (e.g. "Who is digging?")	**Response:** Individual will answer using the pronoun "They" or "We" (i.e. "They are" or "We are digging")
Data Collection: Skill acquisition	**Target Criteria:** 80% or above for 3 consecutive days across 2 people
Materials: Action pictures of instructor and individual, action pictures (using the same actions) of random people and reinforcement	

Fading procedure

Maintenance Criteria: 2W = 4 consecutive scores of 100%; 1W = 4 consecutive scores of 100%; M = 3 consecutive scores of 100%	**Natural Environment (NE) Criterion:** Target has been generalized in NE across 3 novel naturally occurring activities	**Archive Criteria:** Target, maintenance and NE criteria have been met

Target list

Suggestions for targets and probe results

Suggestions for Targets: We and They. *Action*: Digging, clapping, jumping, drinking, blowing bubbles, painting, playing a game, coloring and swinging.
Probe Results (targets in repertoire):

Target	Baseline %	Date Introduced	Date Criteria Met	*Fading Procedure*		
				Maintenance	Date NE Introduced	Date Archived
1. Target 1: We						
2. Target 2: They						
3. Targets that met criteria: random rotation						
4. Generalize to another environment Environment 1:						
5. Generalize to another environment Environment 2:						

6. Maintenance: Assess in varied environments				2W 1W M		

Specific tips for running this task analysis

- Ensure pre-requisite skills have been taught for this TA. Examples of pre-requisite skills for "Pronouns (We/They)" include receptive and expressive labels of action (TA found in the first book of the Journey of Development ABA Curriculum series) and mastery of receptive "Pronouns (Theirs/Ours)" (TA found in this curriculum book).
- Generalize this skill to asking the individual "Who is [action]?" while you are engaging in the action. You can also generalize the S^D to "What's happening?"

PROVIDING SIMPLE DIRECTIONS TO ANOTHER

LEVEL: □ 1 □ 2 □ 3

S^D: "Tell [person] [direction]" (e.g. "Tell Danika to go to lunch")	**Response:** Individual will find the person and convey the direction
Data Collection: Skill acquisition	**Target Criteria:** 80% or above for 3 consecutive days across 2 people
Materials: Other adults/peers and reinforcement	

Fading procedure

Maintenance Criteria: 2W = 4 consecutive scores of 100%; 1W = 4 consecutive scores of 100%; M = 3 consecutive scores of 100%	**Natural Environment (NE) Criterion:** Target has been generalized in NE across 3 novel naturally occurring activities	**Archive Criteria:** Target, maintenance and NE criteria have been met

Target list

Suggestions for targets and probe results

Suggestions for Targets: "Go to [location]," "Get me [item]" (e.g. get me a spoon), "It's time for [activity]," "You need [object]," "Come to [location]," "Play [a game]," "Get your [object]," "I need [item]," "Go to [person]," "Get [item] and [perform action] (e.g. get your pencil and write your name).
Probe Results (targets in repertoire):

Target	Baseline %	Date Introduced	Date Criteria Met	*Fading Procedure*		
				Maintenance	**Date NE Introduced**	**Date Archived**
1. Target 1:						
2. Target 2:						
3. Targets 1 and 2 random rotation						
4. Target 3:						
5. Target 4:						

6. Targets that met criteria: random rotation						
7. Target 5:						
8. Target 6:						
9. Targets that met criteria: random rotation						
10. Target 7:						
11. Target 8:						
12. Targets that met criteria: random rotation						
13. Target 9:						
14. Target 10:						
15. Targets that met criteria: random rotation						
16. Generalize to another environment Environment 1:						
17. Generalize to another environment Environment 2:						
18. Maintenance: Assess in varied environments				2W 1W M		

Specific tips for running this task analysis

- Ensure pre-requisite skills have been taught for this TA. Examples of pre-requisite skills for "Providing Simple Directions to Another" include mastery of verbal imitation programs and receptive and expressive labels of people (TAs found in the first book of the Journey of Development ABA Curriculum series). Progress should have been made towards gaining adult attention and eye contact (TAs also found in the first book of the series).
- Data collection for this TA should be taken on the individual delivering the message appropriately and not on the other peer or instructor responding correctly.

RECIPROCATING INFORMATION

LEVEL: □ 1 □ 2 □ 3

S^D: Present individual with various social statements (e.g. "My favorite color is green")	**Response:** Individual will respond by correctly reciprocating the social statement with their personal information (e.g. "My favorite color is blue")
Data Collection: Skill acquisition	**Target Criteria:** 80% or above for 3 consecutive days across 2 people
Materials: Reinforcement	

Fading procedure

Maintenance Criteria: 2W = 4 consecutive scores of 100%; 1W = 4 consecutive scores of 100%; M = 3 consecutive scores of 100%	**Natural Environment (NE) Criterion:** Target has been generalized in NE across 3 novel naturally occurring activities	**Archive Criteria:** Target, maintenance and NE criteria have been met

Target list

Suggestions for targets and probe results

Suggestions for Targets: I have [x]; My favorite color is [x]; My name is [x]; I am ______ years old; I live at ______; My brother's name is ______; I have a pet ______; I like to play with ______; I like to watch _______; I go to ______ school.
Probe Results (targets in repertoire):

Target	Baseline %	Date Introduced	Date Criteria Met	*Fading Procedure*		
				Maintenance	Date NE Introduced	Date Archived
1. Target 1:						
2. Target 2:						
3. Targets 1 and 2 random rotation						

4. Target 3:						
5. Target 4:						
6. Targets that met criteria: random rotation						
7. Target 5:						
8. Target 6:						
9. Targets that met criteria: random rotation						
10. Target 7:						
11. Target 8:						
12. Targets that met criteria: random rotation						
13. Target 9:						
14. Target 10:						
15. Targets that met criteria: random rotation						
16. Generalize to another environment Environment 1:						
17. Generalize to another environment Environment 2:						

18. Maintenance: Assess in varied environments				2W 1W M		

Specific tips for running this task analysis

- Ensure pre-requisite skills have been taught for this TA. Examples of pre-requisite skills for "Reciprocating Information" include verbal imitation, "Reciprocating a Greeting and Farewell" and "Answering Simple Social Questions" (TAs found in the first book of the Journey of Development ABA Curriculum series).
- If you ran the "Answering Simple Social Questions" program, use these questions for developing the social information the individual will have to reciprocate.
- It is often helpful to choose the first target to be "I have_____." To run this target, you need to hold and show an object. The individual must also have an object. The object is concrete and provides a visual prompt, often making the target easier to master.

REQUESTING NEEDED OR MISSING MATERIALS

LEVEL: □ 1 □ 2 □ 3

S^D: Give individual a S^D that cannot be followed because materials are missing. (e.g. "Sit down" without a chair or "Color" without crayons)	**Response:** Individual will ask (i.e. verbally, by PECS (Bondy and Frost 2002) or by by sign) for needed materials to follow through with directions
Data Collection: Skill acquisition	**Target Criteria:** 80% or above for 3 consecutive days across 2 people
Materials: Missing items (after individual requests them) and reinforcement	

Fading procedure

Maintenance Criteria: 2W = 4 consecutive scores of 100%; 1W = 4 consecutive scores of 100%; M = 3 consecutive scores of 100%	**Natural Environment (NE) Criterion:** Target has been generalized in NE across 3 novel naturally occurring activities	**Archive Criteria:** Target, maintenance and NE criteria have been met

Target list

Suggestions for targets and probe results

Suggestions for Targets: "Sit down" without a chair, "Color" without crayons, "Play with cars" without cars, "Put in your book bag" without a book bag, "Get your socks" without socks, "Drink" without cup, "Put on your shoes" without shoes, "Brush your teeth" without toothpaste, "Let's play Yahtzee" without dice and "Cut this out" without scissors.

Probe Results (targets in repertoire):

Target	Baseline %	Date Introduced	Date Criteria Met	*Fading Procedure*		
				Maintenance	Date NE Introduced	Date Archived
1. Target 1:						
2. Target 2:						
3. Targets 1 and 2 random rotation						
4. Target 3:						

5. Target 4:						
6. Targets that met criteria: random rotation						
7. Target 5:						
8. Target 6:						
9. Targets that met criteria: random rotation						
10. Target 7:						
11. Target 8:						
12. Targets that met criteria: random rotation						
13. Target 9:						
14. Target 10:						
15. Targets that met criteria: random rotation						
16. Generalize to another environment Environment 1:						
17. Generalize to another environment Environment 2:						
18. Maintenance: Assess in varied environments				2W 1W M		

Specific tips for running this task analysis

- Ensure pre-requisite skills have been taught for this TA. Examples of pre-requisite skills for "Requesting Needed or Missing Materials" include mastering "Receptive Instructions (One-Step)," simple requests and expressive labels programs (TAs found in the first book of the Journey of Development ABA Curriculum series) and "Answering Simple 'What' Questions" (e.g. "What do you need?") in this curriculum book.

SIMPLE REQUESTS USING QUESTIONS

LEVEL: □ 1 □ 2 □ 3

S^D: Present individual with a preferred item or visual representation of an activity	**Response:** Individual will request "Can I/you [x]?" (e.g. "Can I have candy" "Can you hand me the toy?")
Data Collection: Skill acquisition	**Target Criteria:** 80% or above for 3 consecutive days across 2 people
Materials: Preferred items, visual representations of activities and reinforcement	

Fading procedure

Maintenance Criteria: 2W = 4 consecutive scores of 100%; 1W = 4 consecutive scores of 100%; M = 3 consecutive scores of 100%	**Natural Environment (NE) Criterion:** Target has been generalized in NE across 3 novel naturally occurring activities	**Archive Criteria:** Target, maintenance and NE criteria have been met

Target list

Suggestions for targets and probe results

Suggestions for Targets: "Can I have [x]? ("Can I have the ball?"), "Can you hand me [x]?" "Can I play [x]?" "Can you show me the [x]?" "Can you give me some [x]?" ("Can you give me some candy?") "Can I take a break?" "Can I go for a walk?" "Can I use the restroom?" "Can I eat [x]?"and "Can we go [x]?"

Probe Results (targets in repertoire):

Target	Baseline %	Date Introduced	Date Criteria Met	*Fading Procedure*		
				Maintenance	**Date NE Introduced**	**Date Archived**
1. Target 1:						
2. Target 2:						
3. Targets 1 and 2 random rotation						
4. Target 3:						

5. Target 4:						
6. Targets that met criteria: random rotation						
7. Target 5:						
8. Target 6:						
9. Targets that met criteria: random rotation						
10. Target 7:						
11. Target 8:						
12. Targets that met criteria: random rotation						
13. Target 9:						
14. Target 10:						
15. Targets that met criteria: random rotation						
16. Generalize to another environment Environment 1:						
17. Generalize to another environment Environment 2:						
18. Maintenance: Assess in varied environments				2W 1W M		

Specific tips for running this task analysis

- Ensure pre-requisite skills have been taught for this TA. Examples of pre-requisite skills for "Simple Requests using Questions" include "Answering Simple Yes/No Questions" and "Simple Requests" (TAs found in the first book of the Journey of Development ABA Curriculum series).

SIMPLE REQUESTS USING SENTENCES

LEVEL: □ 1 □ 2 □ 3

S^D: Present individual with preferred food items, toys or visual representation of a preferred activity	**Response:** Individual will request "I want [x]" (e.g. "I want chips")
Data Collection: Skill acquisition	**Target Criteria:** 80% or above for 3 consecutive days across 2 people
Materials: Preferred food items, visual representations of activities, toys and reinforcement	

Fading procedure

Maintenance Criteria: 2W = 4 consecutive scores of 100%; 1W = 4 consecutive scores of 100%; M = 3 consecutive scores of 100%	**Natural Environment (NE) Criterion:** Target has been generalized in NE across 3 novel naturally occurring activities	**Archive Criteria:** Target, maintenance and NE criteria have been met

Target list

Suggestions for targets and probe results

Suggestions for Targets: Crackers, candy, cookies, gummies, chips, pretzels, chocolate, Graham crackers, raisins, fruit and pudding.
Probe Results (targets in repertoire):

Target	Baseline %	Date Introduced	Date Criteria Met	*Fading Procedure*		
				Maintenance	Date NE Introduced	Date Archived
1. Target 1:						
2. Target 2:						
3. Targets that met criteria: random rotation						
4. Target 3:						
5. Target 4:						

6. Targets that met criteria: random rotation						
7. Target 5:						
8. Target 6:						
9. Targets that met criteria: random rotation						
10. Target 7:						
11. Target 8:						
12. Targets that met criteria: random rotation						
13. Target 9:						
14. Target 10:						
15. Targets that met criteria: random rotation						
16. Generalize to another environment Environment 1:						
17. Generalize to another environment Environment 2:						
18. Maintenance: Assess in varied environments				2W 1W M		

Specific tips for running this task analysis

- Ensure pre-requisite skills have been taught for this TA. Examples of pre-requisite skills for "Simple Requests Using Sentences" include "Simple requests," "Answering Yes/No Questions" and expressive labels programs (TAs found in the first book of the Journey of Development ABA Curriculum series).
- Shape the individual's responses to include variations of "I want [x]" such as "I want to eat [x]," "I want to get [x]," "I want to have [x]," and "I want to drink [x]."

VERBAL IMITATION OF PHRASES

LEVEL: □ 1 □ 2 □ 3

S^D: "Say [phrase]"	**Response:** Individual will repeat the phrase
Data Collection: Skill acquisition	**Target Criteria:** 80% or above for 3 consecutive days across 2 people
Materials: Reinforcement	

Fading procedure

Maintenance Criteria: 2W = 4 consecutive scores of 100%; 1W = 4 consecutive scores of 100%; M = 3 consecutive scores of 100%	**Natural Environment (NE) Criterion:** Target has been generalized in NE across 3 novel naturally occurring activities	**Archive Criteria:** Target, maintenance and NE criteria have been met

Target list

Suggestions for targets and probe results

Suggestions for Targets: Help me, eat [x], drink [x], play with [x], want [x], read book, all done, more please, do it again, and move please.
Probe Results (targets in repertoire):

Target	Baseline %	Date Introduced	Date Criteria Met	*Fading Procedure*		
				Maintenance	**Date NE Introduced**	**Date Archived**
1. Target 1:						
2. Target 2:						
3. Targets 1 and 2 random rotation						
4. Target 3:						
5. Target 4:						

6. Targets that met criteria: random rotation						
7. Target 5:						
8. Target 6:						
9. Targets that met criteria: random rotation						
10. Target 7:						
11. Target 8:						
12. Targets that met criteria: random rotation						
13. Target 9:						
14. Target 10:						
15. Targets that met criteria: random rotation						
16. Generalize to another environment Environment 1:						
17. Generalize to another environment Environment 2:						
18. Maintenance: Assess in varied environments				2W 1W M		

Specific tips for running this task analysis

- Ensure pre-requisite skills have been taught for this TA. Examples of pre-requisite skills for "Verbal Imitation of Phrases" include mastery of "Appropriate Sitting," "Gross Motor Imitation," "Fine Motor Imitation" and "Oral Motor Imitation" (TAs found in the first book of the Journey of Development ABA Curriculum series).
- You can run this program using a mirror so the individual can see their placement of lips, tongue or jaw.
- It is suggested that you choose targets that are functional and will lead to the individual being able to have wants and needs met by using the phrase.

Chapter 14

ACADEMIC SKILLS SKILLS

- Connecting the Dots
- Cutting
- Expressive Labels of 3-Dimensional Shapes
- Expressive Labels of Beginning Sounds of Letters
- Expressive Labels of Money
- Expressive Labels of Opposites
- Folding Paper
- Part/Whole Relationships
- Painting
- Pasting and Gluing
- Quantitative Concepts
- Receptive Labels of 3-Dimensional Shapes
- Receptive Labels of Beginning Sounds of Letters
- Receptive Labels of Money
- Receptive Labels of Opposites
- Reading: Matching Letter Sounds to Pictures
- Reading: Matching Words to Pictures
- Rhyming
- Task Duration

CONNECTING THE DOTS

LEVEL: □ 1 □ 2 □ 3

S^D: Present a "Connect the Dots" worksheet and say "Connect the Dots"	**Response:** Individual will connect the dots in sequential order
Data Collection: Prompt data (number and type of prompts used)	**Target Criteria:** 0 prompts for 3 consecutive days across 2 people
Materials: "Connect the Dots" worksheets and reinforcement. Alternative materials include a number line (use S^D "Connect the numbers")	

Fading procedure

Maintenance Criteria: 2W = 4 consecutive scores of 0 prompts; 1W = 4 consecutive scores of 0 prompts; M = 3 consecutive scores of 0 prompts	**Natural Environment (NE) Criterion:** Target has been generalized in NE across 3 novel naturally occurring activities	**Archive Criteria:** Target, maintenance and NE criteria have been met

Target list

Suggestions for targets and probe results

Suggestions for Targets: Various "Connect the Dots" worksheets or games on the internet.
Probe Results (targets in repertoire):

Target	Baseline: Number and Type of Prompts	Date Introduced	Date Criteria Met	*Fading Procedure*		
				Maintenance	Date NE Introduced	Date Archived
1. Target 1: Connect the dots, numbers 1–5						
2. Target 2: Connect the dots, numbers 1–10						
3. Target 3: Connect the dots, numbers 1–15						
4. Target 4: Connect the dots, numbers 1–20						

5. Target 5: Connect the dots, numbers 1–25						
6. Generalize to another environment Environment 1:						
7. Generalize to another environment Environment 2:						
8. Maintenance: Assess in varied environments.				2W 1W M		

Specific tips for running this task analysis

- Ensure pre-requisite skills have been taught for this TA. Examples of pre-requisite skills for "Connecting the Dots" include mastering receptive labels of numbers, rote counting and pre-handwriting skills (TAs found in the first book of the Journey of Development ABA Curriculum series).
- Start with worksheets that are simple and do not require the individual to scan far distances across the worksheet.
- If the individual has difficulty grasping and writing with a pencil, use games on the internet for connecting the dots that require the individual to click on the number and a line is drawn for them.
- You can create your own "Connecting the Dots" worksheets by simply drawing dots with numbers next to them on a sheet of paper.

CUTTING

LEVEL: □ 1 □ 2 □ 3

S^D: Present individual with scissors and shape to cut out, and say "Cut"	**Response:** Individual will correctly cut out the shape
Data Collection: Prompt data (number and type of prompts used)	**Target criteria:** 0 prompts for 3 consecutive days across 2 people
Materials: Scissors, simple shapes and reinforcement	

Fading procedure

Maintenance Criteria: 2W = 4 consecutive scores of 100%; 1W = 4 consecutive scores of 100%; M = 3 consecutive scores of 100%	**Natural Environment (NE) Criterion:** Target has been generalized in NE across 3 novel naturally occurring activities	**Archive Criteria:** Target, maintenance and NE criteria have been met

Target list

Suggestions for targets and probe results

Suggestions for Targets: Straight line, curved line, diagonal line, 90-degree angle, "V", square, circle, triangle, diamond and heart.
Probe Results (targets in repertoire):

Target	Baseline: Number and Type of Prompts	Date Introduced	Date Criteria Met	*Fading Procedure*		
				Maintenance	Date NE Introduced	Date Archived
1. Target 1:						
2. Target 2:						
3. Targets 1 and 2 random rotation						
4. Target 3:						

5. Target 4:						
6. Targets that met criteria: random rotation						
7. Target 5:						
8. Target 6:						
9. Targets that met criteria: random rotation						
10. Target 7:						
11. Target 8						
12. Targets that met criteria: random rotation						
13. Target 9:						
14. Target 10:						
15. Targets that met criteria: random rotation						
16. Generalize to another environment Environment 1:						
17. Generalize to another environment Environment 2:						
18. Maintenance: Assess in varied environments				2W 1W M		

Specific tips for running this task analysis

- Ensure pre-requisite skills have been taught for this TA. Examples of pre-requisite skills for "Cutting" include "Receptive Instructions (One-Step)"; TA found in the first book of the Journey of Development ABA Curriculum series. The individual should also have the ability to engage in fine motor movements involving the hands.
- For individuals who struggle with this program, you may want to consider using spring-loaded scissors or changing to a heavier-duty paper (i.e. card stock vs. construction paper vs. worksheets on copy paper).

EXPRESSIVE LABELS OF 3-DIMENSIONAL SHAPES

LEVEL: □ 1 □ 2 □ 3

S^D: Present individual with a picture or object of a 3-dimensional shape and say "What shape is this?"	**Response:** Individual will label the object or picture
Data Collection: Skill acquisition	**Target Criteria:** 80% or above for 3 consecutive days across 2 people
Materials: Objects or picture cards depicting various 3-dimensional shapes and reinforcement (picture cards can be found on accompanying CD)	

Fading procedure

Maintenance Criteria: 2W = 4 consecutive scores of 100%; 1W = 4 consecutive scores of 100%; M = 3 consecutive scores of 100%	**Natural Environment (NE) Criterion:** Target has been generalized in NE across 3 novel naturally occurring activities	**Archive Criteria:** Target, maintenance and NE criteria have been met

Target list

Suggestions for targets and probe results

Suggestions for Targets: Cone, cube, pyramid, sphere and cylinder
Probe Results (targets in repertoire):

Target	Baseline %	Date introduced	Date Criteria Met	*Fading Procedure*		
				Maintenance	Date NE Introduced	Date Archived
1. Target 1:						
2. Target 2:						
3. Targets 1 and 2 random rotation						
4. Target 3:						
5. Target 4:						

6. Target 5:						
7. Targets that met criteria: random rotation						
8. Generalize to another environment Environment 1:						
9. Generalize to another environment Environment 2:						
10. Maintenance: Assess in varied environments				2W 1W M		

Specific tips for running this task analysis

- Ensure pre-requisite skills have been taught for this TA. Examples of pre-requisite skills for "Expressive Labels of 3-Dimensional Shapes" include expressive and receptive "Labels of Shapes" (TAs found in the first book of the Journey of Development ABA Curriculum series) and "Receptive Labels of 3-Dimensional Shapes" (TA found in this curriculum book).
- For generalization and higher-level teaching, you can target objects that are 3-dimensional (i.e. ice-cream cone = cone, dice = cube, Play-Doh container = cylinder, etc.).

EXPRESSIVE LABELS OF BEGINNING SOUNDS OF LETTERS

LEVEL: □ 1 □ 2 □ 3

S^D: A. "What sound does [letter] make?" (e.g. "What sound does B make?") B. "What letter says [sound]?" (e.g. "What letter says 'ba'?")	**Response:** A. Individual will make the appropriate sound B. Individual will state the appropriate letter
Data Collection: Skill acquisition	**Target Criteria:** 80% or above for 3 consecutive days across 2 people
Materials: Reinforcement	

Fading procedure

Maintenance Criteria: 2W = 4 consecutive scores of 100%; 1W = 4 consecutive scores of 100%; M = 3 consecutive scores of 100%	**Natural Environment (NE) Criterion:** Target has been generalized in NE across 3 novel naturally occurring activities	**Archive Criteria:** Target, maintenance and NE criteria have been met

Target list

Suggestions for targets and probe results

Suggestions for Targets: All letters of the alphabet.
Probe Results (targets in repertoire):

Target	Baseline %	Date Introduced	Date Criteria Met	*Fading Procedure*		
				Maintenance	Date NE Introduced	Date Archived
Letter Sounds						
1. S^D A: Target 1: A						
2. S^D A: Target 2: B						
3. Targets 1 and 2 random rotation						
4. S^D A: Target 3: C						

5. S^D A: Target 4: D						
6. Targets that met criteria: random rotation						
7. S^D A: Target 5: E						
8. S^D A: Target 6: F						
9. Targets that met criteria: random rotation						
10. S^D A: Target 7: G						
11. S^D A: Target 8: H						
12. Targets that met criteria: random rotation						
13. S^D A: Target 9: I						
14. S^D A: Target 10: J						
15. Targets that met criteria: random rotation						
16. S^D A: Target 11: K						
17. S^D A: Target 12: L						
18. Targets that met criteria: random rotation						
19. S^D A: Target 13: M						
20. S^D A: Target 14: N						

21. Targets that met criteria: random rotation						
22. S^D A: Target 15: O						
23. S^D A: Target 16: P						
24. Targets that met criteria: random rotation						
25. S^D A: Target 17: Q						
26. S^D A: Target 18: R						
27. Targets that met criteria: random rotation						
28. S^D A: Target 19: S						
29. S^D A: Target 20: T						
30. Targets that met criteria: random rotation						
31. S^D A: Target 21: U						
32. S^D A: Target 22: V						
33. Targets that met criteria: random rotation						
34. S^D A: Target 23: W						
35. S^D A: Target 24: X						
36. Targets that met criteria: random rotation						

37. S^D A: Target 25: Y						
38. S^D A: Target 26: Z						
39. Targets that met criteria: random rotation						
40. Generalize to another environment Environment 1:						
41. Generalize to another environment Environment 2:						
42. Maintenance: Assess in varied environments				2W 1W M		
Letter						
1. S^D B: Target 1: A						
2. S^D B: Target 2: B						
3. S^D B: Targets 1 and 2 random rotation						
4. S^D B: Target 3: C						
5. S^D B: Target 4: D						
6. S^D B: Targets that met criteria: random rotation						
7. S^D B: Target 5: E						
8. S^D B: Target 6: F						
9. S^D B: Targets that met criteria: random rotation						
10. S^D B: Target 7: G						

11. S^D B: Target 8: H						
12. S^D B: Targets that met criteria: random rotation						
13. S^D B: Target 9: I						
14. S^D B: Target 10: J						
15. S^D B: Targets that met criteria: random rotation						
16. S^D B: Target 11: K						
17. S^D B: Target 12: L						
18. S^D B: Targets that met criteria: random rotation						
19. S^D B: Target 13: M						
20. S^D B: Target 14: N						
21. S^D B: Targets that met criteria: random rotation						
22. S^D B: Target 15: O						
23. S^D B: Target 16: P						
24. S^D B: Targets that met criteria: random rotation						
25. S^D B: Target 17: Q						
26. S^D B: Target 18: R						

27. S^D B: Targets that met criteria: random rotation						
28. S^D B: Target 19: S						
29. S^D B: Target 20: T						
30. S^D B: Targets that met criteria: random rotation						
31. S^D B: Target 21: U						
32. S^D B: Target 22: V						
33. S^D B: Targets that met criteria: random rotation						
34. S^D B: Target 23: W						
35. S^D B: Target 24: X						
36. S^D B: Targets that met criteria: random rotation						
37. S^D B: Target 25: Y						
38. S^D B: Target 26: Z						
39. S^D B: Targets that met criteria: random rotation						
40. Generalize to another environment. Environment 1						
41. Generalize to another environment. Environment 2:						
42. Maintenance: Assess in varied environments				2W 1W M		

Specific tips for running this task analysis

- Ensure pre-requisite skills have been taught for this TA. Examples of pre-requisite skills for "Expressive Labels of Beginning Sounds of Letters" include mastering receptive and expressive labels of letters and "Answering Simple 'What' Questions" (TAs found in the first book of the Journey of Development ABA Curriculum series). In addition, the individual should have mastered receptive labels of beginning sounds of letters (TA found in this curriculum book).
- For vowels, target the short vowel sound, as the long vowel sound is the letter name.
- It may be easier for the individual to identify the sounds for consonants first followed by vowels.

EXPRESSIVE LABELS OF MONEY

LEVEL: □ 1 □ 2 □ 3

S^D: Present individual with a picture card of a coin or dollar bill, or present a real or pretend coin/dollar bill and ask "What is it?"	**Response:** Individual will label the coin or dollar bill
Data Collection: Skill acquisition	**Target Criteria:** 80% or above for 3 consecutive days across 2 people
Materials: Real or pretend coins and dollar bills, and reinforcement (picture cards can be found on accompanying CD)	

Fading procedure

Maintenance Criteria: 2W = 4 consecutive scores of 100%; 1W = 4 consecutive scores of 100%; M = 3 consecutive scores of 100%	**Natural Environment (NE) Criterion:** Target has been generalized in NE across 3 novel naturally occurring activities	**Archive Criteria:** Target, maintenance and NE criteria have been met

Target list

Suggestions for targets and probe results

Suggestions for Targets: Penny, nickel, dime, quarter, 1-dollar bill, 5-dollar bill, 10-dollar bill and 20-dollar bill.
Probe Results (targets in repertoire):

Target	Baseline %	Date Introduced	Date Criteria Met	*Fading Procedure* Maintenance	Date NE Introduced	Date Archived
1. Target 1:						
2. Target 2:						
3. Targets 1 and 2 random rotation						
4. Target 3:						
5. Target 4:						

6. Targets that met criteria: random rotation						
7. Target 5:						
8. Target 6:						
9. Targets that met criteria: random rotation						
10. Target 7:						
11. Target 8:						
12. Targets that met criteria: random rotation						
13. Generalize to another environment Environment 1:						
14. Generalize to another environment Environment 2:						
15. Maintenance: Assess in varied environments				2W 1W M		

EXPRESSIVE LABELS OF OPPOSITES

LEVEL: □ 1 □ 2 □ 3

S^D: Present two objects or pictures of objects that represent opposites. Say "This one is [x] and this one is…" (e.g. "This one is tall and this one is (short)"	**Response:** Individual will label the picture or objects using the opposite (e.g. "cold" vs. "hot")
Data Collection: Skill acquisition	**Target Criteria:** 80% or above for 3 consecutive days across 2 people
Materials: Objects and/or picture cards of opposite pairs and reinforcement (picture cards can be found on accompanying CD)	

Fading procedure

Maintenance Criteria: 2W = 4 consecutive scores of 100%; 1W = 4 consecutive scores of 100%; M = 3 consecutive scores of 100%	**Natural Environment (NE) Criterion:** Target has been generalized in NE across 3 novel naturally occurring activities	**Archive Criteria:** Target, maintenance and NE criteria have been met

Target list

Suggestions for targets and probe results

Suggestions for Targets: Big/little, light/dark, day/night, on/off, open/close, tall/short, thick/thin, deep/shallow, happy/sad and sisters/brothers.

Probe Results (targets in repertoire):

Target	Baseline %	Date Introduced	Date Criteria Met	*Fading Procedure*		
				Maintenance	Date NE Introduced	Date Archived
1. Target 1:						
2. Target 2:						
3. Targets that met criteria: random rotation						
4. Target 3:						
5. Target 4:						

6. Targets that met criteria: random rotation						
7. Target 5:						
8. Target 6:						
9. Targets that met criteria: random rotation						
10. Target 7:						
11. Target 8:						
12. Targets that met criteria: random rotation						
13. Target 9:						
14. Target 10:						
15. Targets that met criteria: random rotation						
16. Generalize to another environment Environment 1:						
17. Generalize to another environment Environment 2:						
18. Maintenance: Assess in varied environments				2W 1W M		

Specific tips for running this task analysis

- Ensure pre-requisite skills have been taught for this TA. Examples of pre-requisite skills for "Expressive Labels of Opposites" include receptive and expressive labels programs found in the first book of the Journey of Development ABA Curriculum series. In addition, progress should be made toward receptive and expressive labels of attributes (TA found in this curriculum book).
- If individual is on Level 3 learning, you can change S^D to say "What is the opposite of [x]?"

FOLDING PAPER

LEVEL: □ 1 □ 2 □ 3

S^D: Present individual with paper to fold and example of folded paper. Point to the paper that needs folding and say "Fold the paper."	**Response:** Individual will fold the paper
Data Collection: Skill acquisition	**Target criteria:** 80% or above for 3 consecutive days across 2 people.
Materials: Paper and reinforcement	

Fading procedure

Maintenance Criteria: 2W = 4 consecutive scores of 100%; 1W = 4 consecutive scores of 100%; M = 3 consecutive scores of 100%	**Natural Environment (NE) Criterion:** Target has been generalized in NE across 3 novel naturally occurring activities	**Archive Criteria:** Target, maintenance and NE criteria have been met

Target list

Suggestions for targets and probe results

Suggestions for Targets: Fold a paper that is pre-folded, fold the paper on a given line, fold paper like a hotdog on a given line, fold paper like a hotdog (without a line), fold paper like a hamburger on a line, fold paper like a hamburger (without a line), fold paper into a triangle (matching corners) on a given line, fold paper into a triangle (matching corners without a line), fold a paper in 3s (trifold) on a given line, and fold paper into 3s (trifold) without a line.

Probe Results (targets in repertoire):

				Fading Procedure		
Target	**Baseline %**	**Date Introduced**	**Date Criteria Met**	**Maintenance**	**Date NE Introduced**	**Date Archived**
1. Target 1:						
2. Target 2:						
3. Targets 1 and 2 random rotation						
4. Target 3:						

5. Target 4:						
6. Targets that met criteria: random rotation						
7. Target 5:						
8. Target 6:						
9. Targets that met criteria: random rotation						
10. Target 7:						
11. Target 8:						
12. Targets that met criteria: random rotation						
13. Target 9:						
14. Target 10:						
15. Targets that met criteria: random rotation						
16. Generalize to another environment Environment 1:						
17. Generalize to another environment Environment 2:						
18. Maintenance: Assess in varied environments				2W 1W M		

Specific tips for running this task analysis

- Ensure pre-requisite skills have been taught for this TA. Examples of pre-requisite skills for "Folding Paper" include fine motor imitation (TA found in the first book of the Journey of Development ABA Curriculum series). The individual should also possess some bilateral coordination.
- Make this program fun and functional by running it during a craft or art project.

PART/WHOLE RELATIONSHIPS

LEVEL: □ 1 □ 2 □ 3

S^D: Present individual with a field of 3 picture cards representing half and whole portions, and a distractor portion (e.g. quarter). Say "Touch [x]," "Give me [x]" or "Point to [x]." (e.g. "Give me half of the pie" or "Point to the whole pizza")	**Response:** Individual will touch, give or point to the specified portion (e.g. half of the pie)
Data Collection: Skill acquisition	**Target Criteria:** 80% or above for 3 consecutive days across 2 people
Materials: Picture cards of symmetrical objects each depicting a half and the whole object, and reinforcement (picture cards can be found on accompanying CD)	

Fading procedure

Maintenance Criteria: 2W = 4 consecutive scores of 100%; 1W = 4 consecutive scores of 100%; M = 3 consecutive scores of 100%	**Natural Environment (NE) Criterion:** Target has been generalized in NE across 3 novel naturally occurring activities	**Archive Criteria:** Target, maintenance and NE criteria have been met

Target list

Suggestions for targets and probe results

Suggestions for Targets: Pie, person, pizza, cake, butterfly, house, face, square, triangle and circle.

Probe Results (targets in repertoire):

Target	Baseline %	Date Introduced	Date Criteria Met	*Fading Procedure* Maintenance	Date NE Introduced	Date Archived
1. Target 1 (isolation):						
2. Target 1 (FO2/target and distractor):						
3. Target 1 (FO3/target and 2 distractors)						
4. Target 2 (isolation):						

5. Target 2 (FO2/target and distractor):						
6. Target 2 (FO3/target and 2 distractors)						
7. Targets 1 and 2 random rotation						
8. Target 3 (isolation):						
9. Target 3 (FO2/target and distractor):						
10. Target 3 (FO3/target and 2 distractors)						
11. Target 4 (isolation):						
12. Target 4 (FO2/target and distractor):						
13. Target 4 (FO3/target and 2 distractors)						
14. Targets that met criteria: random rotation						
15. Target 5 (isolation):						
16. Target 5 (FO2/target and distractor):						
17. Target 5 (FO3/target and 2 distractors)						
18. Target 6 (isolation):						
19. Target 6 (FO2/target and distractor):						
20. Target 6 (FO3/target and 2 distractors)						

21. Targets that met criteria: random rotation						
22. Target 7 (isolation):						
23. Target 7 (FO2/target and distractor):						
24. Target 7 (FO3/target and 2 distractors)						
25. Target 8 (isolation):						
26. Target 8 (FO2/target and distractor):						
27. Target 8 (FO3/target and 2 distractors)						
28. Targets that met criteria: random rotation						
29. Target 9 (isolation):						
30. Target 9 (FO2/target and distractor):						
31. Target 9 (FO3/target and 2 distractors)						
32. Target 10 (isolation):						
33. Target 10 (FO2/target and distractor):						
34. Target 10 (FO3/target and 2 distractors)						
35. Targets that met criteria: random rotation						
36. Generalize to another environment Environment 1:						

37. Generalize to another environment Environment 2:						
38. Maintenance: Assess in varied environments				2W 1W M		

Specific tips for running this task analysis

- Ensure pre-requisite skills have been taught for this TA. Examples of pre-requisite skills for "Part/Whole Relationships" include mastering the receptive and expressive labels of objects, food, shapes and body parts (TAs found in the first book of the Journey of Development ABA Curriculum series).
- Isolation is the fraction being targeted. FO2 and FO3 include distracters of other fractions: a third, a quarter, whole and a shaded-out picture (representing none). Then random rotation should only include half vs. whole.

PAINTING

LEVEL: □ 1 □ 2 □ 3

S^D: Present individual with a simple shape or picture to paint, and say "Paint"	**Response:** Individual will respond by painting 75% of a simple shape or picture (painting outside of lines is acceptable)
Data Collection: Prompt data (number and type of prompts used)	**Target criteria:** 0 prompts for 3 consecutive days across 2 people
Materials: Paint, paintbrushes, simple shapes in varying sizes (1 inch, 2 inches and 3 inches), pictures and reinforcement	

Fading procedure

Maintenance Criteria: 2W = 4 consecutive scores of 0 prompts; 1W = 4 consecutive scores of 0 prompts; M = 3 consecutive scores of 0 prompts	**Natural Environment (NE) Criterion:** Target has been generalized in NE across 3 novel naturally occurring activities	**Archive Criteria:** Target, maintenance and NE criteria have been met

Target list

Suggestions for targets and probe results

Suggestions for Targets: Triangle, circle, square, rectangle, boat, train, apple, bird, rainbow and ice-cream cone.
Probe Results (targets in repertoire):

Target	Baseline: Number and Type of Prompts	Date Introduced	Date Criteria Met	*Fading Procedure*		
				Maintenance	Date NE Introduced	Date Archived
1. Target 1:						
2. Target 2:						
3. Targets 1 and 2 random rotation						
4. Target 3:						

5. Target 4:						
6. Targets that met criteria: random rotation						
7. Target 5:						
8. Target 6:						
9. Targets that met criteria: random rotation						
10. Target 7:						
11. Target 8:						
12. Targets that met criteria: random rotation						
13. Target 9:						
14. Target 10:						
15. Targets that met criteria: random rotation						
16. Generalize to another environment Environment 1:						
17. Generalize to another environment Environment 2:						
18. Maintenance: Assess in varied environments				2W 1W M		

Specific tips for running this task analysis

- Ensure pre-requisite skills have been taught for this TA. Examples of pre-requisite skills for "Painting" include "Fine Motor Imitation" and progress made toward "Coloring" (TAs found in the first book of the Journey of Development ABA Curriculum series).
- Having the individual choose the color(s) they want to paint with or a picture that they want to paint may help keep motivation high.

PASTING AND GLUING

LEVEL: □ 1 □ 2 □ 3

S^D: Present individual with items to glue or paste, and say "Glue" or "Paste"	**Response:** Individual will glue or paste the items onto a location
Data Collection: Prompt data (number and type of prompts used)	**Target criteria:** 0 prompts for 3 consecutive days across 2 people
Materials: Paper, glue/glue stick, items to glue and reinforcement	

Fading procedure

Maintenance Criteria: 2W = 4 consecutive scores of 0 prompts; 1W = 4 consecutive scores of 0 prompts; M = 3 consecutive scores of 0 prompts	**Natural Environment (NE) Criterion:** Target has been generalized in NE across 3 novel naturally occurring activities	**Archive Criteria:** Target, maintenance and NE criteria have been met

Target list

Suggestions for targets and probe results

Suggestions for targets: Glue stick and glue bottle.
Probe Results (targets in repertoire):

Target	Baseline: Number and Type of Prompts	Date Introduced	Date Criteria Met	*Fading Procedure*		
				Maintenance	Date NE Introduced	Date Archived
Total Task Analysis – Glue Stick						
1. Target 1: Individual will retrieve glue stick.						
2. Target 2: Individual will remove the cap of the glue stick.						
3. Target 3: Individual will turn the crank to raise the glue stick.						
4. Target 4: Individual will place glue on the larger stationery item.						

5. Target 5: Place the smaller movable item onto the glued area.						
6. Target 6: Individual will turn crank to lower the glue stick.						
7. Target 7: Individual will replace cap.						
8. Generalize to another environment Environment 1:						
9. Generalize to another environment Environment 2:						
10. Maintenance: Assess in varied environments				2W 1W M		
Total Task Analysis – Glue Bottle						
11. Target 1: Individual will retrieve glue bottle.						
12. Target 2: Individual will turn the top of the bottle to open the glue bottle.						
13. Target 3: Individual will turn the glue bottle upside down.						
14. Target 4: Squeeze glue bottle to make dots on larger stationery item.						
15. Target 5: Place the smaller movable item onto the glue dots.						
16. Target 6: Individual will turn top to close the glue bottle.						
17. Generalize to another environment Environment 1:						
18. Generalize to another environment Environment 2:						
19. Maintenance: Assess in varied environments				2W 1W M		

Specific tips for running this task analysis

- Ensure pre-requisite skills have been taught for this TA. Examples of pre-requisite skills for "Pasting and Gluing" include mastering "Fine Motor Imitation" and "Receptive Instructions (One-Step)," both TAs found in the first book of the Journey of Development ABA Curriculum series. In addition, the individual should be able to engage in the fine motor tasks required of this program (i.e. removing/replacing the lid, squeezing the bottle, opening the glue bottle, etc.).
- This program is designed to teach the individual how to use craft supplies appropriately using a total TA. This requires the individual to engage in all steps of the procedure every therapy session, instructor provides assistance (prompts) with any step the individual is not able to perform. Instructor should record the number and type of prompts required for each step, until all steps of the task are completed.
- It is best to begin gluing items that are 3-D to 2-D (i.e. pom poms to paper plate, cotton balls to paper, etc.) This will help with grasping the smaller items and placing them on the glue. Then move on to gluing paper to paper.

QUANTITATIVE CONCEPTS

LEVEL: □ 1 □ 2 □ 3

S^D: A. Present field of two objects or pictures and say "Touch [describe picture or object in few words and include quantity concept]." (e.g. "Touch the individual who has more cake") B. Present two pictures or objects and say "[description of one of the pictures/objects with quantity concept, then a lead for the other object/picture.]" (e.g. This boy has some toys, this boy has…")	**Response:** A. Individual will touch the picture or object representing the quantity concept B. Individual will label the quantity concept in the picture or object
Data Collection: Skill acquisition	**Target Criteria:** 80% or above for 3 consecutive days across 2 people
Materials: Pictures/objects displaying different quantity concepts, and reinforcement (picture cards can be found on accompanying CD)	

Fading procedure

Maintenance Criteria: 2W = 4 consecutive scores of 100%; 1W = 4 consecutive scores of 100%; M = 3 consecutive scores of 100%	**Natural Environment (NE) Criterion:** Target has been generalized in NE across 3 novel naturally occurring activities	**Archive Criteria:** Target, maintenance and NE criteria have been met

Target list

Suggestions for targets and probe results

Suggestions for Targets: One, all, another one, more, less, none, few, some, same, double, triple, first, last and third.
Probe Results (targets in repertoire):

Target	Baseline %	Date Introduced	Date Criteria Met	*Fading Procedure*		
				Maintenance	Date NE Introduced	Date Archived
1. S^D A: Target 1:						
2. S^D A: Target 2:						
3. Targets 1 and 2 random rotation						

4. S^D A: Target 3:						
5. S^D A: Target 4:						
6. Targets that met criteria: random rotation						
7. S^D A: Target 5:						
8. S^D A: Target 6:						
9. Targets that met criteria: random rotation						
10. S^D A: Target 7:						
11. S^D A: Target 8:						
12. Targets that met criteria: random rotation						
13. S^D A: Target 9:						
14. S^D A: Target 10:						
15. Targets that met criteria: random rotation						
16. Generalize to another environment Environment 1:						
17. Generalize to another environment Environment 2:						
18. Maintenance: Assess in varied environments				2W 1W M		
19. S^D B: Target 1:						

20. S^D B: Target 2:						
21. Targets 1 and 2 random rotation						
22. S^D B: Target 3:						
23. S^D B: Target 4:						
24. Targets that met criteria: random rotation						
25. S^D B: Target 5:						
26. S^D B: Target 6:						
27. Targets that met criteria: random rotation						
28. S^D B: Target 7:						
29. S^D B: Target 8:						
30. Targets that met criteria: random rotation						
31. S^D B: Target 9:						
32. S^D B: Target 10:						
33. Targets that met criteria: random rotation						
34. Generalize to another environment Environment 1:						
35. Generalize to another environment Environment 2:						
36. Maintenance: Assess in varied environments				2W 1W M		

RECEPTIVE LABELS OF 3-DIMENSIONAL SHAPES

LEVEL: □ 1 □ 2 □ 3

S^D: Present individual with a field of 1, 2 or 3 objects or picture cards and say "Touch [3-D shape]" or "Give me [3-D shape]" (e.g. "Touch Cone")	**Response:** Individual will [touch or give] the specified object or picture
Data Collection: Skill acquisition	**Target Criteria:** 80% or above for 3 consecutive days across 2 people
Materials: Objects or picture cards depicting various 3-dimensional shapes and reinforcement (picture cards can be found on accompanying CD)	

Fading procedure

Maintenance Criteria: 2W = 4 consecutive scores of 100%; 1W = 4 consecutive scores of 100%; M = 3 consecutive scores of 100%	**Natural Environment (NE) Criterion:** Target has been generalized in NE across 3 novel naturally occurring activities	**Archive Criteria:** Target, maintenance and NE criteria have been met

Target list

Suggestions for targets and probe results

Suggestions for Targets: Cone, cube, pyramid, sphere and cylinder
Probe Results (targets in repertoire):

Target	Baseline %	Date Introduced	Date Criteria Met	*Fading Procedure*		
				Maintenance	Date NE Introduced	Date Archived
1. Target 1 (isolation):						
2. Target 1 (FO2/target and distractor):						
3. Target 1 (FO3/target and 2 distractors):						
4. Target 2 (isolation):						
5. Target 2 (FO2/target and distractor):						

6. Target 2 (FO3/target and 2 distractors):						
7. Targets 1 and 2 random rotation						
8. Target 3 (isolation):						
9. Target 3 (FO2/target and distractor):						
10. Target 3 (FO3/target and 2 distractors):						
11. Target 4 (isolation):						
12. Target 4 (FO2/target and distractor):						
13. Target 4 (FO3/target and 2 distractors):						
14. Target 5 (isolation):						
15. Target 5 (FO2/target and distractor):						
16. Target 5 (FO3/target and 2 distractors):						
17. Targets that met criteria: random rotation						
18. Generalize to another environment Environment 1:						
19. Generalize to another environment Environment 2:						
20. Maintenance: Assess in varied environments				2W 1W M		

Specific tips for running this task analysis

- Ensure pre-requisite skills have been taught for this TA. Examples of pre-requisite skills for "Receptive Labels of 3-Dimensional Shapes" include "Receptive Instructions (One-Step)" and "Receptive Labels of Shapes" (TAs found in the first book of the Journey of Development ABA Curriculum series).
- For generalization and higher-level teaching, you can also target objects that are 3-dimensional (i.e. ice-cream cone = cone, dice = cube, Play-Doh container = cylinder, etc.).

RECEPTIVE LABELS OF BEGINNING SOUNDS OF LETTERS

LEVEL: □ 1 □ 2 □ 3

S^D: Present individual with a field of 1, 2 or 3 letters and say "Touch the letter that says [x]" or "Give me the letter that says [x]" (e.g. "Touch the letter that says ba")	**Response:** Individual will touch or give the correct letter
Data Collection: Skill acquisition	**Target Criteria:** 80% or above for 3 consecutive days across 2 people
Materials: Pictures of letters, 3-dimensional letters (plastic letters or puzzle piece letters) and reinforcement (picture cards can be found on accompanying CD)	

Fading procedure

Maintenance Criteria: 2W = 4 consecutive scores of 100%; 1W = 4 consecutive scores of 100%; M = 3 consecutive scores of 100%	**Natural Environment (NE) Criterion:** Target has been generalized in NE across 3 novel naturally occurring activities	**Archive Criteria:** Target, maintenance and NE criteria have been met

Target list

Suggestions for targets and probe results

Suggestions for Targets: All letters of the alphabet.
Probe Results (targets in repertoire):

Target	Baseline %	Date Introduced	Date Criteria Met	*Fading Procedure* Maintenance	Date NE Introduced	Date Archived
1. Target 1 (isolation):						
2. Target 1 (FO2/target and distractor):						
3. Target 1 (FO3/target and 2 distractors):						
4. Target 2 (isolation):						
5. Target 2 (FO2/target and distractor):						

6. Target 2 (FO3/target and 2 distractors):						
7. Targets that met criteria: random rotation						
8. Target 3 (isolation):						
9. Target 3 (FO2/target and distractor):						
10. Target 3 (FO3/target and 2 distractors):						
11. Target 4 (isolation):						
12. Target 4 (FO2/target and distractor):						
13. Target 4 (FO3/target and 2 distractors):						
14. Targets that met criteria: random rotation						
15. Target 5 (isolation):						
16. Target 5 (FO2/target and distractor):						
17. Target 5 (FO3/target and 2 distractors):						
18. Target 6 (isolation):						
19. Target 6 (FO2/target and distractor):						
20. Target 6 (FO3/target and 2 distractors):						
21. Targets that met criteria: random rotation						

22. Target 7 (isolation):						
23. Target 7 (FO2/target and distractor):						
24. Target 7 (FO3/target and 2 distractors):						
25. Target 8 (isolation):						
26. Target 8 (FO2/target and distractor):						
27. Target 8 (FO3/target and 2 distractors):						
28. Targets that met criteria: random rotation						
29. Target 9 (isolation):						
30. Target 9 (FO2/target and distractor):						
31. Target 9 (FO3/target and 2 distractors):						
32. Target 10 (isolation):						
33. Target 10 (FO2/target and distractor):						
34. Target 10 (FO3/target and 2 distractors):						
35. Targets that met criteria: random rotation						
36. Target 11 (isolation):						
37. Target 11 (FO2/target and distractor):						

38. Target 11 (FO3/target and 2 distractors):						
39. Target 12 (isolation):						
40. Target 12 (FO2/target and distractor):						
41. Target 12 (FO3/target and 2 distractors):						
42. Targets that met criteria: random rotation						
43. Target 13 (isolation):						
44. Target 13 (FO2/target and distractor):						
45. Target 13 (FO3/target and 2 distractors):						
46. Target 14 (isolation):						
47. Target 14 (FO2/target and distractor):						
48. Target 14 (FO3/target and 2 distractors):						
49. Targets that met criteria: random rotation						
50. Target 15 (isolation):						
51. Target 15 (FO2/target and distractor):						
52. Target 15 (FO3/target and 2 distractors):						
53. Target 16 (isolation):						

54. Target 16 (FO2/target and distractor):						
55. Target 16 (FO3/target and 2 distractors):						
56. Targets that met criteria: random rotation						
57. Target 17 (isolation):						
58. Target 17 (FO2/target and distractor):						
59. Target 17 (FO3/target and 2 distractors):						
60. Target 18 (isolation):						
61. Target 18 (FO2/target and distractor):						
62. Target 18 (FO3/target and 2 distractors):						
63. Targets that met criteria: random rotation						
64. Target 19 (isolation):						
65. Target 19 (FO2/target and distractor):						
66. Target 19 (FO3/target and 2 distractors):						
67. Target 20 (isolation):						
68. Target 20 (FO2/target and distractor):						
69. Target 20 (FO3/target and 2 distractors):						

70. Targets that met criteria: random rotation						
71. Target 21 (isolation):						
72. Target 21 (FO2/target and distractor):						
73. Target 21 (FO3/target and 2 distractors):						
74. Target 22 (isolation):						
75. Target 22 (FO2/target and distractor):						
76. Target 22 (FO3/target and 2 distractors):						
77. Targets that met criteria: random rotation						
78. Target 23 (isolation):						
79. Target 23 (FO2/target and distractor):						
80. Target 23 (FO3/target and 2 distractors):						
81. Target 24 (isolation):						
82. Target 24 (FO2/target and distractor):						
83. Target 24 (FO3/target and 2 distractors):						
84. Targets that met criteria: random rotation						
85. Target 25 (isolation):						

86. Target 25 (FO2/target and distractor):						
87. Target 25 (FO3/target and 2 distractors):						
88. Target 26 (isolation):						
89. Target 26 (FO2/target and distractor):						
90. Target 26 (FO3/target and 2 distractors):						
91. Targets that met criteria: random rotation						
92. Generalize to another environment Environment 1:						
93. Generalize to another environment Environment 2:						
94. Maintenance: Assess in varied environments				2W 1W M		

Specific tips for running this task analysis

- Ensure pre-requisite skills have been taught for this TA. Examples of pre-requisite skills for "Receptive Labels of Beginning Sounds of Letters" include mastering the "Receptive Labels of Letters" (TA found in the first book of the Journey of Development ABA Curriculum series) and "Answering Simple 'What' Questions" (TA found in this curriculum book).
- For vowels, target the short vowel sound, as the long vowel sound is the letter name.

RECEPTIVE LABELS OF MONEY

LEVEL: □ 1 □ 2 □ 3

S^D: Present individual with a field of 1, 2 or 3 picture cards of money, or real or pretend coins/dollar bills. Say "Touch [x]" "Give me [x]" or "Point to [x]" (e.g. "Touch penny")	**Response:** Individual will touch, give or point to correct picture card or correct coin/dollar bill
Data Collection: Skill acquisition	**Target Criteria:** 80% or above for 3 consecutive days across 2 people
Materials: Picture cards of money, real or pretend coins/dollar bills and reinforcement (picture cards can be found on accompanying CD)	

Fading procedure

Maintenance Criteria: 2W = 4 consecutive scores of 100%; 1W = 4 consecutive scores of 100%; M = 3 consecutive scores of 100%	**Natural Environment (NE) Criterion:** Target has been generalized in NE across 3 novel naturally occurring activities	**Archive Criteria:** Target, maintenance and NE criteria have been met

Target list

Suggestions for targets and probe results

Suggestions for Targets: Penny, nickel, dime, quarter, 1-dollar bill, 5-dollar bill, 10-dollar bill and 20-dollar bill.
Probe Results (targets in repertoire):

Target	Baseline %	Date Introduced	Date Criteria Met	*Fading Procedure*		
				Maintenance	Date NE Introduced	Date Archived
1. Target 1 (isolation):						
2. Target 1 (FO2/target and distractor):						
3. Target 1 (FO3/target and 2 distractors):						
4. Target 2 (isolation):						

5. Target 2 (FO2/target and distractor):						
6. Target 2 (FO3/target and 2 distractors):						
7. Targets 1 and 2 random rotation						
8. Target 3 (isolation):						
9. Target 3 (FO2/target and distractor):						
10. Target 3 (FO3/target and 2 distractors):						
11. Target 4 (isolation):						
12. Target 4 (FO2/target and distractor):						
13. Target 4 (FO3/target and 2 distractors):						
14. Targets that met criteria: random rotation						
15. Target 5 (isolation):						
16. Target 5 (FO2/target and distractor):						
17. Target 5 (FO3/target and 2 distractors):						
18. Target 6 (isolation):						
19. Target 6 (FO2/target and distractor):						
20. Target 6 (FO3/target and 2 distractors):						

21. Targets that met criteria: random rotation						
22. Target 7 (isolation):						
23. Target 7 (FO2/target and distractor):						
24. Target 7 (FO3/target and 2 distractors):						
25. Target 8 (isolation):						
26. Target 8 (FO2/target and distractor):						
27. Target 8 (FO3/target and 2 distractors):						
28. Targets that met criteria: random rotation						
29. Generalize to another environment Environment 1:						
30. Generalize to another environment Environment 2:						
31. Maintenance: Assess in varied environments				2W 1W M		

RECEPTIVE LABELS OF OPPOSITES

LEVEL: □ 1 □ 2 □ 3

S^D: Present a field of 1 or 2 objects or pictures representing opposite pairs and say, "Touch [opposite]" (e.g. "Touch cold" vs. "Touch hot")	**Response:** Individual will touch the specified opposite in the pictures or objects
Data Collection: Skill acquisition	**Target Criteria:** 80% or above for 3 consecutive days across 2 people
Materials: Objects and/or picture cards of opposite pairs and reinforcement (picture cards can be found on accompanying CD)	

Fading procedure

Maintenance Criteria: 2W = 4 consecutive scores of 100%; 1W = 4 consecutive scores of 100%; M = 3 consecutive scores of 100%	**Natural Environment (NE) Criterion:** Target has been generalized in NE across 3 novel naturally occurring activities	**Archive Criteria:** Target, maintenance and NE criteria have been met

Target list

Suggestions for targets and probe results

Suggestions for Targets: Big/little, light/dark, day/night, on/off, open/close, tall/short, thick/thin, deep/shallow, happy/sad and sisters/brothers.
Probe Results (targets in repertoire):

Target	Baseline %	Date Introduced	Date Criteria Met	*Fading Procedure*		
				Maintenance	Date NE Introduced	Date Archived
1. Target 1 (isolation):						
2. Target 1 (FO2/target and distractor):						
3. Target 2 (isolation):						
4. Target 2 (FO2/target and distractor):						
5. Targets that met criteria: random rotation						

6. Target 3 (isolation):						
7. Target 3 (FO2/target and distractor):						
8. Target 4 (isolation):						
9. Target 4 (FO2/target and distractor):						
10. Targets that met criteria: random rotation						
11. Target 5 (isolation):						
12. Target 5 (FO2/target and distractor):						
13. Target 6 (isolation):						
14. Target 6 (FO2/target and distractor):						
15. Targets that met criteria: random rotation						
16. Target 7 (isolation):						
17. Target 7 (FO2/target and distractor):						
18. Target 8 (isolation):						
19. Target 8 (FO2/target and distractor):						
20. Targets that met criteria: random rotation						
21. Target 9 (isolation):						

22. Target 9 (FO2/target and distractor):						
23. Target 10 (isolation):						
24. Target 10 (FO2/target and distractor):						
25. Targets that met criteria: random rotation						
26. Generalize to another environment Environment 1:						
27. Generalize to another environment Environment 2:						
28. Maintenance: Assess in varied environments				2W 1W M		

Specific tips for running this task analysis

- Ensure pre-requisite skills have been taught for this TA. Examples of pre-requisite skills for “Receptive Labels of Opposites” include receptive and expressive labels programs found in the first book of the Journey of Development ABA Curriculum series. In addition, progress should be made toward “Receptive Labels of Attributes” (TA found in this curriculum book).

READING: MATCHING LETTER SOUNDS TO PICTURES

LEVEL: □ 1 □ 2 □ 3

S^D: Present individual with a letter and a field of 1, 2 or 3 pictures (one picture matching the letter sound) and say "Match" (i.e., present the letter A with a picture of car, apple and train, say "Match")	**Response:** Individual will match the letter sound to its appropriate picture
Data Collection: Skill acquisition	**Target Criteria:** 80% or above for 3 consecutive days across 2 people
Materials: Letter cards, picture cards, and reinforcement (picture cards can be found on accompanying CD)	

Fading procedure

Maintenance Criteria: 2W = 4 consecutive scores of 100%; 1W = 4 consecutive scores of 100%; M = 3 consecutive scores of 100%	**Natural Environment (NE) Criterion:** Target has been generalized in NE across 3 novel naturally occurring activities	**Archive Criteria:** Target, maintenance and NE criteria have been met

Target list

Suggestions for targets and probe results

Suggestions for Targets: A/apple, B/boy, C/car, D/dog, E/elephant, F/fruit, G/game, H/home, I/ice, J/jar, K/kite, L/lion, M/man, etc.

Probe Results (targets in repertoire):

Target	Baseline %	Date Introduced	Date Criteria Met	*Fading Procedure*		
				Maintenance	Date NE Introduced	Date Archived
1. Target 1 (isolation):						
2. Target 1 (FO2/target and distractor):						
3. Target 1 (FO3/target and 2 distractors):						
4. Target 2 (isolation):						

5. Target 2 (FO2/target and distractor):						
6. Target 2 (FO3/target and 2 distractors):						
7. Targets that met criteria: random rotation						
8. Target 3 (isolation):						
9. Target 3 (FO2/target and distractor):						
10. Target 3: FO3/target and 2 distractors:						
11. Target 4 (isolation):						
12. Target 4 (FO2/target and distractor):						
13. Target 4 (FO3/target and 2 distractors):						
14. Targets that met criteria: random rotation						
15. Target 5 (isolation):						
16. Target 5 (FO2/target and distractor):						
17. Target 5 (FO3/target and 2 distractors):						
18. Target 6 (isolation):						
19. Target 6 (FO2/target and distractor):						
20. Target 6 (FO3/target and 2 distractors):						

21. Targets that met criteria: random rotation						
22. Target 7 (isolation):						
23. Target 7 (FO2/target and distractor):						
24. Target 7 (FO3/target and 2 distractors):						
25. Target 8 (isolation):						
26. Target 8 (FO2/target and distractor):						
27. Target 8 (FO3/target and distractors):						
28. Targets that met criteria: random rotation						
29. Target 9 (isolation):						
30. Target 9 (FO2/target and distractor):						
31. Target 9 (FO3/target and 2 distractors):						
32. Target 10 (isolation):						
33. Target 10 (FO2/target and distractor):						
34. Target 10 (FO3/target and 2 distractors):						
35. Targets that met criteria: random rotation						
36. Generalize to another environment Environment 1:						

37. Generalize to another environment Environment 2:						
38. Maintenance: Assess in varied environments				2W 1W M		

Specific tips for running this task analysis

- Ensure pre-requisite skills have been taught for this TA. Examples of pre-requisite skills for "Reading: Matching Letter Sounds to Pictures" include mastery of "Appropriate Sitting" and attending skills, mastery of "Receptive Labels of Letters" (TAs found in the first book of the Journey of Development ABA Curriculum series). In addition, the individual should master "Receptive Labels of Beginning Sounds of Letters" (TA found in this curriculum book).

READING: MATCHING WORDS TO PICTURES

LEVEL: □ 1 □ 2 □ 3

S^D: Present individual with a picture and a field of 1, 2 or 3 words (one word matches the picture) and say "Match" (e.g. present a picture of a cat with the word "cat" and 2 distractor words such as "dog" and "mom" and say "Match")	**Response:** Individual will match the word to its picture
Data Collection: Skill acquisition	**Target Criteria:** 80% or above for 3 consecutive days across 2 people
Materials: Pictures corresponding to the target word, word written out, distractor words and reinforcement (picture cards can be found on accompanying CD)	

Fading procedure

Maintenance Criteria: 2W = 4 consecutive scores of 100%; 1W = 4 consecutive scores of 100%; M = 3 consecutive scores of 100%	**Natural Environment (NE) Criterion:** Target has been generalized in NE across 3 novel naturally occurring activities	**Archive Criteria:** Target, maintenance and NE criteria have been met

Target list

Suggestions for targets and probe results

Suggestions for Targets: Use words representing the individual's interest to increase motivation, then move on to targets that resemble their interests. For example, if the individual is interested in trains, begin with words of trains then move on to cars, planes and other transportation. As reading improves, choose targets that may be more functional (this involves safety words, daily living skills, leisure items, etc.).

Probe Results (targets in repertoire):

Target	Baseline %	Date Introduced	Date Criteria Met	*Fading Procedure*		
				Maintenance	Date NE Introduced	Date Archived
1. Target 1 (isolation):						
2. Target 1 (FO2/target and distractor):						
3. Target 1 (FO3/target and 2 distractors):						

4. Target 2 (isolation):						
5. Target 2 (FO2/target and distractor):						
6. Target 2 (FO3/target and 2 distractors):						
7. Targets that met criteria: random rotation						
8. Target 3 (isolation):						
9. Target 3 (FO2/target and distractor):						
10. Target 3 (FO3/target and 2 distractors):						
11. Target 4 (isolation):						
12. Target 4 (FO2/target and distractor):						
13. Target 4 (FO3/target and 2 distractors):						
14. Targets that met criteria: random rotation						
15. Target 5 (isolation):						
16. Target 5 (FO2/target and distractor):						
17. Target 5 (FO3/target and 2 distractors):						
18. Target 6 (isolation):						
19. Target 6 (FO2/target and distractor):						

20. Target 6 (FO3/target and 2 distractors):						
21. Targets that met criteria: random rotation						
22. Target 7 (isolation):						
23. Target 7 (FO2/target and distractor):						
24. Target 7 (FO3/target and 2 distractors):						
25. Target 8 (isolation):						
26. Target 8 (FO2/target and distractor):						
27. Target 8 (FO3/target and 2 distractors):						
28. Targets that met criteria: random rotation						
29. Target 9 (isolation):						
30. Target 9 (FO2/target and distractor):						
31. Target 9 (FO3/target and 2 distractors):						
32. Target 10 (isolation):						
33. Target 10 (FO2/target and distractor):						
34. Target 10 (FO3/target and 2 distractors):						
35. Targets that met criteria: random rotation						

36. Generalize to another environment Environment 1:						
37. Generalize to another environment Environment 2:						
38. Maintenance: Assess in varied environments				2W 1W M		

Specific tips for running this task analysis

- Ensure pre-requisite skills have been taught for this TA. Pre-requisite skills for "Reading: Matching Words to Pictures" include mastery of receptive/expressive labels of letters (TAs found in the first book of the Journey of Development ABA Curriculum series), and "Receptive Labels of Beginning Sounds of Letters" and "Reading: Matching Letter Sounds to Pictures" (TAs found in this curriculum book).

RHYMING

LEVEL: □ 1 □ 2 □ 3

S^D: Say "What rhymes with [x]?"	**Response:** Individual will respond with a word that rhymes with the word presented
Data Collection: Skill acquisition	**Target Criteria:** 80% or above for 3 consecutive days across 2 people
Materials: Reinforcement	

Fading procedure

Maintenance Criteria: 2W = 4 consecutive scores of 100%; 1W = 4 consecutive scores of 100%; M = 3 consecutive scores of 100%	**Natural Environment (NE) Criterion:** Target has been generalized in NE across 3 novel naturally occurring activities	**Archive Criteria:** Target, maintenance and NE criteria have been met

Target list

Suggestions for targets and probe results

Suggestions for Targets: Cat/hat, dog/log, sky/bye, car/far, toy/boy, book/look, boat/coat, pen/hen, cake/lake and bike/like.

Probe Results (targets in repertoire):

Target	Baseline %	Date Introduced	Date Criteria Met	*Fading Procedure*		
				Maintenance	Date NE Introduced	Date Archived
1. Target 1:						
2. Target 2:						
3. Targets 1 and 2 random rotation						
4. Target 3:						
5. Target 4:						

6. Targets that met criteria: random rotation						
7. Target 5:						
8. Target 6:						
9. Targets that met criteria: random rotation						
10. Target 7:						
11. Target 8:						
12. Targets that met criteria: random rotation						
13. Target 9:						
14. Target 10:						
15. Targets that met criteria: random rotation						
16. Generalize to another environment Environment 1:						
17. Generalize to another environment Environment 2:						
18. Maintenance: Assess in varied environments				2W 1W M		

Specific tips for running this task analysis

- Ensure pre-requisite skills have been taught for this TA. Examples of pre-requisite skills for "Rhyming" include mastery of receptive language programs and progress toward expressive language programs (TAs found in the first book of the Journey of Development ABA Curriculum series).
- If the individual requires the use of picture icons as a visual prompt, the instructor can present the same S^D "What rhymes with [x]?" while presenting a field of 3 picture icons (one icon being the correct response). The individual then chooses from that field of picture icons for the correct response. Then work to fade this teaching strategy.
- Allow the opportunity for the individual to express multiple words that rhyme with the word presented to ensure more than rote memorization.

TASK DURATION

LEVEL: □ 1 □ 2 □ 3

S^D: Present individual with instructions on work to complete (i.e. verbal instructions, visual schedule, work system, etc.)	**Response:** Individual will work for up to 30 minutes
Data Collection: Prompt data (number and type of prompts used)	**Target criteria:** 0 prompts for 3 consecutive days across 2 people
Materials: Worksheets, file folders, close-ended table activities (i.e. sorting objects, pattern blocks, etc.) and reinforcement	

Fading procedure

Maintenance Criteria: 2W = 4 consecutive scores of 0 prompts; 1W = 4 consecutive scores of 0 prompts; M = 3 consecutive scores of 0 prompts	**Natural Environment (NE) Criterion:** Target has been generalized in NE across 3 novel naturally occurring activities	**Archive Criteria:** Target, maintenance and NE criteria have been met

Target list

Suggestions for targets and probe results

Suggestions for Targets: 1–30 minutes.
Probe Results (targets in repertoire):

Target	Baseline: Numbe and Type of Prompts	Date Introduced	Date Criteria Met	*Fading Procedure*		
				Maintenance	Date NE Introduced	Date Archived
1. Target 1:						
2. Target 2:						
3. Targets 1 and 2 random rotation						
4. Target 3:						
5. Target 4:						

6. Targets that met criteria: random rotation						
7. Target 5:						
8. Target 6:						
9. Targets that met criteria: random rotation						
10. Target 7:						
11. Target 8:						
12. Targets that met criteria: random rotation						
13. Target 9:						
14. Target 10:						
15. Targets that met criteria: random rotation						
16. Generalize to another environment Environment 1:						
17. Generalize to another environment Environment 2:						
18. Maintenance: Assess in varied environments				2W 1W M		

Specific tips for running this task analysis

- Ensure pre-requisite skills have been taught for this TA. Examples of pre-requisite skills for "Task Duration" include mastering the attending skills programs (TAs in the first book of the Journey of Development ABA Curriculum series), ability to follow a visual schedule, and ability to follow "Receptive Instructions (Two-Step)" (TA found in this curriculum book).
- When the individual stops working for longer than a 10-second interval, the instructor should prompt the individual back to task.
- The individual targets can be increased by any increment (i.e. begin at 1 minute of work then increase each time by 2 minutes etc.) The targets and increments of increasing targets should be determined by the team, based on individual's age and baseline task duration.

Chapter 15

PLAY/SOCIAL SKILLS

- Duck Duck Goose
- Independent Play via a Play Schedule
- Participation in Complex Songs and Games with Actions
- Playground: Ladder
- Playground: Merry Go Round
- Playground: Monkey Bars
- Playground: Sliding Board
- Playground: Swing
- Playground: Teeter Totter
- Playground: Tunnel
- Pretend Play: Birthday Party
- Pretend Play: Detective
- Pretend Play: Doctor
- Pretend Play: Kitchen
- Pretend Play: Mommy and Daddy
- Pretend Play: School
- Pretend Play (No Props)
- Pretend Play: Same Role—Dancers
- Pretend Play: Same Role—Pirates
- Pretend Play: Same Role—Princesses
- Pretend Play: Same Role—Race Car Driver
- Pretend Play: Same Role—Train Engineers
- Swimming: Level 1
- Symbolic Play
- Turn-Taking

DUCK DUCK GOOSE

LEVEL: □ 1 □ 2 □ 3

S^D: A. (Individual is ducker). "Play duck duck goose" B. (Individual is goose). "Play duck duck goose"	**Response:** A. Individual will walk around the circle touching tops of peers' heads while saying "duck, duck, duck." Individual will choose a peer to be the "goose" and run in a circle taking the "goose" spot in the circle B. Individual will chase the "ducker" around the circle until the ducker sits down or they catch the ducker
Data Collection: Prompt data (number and type of prompts used)	**Target criteria:** 0 prompts for 3 consecutive days across 2 people
Materials: Peers and reinforcement	

Fading procedure

Maintenance Criteria: 2W = 4 consecutive scores of 0 prompts; 1W = 4 consecutive scores of 0 prompts; M = 3 consecutive scores of 0 prompts	**Natural Environment (NE) Criterion:** Target has been generalized in NE across 3 novel naturally occurring activities	**Archive Criteria:** Target, maintenance and NE criteria have been met

Target list

Target	Baseline: Number and Type of Prompts	Date Introduced	Date Criteria Met	*Fading Procedure*		
				Maintenance	Date NE Introduced	Date Archived
Total Task Analysis—Ducker						
1. S^D A: Target 1: Individual will walk around the circle.						
2. S^D A: Target 2: Individual will gently touch each peer on the head stating either duck or goose.						
3. S^D A: Target 3: Individual will choose a peer to be the goose.						

4. S^D A: Target 4: Individual will run around the circle (running away from the "goose")						
5. S^D A: Target 5: Individual will sit down in the "goose" spot.						
6. Generalize to another environment Environment 1:						
7. Generalize to another environment Environment 2:						
8. Maintenance: Assess in varied environments				2W 1W M		
Total Task Analysis—Goose						
9. S^D B: Target 1: Individual will sit in the circle.						
10. S^D B: Target 2: When picked by the ducker, the individual (goose) will stand up.						
11. S^D B: Target 3: Individual will chase the ducker around the circle trying to tag them.						
12. Generalize to another environment Environment 1:						
13. Generalize to another environment Environment 2:						
14. Maintenance: Assess in varied environments				2W 1W M		

Specific tips for running this task analysis

- Ensure pre-requisite skills have been taught for this TA. Examples of pre-requisite skills for "Duck Duck Goose" include mastering "Gross Motor Imitation" and "Receptive Instructions (One-Step)" (TAs found in the first book of the Journey of Development ABA Curriculum series) and the "Waiting" program (TA found in this curriculum book). In addition, the individual should have the ability to engage in gross motor skills required of this program such as running.

- This program is designed to teach the individual how to play childhood games using a total TA. This requires the individual to engage in all steps of the procedure every therapy session. The instructor provides assistance (prompts) with any step the individual is not able to perform. The instructor should record the number and type of prompts required for each step, until all steps of the task are completed.
- Alternative teaching materials for this program includes spot markers to sit on, so the individual is visually prompted where to sit around the circle. As with all visual prompts, this should be faded over time.

INDEPENDENT PLAY VIA A PLAY SCHEDULE

LEVEL: □ 1 □ 2 □ 3

S^D: Present individual with play schedule and say "Go play"	**Response:** Individual will independently complete three play activities that are listed on his/her play schedule
Data Collection: Prompt data (number and type of prompts used)	**Target criteria:** 0 prompts for 3 consecutive days across 2 people
Materials: Play schedule, toys in which individual can engage in appropriate play and reinforcement	

Fading procedure

Maintenance Criteria: 2W = 4 consecutive scores of 0 prompts; 1W = 4 consecutive scores of 0 prompts; M = 3 consecutive scores of 0 prompts	**Natural Environment (NE) Criterion:** Target has been generalized in NE across 3 novel naturally occurring activities	**Archive Criteria:** Target, maintenance and NE criteria have been met

Target list

Suggestions for targets and probe results

Suggestions for Targets: Choose toys the individual can play with functionally and independently.
Probe Results (targets in repertoire):

Target	Baseline: Number and Type of Prompts	Date Introduced	Date Criteria Met	*Fading Procedure*		
				Maintenance	Date NE Introduced	Date Archived
1. Target 1: Individual locates first picture/icon on the schedule.						
2. Target 2: Individual retrieves the toy and brings it to the play area.						
3. Target 3: Individual plays with toy to completion or for 3 minutes.						
4. Target 4: Individual cleans up and replaces toy to original location.						

5. Target 5: Individual returns to the play schedule.						
6. Target 6: Individual locates second picture/icon on the play schedule.						
7. Target 7: Individual retrieves the toy and brings it to the play area.						
8. Target 8: Individual plays with toy to completion or for 3 minutes.						
9. Target 9: Individual cleans up and replaces toy to original location.						
10. Target 10: Individual returns to the play schedule.						
11. Target 11: Individual locates third picture/icon on the play schedule.						
12. Target 12: Individual retrieves the toy and brings it to the play area.						
13. Target 13: Individual plays with toy to completion or for 3 minutes.						
14. Target 14: Individual cleans up and replaces toy to original location.						
15. Target 15: Individual completes play schedule, instructor 1 foot away.						
16. Target 16: Individual completes play schedule, instructor 3 feet away.						
17. Target 17: Individual completes play schedule, instructor at doorway.						
18. Target 18: Individual completes play schedule, instructor out of room.						
19. Generalize to another environment Environment 1:						
20. Generalize to another environment Environment 2:						
21. Maintenance: Assess in varied environments				2W 1W M		

Specific tips for running this task analysis

- Ensure pre-requisite skills have been taught for this TA. Examples of pre-requisite skills for "Independent Play via a Play Schedule" include mastering the matching programs and solitary toy play open ended and closed ended programs (TAs found in the first book of the Journey of Development ABA Curriculum series).
- When creating a play schedule, color code the schedule with three different colors (e.g. green, blue, yellow). When the individual is creating their play schedule they choose one picture from the blue section, one picture/icon from the green section, etc. until the play schedule is complete.
- When presenting the S^D, you can also pair a timer so that the individual understands how long they have to play.
- The last toy on the play schedule should be the most reinforcing toy. The last toy can also be an open-ended toy that the individual knows how to play with for a longer duration.
- This program is designed to teach individuals how to play independently with a visual schedule. This TA uses a forward chaining procedure whereby the TA is taught in order that the steps naturally occur until all steps are completed independently. Thus, for Target 1, the individual displays the target behavior then is prompted through the remaining steps. For Target 2, all steps are prompted except for the previous Target 1. For Target 3, all steps are prompted except for the previous Targets 1 and 2. Continue to follow this procedure until the individual has achieved independent mastery of entire chain.
- The next natural step in this TA is to eventually fade the need of the play schedule. S^D "Go play" and the individual will be able to go play independently without a play schedule for duration of [x] minutes, extending to longer duration.

PARTICIPATION IN COMPLEX SONGS AND GAMES WITH ACTIONS

LEVEL: □ 1 □ 2 □ 3

S^D: Sing a song or play a game with the individual and prompt them through the actions that accompany the song/game (i.e. hand and body movements with Follow the Leader game)	**Response:** Individual will participate in the song or game by demonstrating the accompanying actions (i.e. hand and body movements) and singing or playing along with the instructor
Data Collection: Prompt data (number and type of prompts used)	**Target Criteria:** 0 prompts for 3 consecutive days across 2 people
Materials: Reinforcement	

Fading procedure

Maintenance Criteria: 2W = 4 consecutive scores of 0 prompts; 1W = 4 consecutive scores of 0 prompts; M = 3 consecutive scores of 0 prompts	**Natural Environment (NE) Criterion:** Target has been generalized in NE across 3 novel naturally occurring activities	**Archive Criteria:** Target, maintenance and NE criteria have been met

Target list

Suggestions for targets and probe results

Suggestions for Targets: Follow the leader; leap frog; musical chairs; Duck Duck Goose; Hokie Pokie; Simon Says; Hot Potato; Charades, Farmer and the Dell, and hopscotch.
Probe Results (targets in repertoire):

Target	Baseline: Number and Type of Prompts	Date Introduced	Date Criteria Met	*Fading Procedure*		
				Maintenance	Date NE Introduced	Date Archived
1. Target 1:						
2. Target 2:						
3. Targets that met criteria: random rotation						

4. Target 3:						
5. Target 4:						
6. Targets that met criteria: random rotation						
7. Target 5:						
8. Target 6:						
9. Targets that met criteria: random rotation						
10. Target 7:						
11. Target 8:						
12. Targets that met criteria: random rotation						
13. Target 9:						
14. Target 10:						
15. Targets that met criteria: random rotation						
16. Generalize to another environment Environment 1:						
17. Generalize to another environment Environment 2:						
18. Maintenance: Assess in varied environments				2W 1W M		

Specific tips for running this task analysis

- Ensure pre-requisite skills have been taught for this TA. Examples of pre-requisite skills for "Participation in Complex Songs and Games with Actions" include mastering the easier songs and games and joint attention (TAs found in the first book of the Journey of Development ABA Curriculum series).
- Remember to fade the prompts over teaching trials. Differentially reinforce responses independently demonstrated or those responses requiring lower levels of prompting.
- The complex games/songs listed in this program would be best taught with another person and the ABA instructor prompting the individual through the motions or actions associated with the game or song. The games can initially be taught with a parent and then should be generalized to playing the game with a peer followed by a group of peers.
- If the individual struggles with learning a particular game or song, this target may need to be taught separately via its own TA breaking down each individual step associated with the game or song.

PLAYGROUND: LADDER

LEVEL: □ 1 □ 2 □ 3

S^D: Say "Play on the ladder"	**Response:** Individual will play on the ladder appropriately and safely
Data Collection: Prompt data (number and type of prompts used)	**Target criteria:** 0 prompts for 3 consecutive days across 2 people
Materials: Ladder and reinforcement	

Fading procedure

Maintenance Criteria: 2W = 4 consecutive scores of 0 prompts; 1W = 4 consecutive scores of 0 prompts; M = 3 consecutive scores of 0 prompts	**Natural Environment (NE) Criterion:** Target has been generalized in NE across 3 novel naturally occurring activities	**Archive Criteria:** Target, maintenance and NE criteria have been met

Target list

Suggestions for targets and probe results

Suggestions for Targets: Different types of ladders: Arching ladders, vertical ladders up to a higher platform, rope ladders, and vertical ladders (going up one side and down the other).
Probe Results (targets in repertoire):

Target	Baseline: Number and Type of Prompts	Date Introduced	Date Criteria Met	*Fading Procedure*		
				Maintenance	Date NE Introduced	Date Archived
Total Task Analysis						
1. Target 1: Individual will wait until all people are off the ladder.						
2. Target 2: Individual will hold on to side railings.						

3. Target 3: Individual will climb to the first step of the ladder, while holding on with both hands (side or higher rung).						
4. Target 4: Individual will climb to the second step of the ladder, while holding on with both hands (side or higher rung).						
5. Target 5: Individual will climb to the fifth step of the ladder, while holding on with both hands (side or higher rung).						
6. Target 6: Individual will climb to the eighth step of the ladder, while holding on with both hands (side or higher rung).						
7. Target 7: Individual will climb down ladder						
8. Generalize to another environment Environment 1:						
9. Generalize to another environment Environment 2:						
10. Maintenance: Assess in varied environments				2W 1W M		

Specific tips for running this task analysis

- Ensure pre-requisite skills have been taught for this TA. Examples of pre-requisite skills for "Playground: Ladder" include mastering "Receptive Instructions (One-Step)" (TA found in the first book of the Journey of Development ABA Curriculum series) and "Waiting" (from this book). In addition, the individual should have the ability to engage in the gross motor skills required in this task, such as climbing the steps, holding on to rungs, etc.
- This program is designed to teach the individual how to use playground equipment safely and appropriately using a total TA. This requires the individual to engage in all steps of the procedure every treatment session with the instructor providing assistance (prompts) with any step the individual is not able to perform. Instructor should record the number and type of prompts required for each step until all steps of the task are completed.
- Ladders that are straight up and down are the easiest for the individual to master; rope ladders are next; arching ladders or ladders that require an individual to turn around midway through the course or over the top are typically most difficult.
- It is best for an individual to practice this skill initially by themselves (with the instructor) then gradually add in peers.

PLAYGROUND: MERRY GO ROUND

LEVEL: □ 1 □ 2 □ 3

S^D: Say "Play on the merry go round"	**Response:** Individual will play on the merry go round appropriately and safely
Data Collection: Prompt data (number and type of prompts used)	**Target criteria:** 0 prompts for 3 consecutive days across 2 people
Materials: Merry go round and reinforcement	

Fading procedure

Maintenance Criteria: 2W = 4 consecutive scores of 0 prompts; 1W = 4 consecutive scores of 0 prompts; M = 3 consecutive scores of 0 prompts	**Natural Environment (NE) Criterion:** Target has been generalized in NE across 3 novel naturally occurring activities	**Archive Criteria:** Target, maintenance and NE criteria have been met

Target list

Target	Baseline: Number and Type of Prompts	Date Introduced	Date Criteria Met	*Fading Procedure*		
				Maintenance	Date NE Introduced	Date Archived
Riding the Merry Go Round						
1. Target 1: Individual will get on the merry go round while it is not moving.						
2. Target 2: Individual will hold on to the handlebars while merry go round is moving, with instructor standing next to them, for 30 seconds. Individual will exit the merry go round once it has stopped spinning.						
3. Target 3: Individual will hold on to the handlebars while merry go round is moving with instructor standing next to them, for 1 minute. Individual will exit the merry go round once it has stopped spinning.						

4. Target 4: Individual will hold on to the handlebars while merry go round is moving with instructor standing within 2 feet, for 30 seconds. Individual will exit the merry go round once it has stopped spinning.						
5. Target 5: Individual will hold on to the handlebars while merry go round is moving with instructor standing within 2 feet, for 1 minute. Individual will exit the merry go round once it has stopped spinning.						
6. Target 6: Individual will hold on to the handlebars while merry go round is moving with instructor off the merry go round, for 1 minute. Individual will exit the merry go round once it has stopped spinning.						
Pushing the Merry Go Round						
7. Target 7: Individual will hold on to merry go round handle and run half way around, let go and step away from the merry go round.						
8. Target 8: Individual will hold on to merry go round handle and run all the way around, let go and step away from the merry go round.						
9. Generalize to another environment Environment 1:						
10. Generalize to another environment Environment 2:						
11. Maintenance: Assess in varied environments				2W 1W M		

Specific tips for running this task analysis

- Ensure pre-requisite skills have been taught for this TA. Examples of pre-requisite skills for "Playground: Merry Go Round" include mastering "Receptive Instructions (One-Step)" (TA found in the first book of the Journey of Development ABA Curriculum series) and "Waiting" (TA found in this book). In addition, the individual should have the ability to engage in the gross motor skills required of this task, such as holding on to the railing and running along next to the merry go round.
- This TA gradually fades the instructor support, ensuring that the individual holds on for the duration of the ride and remains still. Gradually the time interval is increased and the instructor support is faded out.
- At this time it is also good to practice appropriate requesting to get off the ride (i.e. "Stop," "I want to get off," etc.).
- It is best for the individual to practice this skill initially by themselves (with the instructor) then gradually add in peers.

PLAYGROUND: MONKEY BARS

LEVEL: □ 1 □ 2 □ 3

S^D: Say "Play on the monkey bars"	**Response:** Individual will play on the monkey bars appropriately and safely
Data Collection: Prompt data (number and type of prompts used)	**Target criteria:** 0 prompts for 3 consecutive days across 2 people
Materials: Monkey bars and reinforcement	

Fading procedure

Maintenance Criteria: 2W = 4 consecutive scores of 0 prompts; 1W = 4 consecutive scores of 0 prompts; M = 3 consecutive scores of 0 prompts	**Natural Environment (NE) Criterion:** Target has been generalized in NE across 3 novel naturally occurring activities	**Archive Criteria:** Target, maintenance and NE criteria have been met

Target list

Target	Baseline: Number and Type of Prompts	Date Introduced	Date Criteria Met	*Fading Procedure*		
				Maintenance	Date NE Introduced	Date Archived
Total Task Analysis						
1. Target 1: Hold on to railings and climb to the top rung.						
2. Target 2: Individual will grab the first rung with their dominant hand.						
3. Target 3: Individual will grab the first rung with nondominant hand.						
4. Target 4: Individual will grab the second rung with their dominant hand.						
5. Target 5: Individual will grab the second rung with nondominant hand.						
6. Target 6: Individual will grab the third rung with their dominant hand.						

7. Target 7: Individual will grab the third rung with nondominant hand.						
8. Target 8: Individual will grab the fourth rung with their dominant hand.						
9. Target 9: Individual will grab the fourth rung with nondominant hand.						
10. Target 10: Individual will grab the fifth rung with their dominant hand.						
11. Target 11: Individual will grab the fifth rung with nondominant hand.						
12. Target 12: Individual will grab the sixth rung with their dominant hand.						
13. Target 13: Individual will grab the sixth rung with nondominant hand.						
14. Target 14: Individual will grab the seventh rung with their dominant hand.						
15. Target 15: Individual will grab the seventh rung with nondominant hand.						
16. Target 16: Individual will grab the eighth rung with their dominant hand.						
17. Target 17: Individual will grab the eighth rung with nondominant hand.						
18. Target 18: Individual will step one foot on top rung of the ladder.						
19. Target 19: Individual will step second foot on top rung of the ladder.						
20. Target 20: Individual will grab on to the side railings and pull self to standing position						
21. Target 21: Individual will climb down ladder.						

22. Generalize to another environment Environment 1:						
23. Generalize to another environment Environment 2:						
24. Maintenance: Assess in varied environments				2W 1W M		

Specific tips for running this task analysis

- Ensure pre-requisite skills have been taught for this TA. Examples of pre-requisite skills for "Playground: Monkey Bars" include mastering "Receptive Instructions (One-Step)" (TA found in the first book of the Journey of Development ABA Curriculum series) and "Waiting" (TA found in this book). In addition, the individual should have the ability to engage in the gross motor skills required of this task, such as climbing the steps and hanging from each rung.
- This program is designed to teach the individual how to use playground equipment safely and appropriately using a total TA. This requires the individual to engage in all steps of the procedure every treatment session with the instructor providing assistance (prompts) with any step the individual is not able to perform. The instructor should record the number and type of prompts required for each step, until all steps of the task are completed.
- Typically individuals will learn to cross monkey bars as this TA is written; when they have more stamina, they will only place one hand on each rung and swing their body to the next rung. If the individual you are working with is at this level, the TA will need to be modified to meet the individual's learning rate and skill level.
- It is best for the individual to practice this skill initially by themselves (with the instructor) then gradually add in peers.

PLAYGROUND: SLIDING BOARD

LEVEL: □ 1 □ 2 □ 3

S^D: Say "Play on the slide"	**Response:** Individual will play on the slide appropriately and safely
Data Collection: Prompt data (number and type of prompts used)	**Target criteria:** 0 prompts for 3 consecutive days across 2 people
Materials: Sliding board and reinforcement	

Fading procedure

Maintenance Criteria: 2W = 4 consecutive scores of 0 prompts; 1W = 4 consecutive scores of 0 prompts; M = 3 consecutive scores of 0 prompts	**Natural Environment (NE) Criterion:** Target has been generalized in NE across 3 novel naturally occurring activities	**Archive Criteria:** Target, maintenance and NE criteria have been met

Target list

Target	Baseline: Number and Type of Prompts	Date Introduced	Date Criteria Met	*Fading Procedure*		
				Maintenance	Date NE Introduced	Date Archived
Total Task Analysis						
1. Target 1: Individual will hold on to railing and climb to the top step.						
2. Target 2: Individual will sit down at the top of the slide.						
3. Target 3: Individual will go down slide without stopping.						
4. Target 4: Once Individual reaches the bottom of the slide, they will stand up within 3 seconds.						
5. Generalize to another environment Environment 1:						

6. Generalize to another environment Environment 2:						
7. Maintenance: Assess in varied environments				2W 1W M		

Specific tips for running this task analysis

- Ensure pre-requisite skills have been taught for this TA. Examples of pre-requisite skills for "Playground: Sliding Board" include mastering "Receptive Instructions (One-Step)" (TA found in the first book of the Journey of Development ABA Curriculum series) and "Waiting" (TA found in this book). In addition, the individual should have the ability to engage in the gross motor skills required in this task, such as climbing the steps.
- This program is designed to teach the individual how to use playground equipment safely and appropriately using a total TA. This requires the individual to engage in all steps of the procedure every treatment session with the instructor providing assistance (prompts) with any step the individual is not able to perform. The instructor should record the number and type of prompts required for each step, until all steps of the task are completed.
- It is best for the individual to practice this skill initially by themselves (with the instructor) then gradually add in peers.

PLAYGROUND: SWING

LEVEL: □ 1 □ 2 □ 3

S^D: Say "Play on the swing"	**Response:** Individual will play on the swing appropriately and safely
Data Collection: Prompt data (number and type of prompts used)	**Target criteria:** 0 prompts for 3 consecutive days across 2 people
Materials: Swings and reinforcement	

Fading procedure

Maintenance Criteria: 2W = 4 consecutive scores of 0 prompts; 1W = 4 consecutive scores of 0 prompts; M = 3 consecutive scores of 0 prompts	**Natural Environment (NE) Criterion:** Target has been generalized in NE across 3 novel naturally occurring activities	**Archive Criteria:** Target, maintenance and NE criteria have been met

Target list

Suggestions for targets and probe results

Suggestions for Targets: Different types of swings: Belt swing, flat swing, tire swing, disk swing and bucket swing.
Probe Results (targets in repertoire):

Target	Baseline: Number and Type of Prompts	Date Introduced	Date Criteria Met	*Fading Procedure*		
				Maintenance	Date NE Introduced	Date Archived
Total Task Analysis						
1. Target 1: Individual will go to an empty swing, walking a safe distance from other swings in use.						
2. Target 2: Individual will hold on to both chains and lift themselves up onto the swing.						
3. Target 3: Individual will lean back and extend legs (first time).						

4. Target 4: Individual will lean forward and bend legs (second time).						
5. Target 5: Individual will lean back and extend legs (third time).						
6. Target 6: Individual will lean forward and bend legs (fourth time).						
7. Target 7: Individual will lean back and extend legs (fifth time).						
8. Target 8: Individual will lean forward and bend legs (sixth time).						
9. Target 9: Individual will lean back and extend legs (seventh time).						
10. Target 10: Individual will lean forward and bend legs (eighth time).						
11. Target 11: Individual will lean back and extend legs (ninth time).						
12. Target 12: Individual will lean forward and bend legs (tenth time).						
13. Target 13: Individual will drag feet on the ground to slow down swing (or stop pumping and wait for swing to slow down).						
14. Target 14: Individual will get down off the seat.						
15. Target 15: Individual will walk away from swing (staying a safe distance away from other swings in use).						
16. Generalize to another environment Environment 1:						
17. Generalize to another environment Environment 2:						
18. Maintenance: Assess in varied environments				2W 1W M		

Specific tips for running this task analysis

- Ensure pre-requisite skills have been taught for this TA. Examples of pre-requisite skills for "Playground: Swing" include mastering "Receptive Instructions (One-Step)" (TA found in the first book of the Journey of Development ABA Curriculum series) and "Waiting" (TA found in this book). In addition, the individual should have the ability to engage in the gross motor skills required in this task, such as holding on to the chain with both hands and pumping legs.
- This program is designed to teach the individual how to use playground equipment safely and appropriately using a total TA. This requires the individual to engage in all steps of the procedure every treatment session with the instructor providing assistance (prompts) with any step the individual is not able to perform. The instructor should record the number and type of prompts required for each step, until all steps of the task are completed.
- An adaptation to this program may start out with giving the individual beginning pushes to get the swing moving, so they get automatically reinforced by the motion of the swing. It is imperative to fade this step out once the individual is more coordinated with pumping their legs. The goal for any TA is for the individual to become independent.
- It is best for the individual to practice this skill initially by themselves (with the instructor) then gradually add in peers.

PLAYGROUND: TEETER TOTTER

LEVEL: □ 1 □ 2 □ 3

S^D: Say "Play on the teeter totter"	**Response:** Individual will play on the teeter totter appropriately and safely
Data Collection: Prompt data (number and type of prompts used)	**Target criteria:** 0 prompts for 3 consecutive days across 2 people
Materials: Teeter totter and reinforcement	

Fading procedure

Maintenance Criteria: 2W = 4 consecutive scores of 0 prompts; 1W = 4 consecutive scores of 0 prompts; M = 3 consecutive scores of 0 prompts	**Natural Environment (NE) Criterion:** Target has been generalized in NE across 3 novel naturally occurring activities	**Archive Criteria:** Target, maintenance and NE criteria have been met

Target list

Target	Baseline: Number and Type of Prompts	Date Introduced	Date Criteria Met	*Fading Procedure*		
				Maintenance	**Date NE Introduced**	**Date Archived**
Total Task Analysis						
1. Target 1: Individual will find a friend to go on teeter totter with.						
2. Target 2: Individual will raise teeter totter to hip level.						
3. Target 3: Individual will lift leg over teeter totter and sit down.						
4. Target 4: Individual will push off the ground so their end rises (first time).						
5. Target 5: Individual will put feet on the ground and bend legs						
6. Target 6: Individual will push off the ground so their end rises (second time).						

7. Target 7: Individual will put feet on the ground and bend legs.						
8. Target 8: Individual will push off the ground so their end rises (third time).						
9. Target 9: Individual will put feet on the ground and bend legs.						
10. Target 10: Individual will push off the ground so their end rises (fourth time).						
11. Target 11: Individual will put feet on the ground and bend legs.						
12. Target 12: Individual will push off the ground so their end rises (fifth time).						
13. Target 13: Individual will put feet on the ground and bend legs.						
14. Target 14: Individual/peer will state they want to get off.						
15. Target 15: individual will stand up while still on the teeter totter.						
16. Target 16: Individual will slide off teeter totter at same time as peer.						
17. Generalize to another environment Environment 1:						
18. Generalize to another environment Environment 2:						
19. Maintenance: Assess in varied environments				2W 1W M		

Specific tips for running this task analysis

- Ensure pre-requisite skills have been taught for this TA. Examples of pre-requisite skills for "Playground: Teeter Totter" include mastering "Receptive Instructions (One-Step)" (TA found in the first book of the Journey of Development ABA Curriculum series) and "Waiting" (TA found in this book). In addition, the individual should have the ability to engage in the gross motor skills required in this task, such holding on to the handle with both hands and pushing off the ground.

- This program is designed to teach the individual how to use playground equipment safely and appropriately using a total TA. This requires the individual to engage in all steps of the procedure every treatment session with the instructor providing assistance (prompts) with any step the individual is not able to perform. The instructor should record the number and type of prompts required for each step, until all steps of the task are completed.
- It may be helpful to have a peer that is a similar weight to ensure that one individual does not weigh down the other. If this happens, the individual will have to be prompted to scoot backward or forward on the teeter totter.

PLAYGROUND: TUNNEL

LEVEL: □ 1 □ 2 □ 3

S^D: Say "Play in the tunnel"	**Response:** Individual will play in the tunnel appropriately and safely
Data Collection: Prompt data (number and type of prompts used)	**Target criteria:** 0 prompts for 3 consecutive days across 2 people
Materials: Tunnels and reinforcement	

Fading procedure

Maintenance Criteria: 2W = 4 consecutive scores of 0 prompts; 1W = 4 consecutive scores of 0 prompts; M = 3 consecutive scores of 0 prompts	**Natural Environment (NE) Criterion:** Target has been generalized in NE across 3 novel naturally occurring activities	**Archive Criteria:** Target, maintenance and NE criteria have been met

Target list

Suggestions for targets and probe results

Suggestions for Targets: Different types of tunnels: Straight tunnels, curvy tunnels and rope tunnels.
Probe Results (targets in repertoire):

Target	Baseline: Number and Type of Prompts	Date Introduced	Date Criteria Met	*Fading Procedure*		
				Maintenance	Date NE Introduced	Date Archived
Total Task Analysis						
1. Target 1: Individual will wait until all people are away from the tunnel opening (either half way through tunnel or out of the tunnel).						
2. Target 2: Individual will duck their head and crouch down (if needed).						
3. Target 3: Individual will climb into the tunnel.						

4. Target 4: Individual will walk/crawl to the center of the tunnel.						
5. Target 5: Individual will walk/crawl the remaining distance to the end of the tunnel.						
6. Target 6: Individual will exit the tunnel						
7. Target 7: Individual will stand up once out of the tunnel.						
8. Generalize to another environment Environment 1:						
9. Generalize to another environment Environment 2:						
10. Maintenance: Assess in varied environments				2W 1W M		

Specific tips for running this task analysis

- Ensure pre-requisite skills have been taught for this TA. Examples of pre-requisite skills for "Playground: Tunnel" include mastering "Receptive Instructions (One-Step)" (TA found in the first book of the Journey of Development ABA Curriculum series) and "Waiting" (TA found in this book). In addition, the individual should have the ability to engage in the gross motor skills required in this task, such as crouching down and walking.
- This program is designed to teach the individual how to use playground equipment safely and appropriately using a total TA. This requires the individual to engage in all steps of the procedure every treatment session with the instructor providing assistance (prompts) with any step the individual is not able to perform. The instructor should record the number and type of prompts required for each step, until all steps of the task are completed.
- It is best for the individual to practice this skill initially by themselves (with the instructor) then gradually add in peers.

PRETEND PLAY: BIRTHDAY PARTY

LEVEL: □ 1 □ 2 □ 3

S^D: A. Model an action associated with a birthday party and say "Pretend [action/object]" (e.g. "Pretend to blow out the candles" or "Pretend to open a present") B. "Play pretend birthday party" C. "Play pretend birthday party"	**Response:** A. Individual will imitate the pretend action B. Individual will chain together three pretend actions C. Individual will chain together three plus pretend actions for a longer duration
Data Collection: S^D A: Skill acquisition; S^D B and C: Prompt data (number and type of prompts used)	**Target Criteria:** S^D A: 80% or above for 3 consecutive days across 2 people, S^D B and C: 0 prompts for 3 consecutive days across 2 people
Materials: 2 sets of pretend birthday items: wrapping paper, gifts, party hats, pretend cake, candles, plates/bowls, utensils, decorations and reinforcement	

Fading procedure

Maintenance Criteria: 2W = 4 consecutive scores of 100% or 0 prompts; 1W = 4 consecutive scores of 100% or 0 prompts; M = 3 consecutive scores of 100% or 0 prompts	**Natural Environment (NE) Criterion:** Target has been generalized in NE across 3 novel naturally occurring activities	**Archive Criteria:** Target, maintenance and NE criteria have been met

Target list

Suggestions for targets and probe results

Suggestions for Targets: Wrap a present, open a present, eat the cake, blow out the candles, wear a party hat, sing "Happy Birthday," cut the cake, make a cake, scoop ice-cream, and decorate (sign, balloon, etc.).
Probe Results (targets in repertoire):

Target	Baseline % or Number and Type of Prompts	Date Introduced	Date Criteria Met	*Fading Procedure* Maintenance	Date NE Introduced	Date Archived
1. S^D A: Target 1:						
2. S^D A: Target 2:						

3. S^D A: Target 3:						
4. S^D A: Target 4:						
5. S^D A: Target 5:						
6. S^D A: Target 6:						
7. S^D A: Target 7:						
8. S^D A: Target 8:						
9. S^D A: Target 9:						
10. S^D A: Target 10:						
11. S^D B: Individual chains 3 pretend actions.						
12. S^D B: Individual chains 3 different pretend actions.						
13. S^D C: Target 1: Duration = 2 minutes						
14. S^D C: Target 1: Duration = 3 minutes						
15. S^D C: Target 1: Duration = 5 minutes						
16. Generalize S^D C of 5 minutes to another environment Environment 1:						
17. Generalize S^D C of 5 minutes to another environment Environment 2:						
18. Maintenance: Assess in varied environments				2W 1W M		

Specific tips for running this task analysis

- Ensure pre-requisite skills have been taught for this TA. Examples of pre-requisite skills for "Pretend Play: Birthday Party" include mastering basic pretend play, "Functional Use of Objects," "Parallel Play," "Receptive Instructions (One-Step)" and fine motor and gross motor imitation programs (TAs found in the first book of the Journey of Development ABA Curriculum series).
- If the individual has difficulty learning this TA, then you may want to start this program out with the S^D "Do this" as written in the imitation programs in the first book of the Journey of Development ABA curriculum series. Once the individual has grasped the imitation of pretend play with S^D "Do this" then move on to S^D "Pretend [action/object]" as written in this TA.
- This curriculum book offers several pretend play TAs; when beginning to teach this to a individual, choose the pretend play scenario that is likely to be the most motivating and interesting to the individual. In addition, if the individual has pretend play props for another pretend play scenario that is not offered in this book (e.g. grocery store), then modify the TA to include the scenario in which there are already props.
- This TA is written so the individual has to "chain" three pretend actions together. In ABA literature, chaining is a method whereby you chain together related behaviors where one behavior acts as a cue for the next behavior. In this example, getting out the pretend cake supplies may act as a cue to bake the cake followed by eating the cake. The instructor should teach the individual by prompting them to use different related actions to form different chains; this will help expand the individual's pretend play repertoire.

PRETEND PLAY: DETECTIVE

LEVEL: □ 1 □ 2 □ 3

S^D:	Response:
A. Model an action associated with playing detective and say "Pretend [action/object]" (e.g. "Pretend to look for a clue" or "Pretend to take finger prints") B. "Play pretend detective" C. "Play pretend detective"	A. Individual will imitate the pretend action B. Individual will chain together three pretend actions C. Individual will chain together three plus pretend actions for a longer duration
Data Collection: S^D A: Skill acquisition; S^D B and C: Prompt data (number and type of prompts used)	**Target Criteria:** S^D A: 80% or above for 3 consecutive days across 2 people, S^D B and C: 0 prompts for 3 consecutive days across 2 people
Materials: 2 sets of pretend detective items: binoculars, badges, handcuffs, finger print material, magnifying glasses, etc. and reinforcement	

Fading procedure

Maintenance Criteria: 2W = 4 consecutive scores of 100% or 0 prompts; 1W = 4 consecutive scores of 100% or 0 prompts; M = 3 consecutive scores of 100% or 0 prompts	**Natural Environment (NE) Criterion:** Target has been generalized in NE across 3 novel naturally occurring activities	**Archive Criteria:** Target, maintenance and NE criteria have been met

Target list

Suggestions for targets and probe results

Suggestions for Targets: Take finger prints, hunt for clues, use magnifying glass, wear a badge, interview a witness, crack mysterious code, use binoculars to spy, collect evidence, arrest bad guy, and take a mug shot.
Probe Results (targets in repertoire):

Target	Baseline % or Number and Type of Prompts	Date Introduced	Date Criteria Met	*Fading Procedure*		
				Maintenance	Date NE Introduced	Date Archived
1. S^D A: Target 1:						

2. S^D A: Target 2:						
3. S^D A: Target 3:						
4. S^D A: Target 4:						
5. S^D A: Target 5:						
6. S^D A: Target 6:						
7. S^D A: Target 7:						
8. S^D A: Target 8:						
9. S^D A: Target 9:						
10. S^D A: Target 10:						
11. S^D B: Individual chains 3 pretend actions.						
12. S^D B: Individual chains 3 different pretend actions.						
13. S^D C: Target 1: Duration = 2 minutes						
14. S^D C: Target 1: Duration = 3 minutes						
15. S^D C: Target 1: Duration = 5 minutes						
16. Generalize S^D C of 5 minutes to another environment Environment 1:						

17. Generalize S^D C of 5 minutes to another environment Environment 2:						
18. Maintenance: Assess in varied environments				2W 1W M		

Specific tips for running this task analysis

- Ensure pre-requisite skills have been taught for this TA. Examples of pre-requisite skills for pretend play with chained actions include mastering basic pretend play, "Functional Use of Objects," "Parallel Play," "Receptive Instructions (One-Step)" and fine motor and gross motor imitation programs (TAs found in the first book of the Journey of Development ABA Curriculum series).
- If the individual has difficulty learning this TA, then you may want to start this program out with the S^D "Do this" as written in the imitation programs in the first book of the Journey of Development ABA Curriculum series. Once the individual has grasped the imitation of pretend play with S^D "Do this" then move on to S^D "Pretend (action/object)" as written in this TA.
- This curriculum book offers several pretend play TAs; when beginning to teach this to a individual, choose the pretend play scenario that is likely to be the most motivating and interesting to the individual. In addition, if the individual has pretend play props for another pretend play scenario that is not offered in this book (e.g. grocery store), then modify the TA to include the scenario in which there are already props.
- This TA is written so the individual has to "chain" three pretend actions together. In ABA literature, chaining is a method whereby you chain together related behaviors where one behavior acts as a cue for the next behavior. In this example, using a magnifying glass may act as a cue to look for clues followed by cracking the code. The instructor should teach the individual by prompting them to use different related actions to form different chains; this will help expand the individual's pretend play repertoire.

PRETEND PLAY: DOCTOR

LEVEL: □ 1 □ 2 □ 3

S^D: A. Model an action associated with playing doctor and say "Pretend [action/object]" (e.g. "Pretend to put on a bandage" or "Pretend to give a shot") B. "Play pretend doctor" C. "Play pretend doctor"	**Response:** A. Individual will imitate the pretend action B. Individual will chain together three pretend actions C. Individual will chain together three plus pretend actions for a longer duration
Data Collection: S^D A: Skill acquisition, S^D B &C: Prompt data (number and type of prompts used)	**Target Criteria:** S^D A: 80% or above for 3 consecutive days across 2 people, S^D B and C: 0 prompts for 3 consecutive days across 2 people
Materials: 2 sets of pretend doctor items: bandages, needles, stethoscopes, patients (e.g. stuffed animal), otoscopes, blood pressure cuffs, thermometers, etc. and reinforcement	

Fading procedure

Maintenance Criteria: 2W = 4 consecutive scores of 100% or 0 prompts; 1W = 4 consecutive scores of 100% or 0 prompts; M = 3 consecutive scores of 100% or 0 prompts	**Natural Environment (NE) Criterion:** Target has been generalized in NE across 3 novel naturally occurring activities	**Archive Criteria:** Target, maintenance and NE criteria have been met

Target list

Suggestions for targets and probe results

Suggestions for Targets: Give a shot, put on a bandage, check blood pressure, check ears, listen to heart, take temperature, look in mouth, take height and weight, pretend to look at eyes with lighted pen, give stitches, and take x-rays.

Probe Results (targets in repertoire):

Target	Baseline % or Number and Type of Prompts	Date Introduced	Date Criteria Met	*Fading Procedure*		
				Maintenance	Date NE Introduced	Date Archived
1. S^D A: Target 1:						

2. S^D A: Target 2:						
3. S^D A: Target 3:						
4. S^D A: Target 4:						
5. S^D A: Target 5:						
6. S^D A: Target 6:						
7. S^D A: Target 7:						
8. S^D A: Target 8:						
9. S^D A: Target 9:						
10. S^D A: Target 10:						
11. S^D B: Individual chains 3 pretend actions.						
12. S^D B: Individual chains 3 different pretend actions.						
13. S^D C: Target 1: Duration = 2 minutes						
14. S^D C: Target 1: Duration = 3 minutes						
15. S^D C: Target 1: Duration = 5 minutes						
16. Generalize S^D C of 5 minutes to another environment Environment 1:						

17. Generalize S^D C of 5 minutes to another environment Environment 2:						
18. Maintenance: Assess in varied environments				2W 1W M		

Specific tips for running this task analysis

- Ensure pre-requisite skills have been taught for this TA. Examples of pre-requisite skills for pretend play with chained actions includes mastering basic pretend play, "Functional Use of Objects," "Parallel Play," "Receptive Instructions (One-Step)" and fine motor and gross motor imitation programs (TAs found in the first book of the Journey of Development ABA Curriculum series).
- If the individual has difficulty learning this TA, then you may want to start this program out with the S^D "Do this" as written in the imitation programs in the first book of the Journey of Development ABA curriculum series. Once the individual has grasped the imitation of pretend play with S^D "Do this" then move on to S^D "Pretend (action/object)" as written in this TA.
- This curriculum book offers several pretend play TAs; when beginning to teach this to a individual, choose the pretend play scenario that is likely to be the most motivating and interesting to the individual. In addition, if the individual has pretend play props for another pretend play scenario that is not offered in this book (e.g. grocery store), then modify the TA to include the scenario in which there are already props.
- This TA is written so the individual has to "chain" three pretend actions together. In ABA literature, chaining is a method whereby you chain together related behaviors where one behavior acts as a cue for the next behavior. In this example, sitting in front of a patient may act as a cue to take care of them (i.e. put on a bandage or give stitches) followed by giving patient a lolly pop. The instructor should teach the individual by prompting them to use different related actions to form different chains; this will help expand the individual's pretend play repertoire.

PRETEND PLAY: KITCHEN

LEVEL: □ 1 □ 2 □ 3

S^D: A. Model an action associated with playing kitchen and say "Pretend [action/object]" (e.g. "Pretend to stir food" or "Pretend to bake a cake") B. "Play pretend kitchen" C. "Play pretend kitchen"	**Response:** A. Individual will imitate the pretend action B. Individual will chain together three pretend actions C. Individual will chain together three plus pretend actions for a longer duration
Data Collection: S^D A: Skill acquisition, S^D B and C: Prompt data (number and type of prompts used)	**Target Criteria:** S^D A: 80% or above for 3 consecutive days across 2 people, S^D B and C: 0 prompts for 3 consecutive days across 2 people
Materials: 2 sets of pretend kitchen items: cups, bowls, spoons, pots, stoves, various food, etc. and reinforcement	

Fading procedure

Maintenance Criteria: 2W = 4 consecutive scores of 100% or 0 prompts; 1W = 4 consecutive scores of 100% or 0 prompts; M = 3 consecutive scores of 100% or 0 prompts	**Natural Environment (NE) Criterion:** Target has been generalized in NE across 3 novel naturally occurring activities	**Archive Criteria:** Target, maintenance and NE criteria have been met

Target list

Suggestions for targets and probe results

Suggestions for Targets: Put food in pot, put food on stove, stir food, put lid on pot, put food in bowl, eat food, put cake mix in bowl, bake cake, make hot soup, put food on plate and serve food.
Probe Results (targets in repertoire):

Target	Baseline % or Number and Type of Prompts	Date Introduced	Date Criteria Met	*Fading Procedure*		
				Maintenance	Date NE Introduced	Date Archived
1. S^D A: Target 1:						
2. S^D A: Target 2:						

3. S^D A: Target 3:						
4. S^D A: Target 4:						
5. S^D A: Target 5:						
6. S^D A: Target 6:						
7. S^D A: Target 7:						
8. S^D A: Target 8:						
9. S^D A: Target 9:						
10. S^D A: Target 10:						
11. S^D B: Individual chains 3 pretend actions.						
12. S^D B: Individual chains 3 different pretend actions.						
13. S^D C: Target 1: Duration = 2 minutes						
14. S^D C: Target 1: Duration = 3 minutes						
15. S^D C: Target 1: Duration = 5 minutes						
16. Generalize S^D C of 5 minutes to another environment Environment 1:						
17. Generalize S^D C of 5 minutes to another environment Environment 2:						
18. Maintenance: Assess in varied environments				2W 1W M		

Specific tips for running this task analysis

- Ensure pre-requisite skills have been taught for this TA. Examples of pre-requisite skills for pretend play with chained actions include mastering basic pretend play, "Functional Use of Objects," "Parallel Play," "Receptive Instructions (One-Step)" and fine motor and gross motor imitation programs (TAs found in the first book of the Journey of Development ABA Curriculum series).
- If the individual has difficulty learning this TA, then you may want to start this program out with the S^D "Do this" as written in the imitation programs in the first book of the Journey of Development ABA Curriculum series. Once the individual has grasped the imitation of pretend play with S^D "Do this" then move on to S^D "Pretend [action/object]" as written in this TA.
- This curriculum book offers several pretend play TAs; when beginning to teach this to a individual, choose the pretend play scenario that is likely to be the most motivating and interesting to the individual. In addition, if the individual has pretend play props for another pretend play scenario that is not offered in this book (e.g. grocery store), then modify the TA to include the scenario in which there are already props.
- This TA is written so the individual has to "chain" three pretend actions together. In ABA literature, chaining is a method whereby you chain together related behaviors where one behavior acts as a cue for the next behavior. In this example, putting food into a pot may act as a cue to put the pot on the stove followed by stirring the food. The instructor should teach the individual by prompting them to use different related actions to form different chains; this will help expand the individual's pretend play repertoire.

PRETEND PLAY: MOMMY AND DADDY

LEVEL: □ 1 □ 2 □ 3

S^D: A. Model an action associated with playing mommy and daddy, and say "Pretend [action/object]" (e.g. "Pretend to put baby to bed" or "Pretend to kiss baby") B. "Play pretend mommy (or daddy)" C. "Play pretend mommy (or daddy)"	**Response:** A. Individual will imitate the pretend action B. Individual will chain together three pretend actions C. Individual will chain together three plus pretend actions for a longer duration
Data Collection: S^D A: Skill acquisition; S^D B and C: Prompt data (number and type of prompts used)	**Target Criteria:** S^D A: 80% or above for 3 consecutive days across 2 people; S^D B and C: 0 prompts for 3 consecutive days across 2 people
Materials: 2 sets of pretend mommy/daddy toys: dolls or stuffed animals, bottles, blankets, food, burp clothes, wash clothes, clothes, etc. and reinforcement	

Fading procedure

Maintenance Criteria: 2W = 4 consecutive scores of 100% or 0 prompts; 1W = 4 consecutive scores of 100% or 0 prompts; M = 3 consecutive scores of 100% or 0 prompts	**Natural Environment (NE) Criterion:** Target has been generalized in NE across 3 novel naturally occurring activities	**Archive Criteria:** Target, maintenance and NE criteria have been met

Target list

Suggestions for targets and probe results

Suggestions for Targets: Feed baby (or stuffed animal), burp baby, put baby to bed, put diaper on baby, rock baby, give baby a bath, dress baby, give baby a hug, tickle baby, and give baby a kiss.
Probe Results (targets in repertoire):

Target	Baseline % or Number and Type of Prompts	Date Introduced	Date Criteria Met	*Fading Procedure*		
				Maintenance	Date NE Introduced	Date Archived
1. S^D A: Target 1:						
2. S^D A: Target 2:						

3. S^D A: Target 3:						
4. S^D A: Target 4:						
5. S^D A: Target 5:						
6. S^D A: Target 6:						
7. S^D A: Target 7:						
8. S^D A: Target 8:						
9. S^D A: Target 9:						
10. S^D A: Target 10:						
11. S^D B: Individual chains 3 pretend actions.						
12. S^D B: Individual chains 3 different pretend actions.						
13. S^D C: Target 1: Duration = 2 minutes						
14. S^D C: Target 1: Duration = 3 minutes						
15. S^D C: Target 1: Duration = 5 minutes						
16. Generalize S^D C of 5 minutes to another environment Environment 1:						
17. Generalize S^D C of 5 minutes to another environment Environment 2:						
18. Maintenance: Assess in varied environments				2W 1W M		

Specific tips for running this task analysis

- Ensure pre-requisite skills have been taught for this TA. Examples of pre-requisite skills for pretend play with chained actions include includes mastering basic pretend play, "Functional Use of Objects," "Parallel Play," "Receptive Instructions (One-Step)" and fine motor and gross motor imitation programs (TAs found in the first book of the Journey of Development ABA Curriculum series).
- If the individual has difficulty learning this TA, then you may want to start this program out with the S^D "Do this" as written in the imitation programs in the first book of the Journey of Development ABA curriculum series. Once the individual has grasped the imitation of pretend play with S^D "Do this" then move on to S^D "Pretend [action/object]" as written in this TA.
- This curriculum book offers several pretend play TAs; when beginning to teach this to a individual, choose the pretend play scenario that is likely to be the most motivating and interesting to the individual. In addition, if the individual has pretend play props for another pretend play scenario that is not offered in this book (e.g. grocery store), then modify the TA to include the scenario in which there are already props.
- This TA is written so the individual has to "chain" three pretend actions together. In ABA literature, chaining is a method whereby you chain together related behaviors where one behavior acts as a cue for the next behavior. In this example, getting a bottle may act as a cue to feed the baby followed by burping the baby. The instructor should teach the individual by prompting them to use different related actions to form different chains; this will help expand the individual's pretend play repertoire.

PRETEND PLAY: SCHOOL

LEVEL: □ 1 □ 2 □ 3

S^D: A. Model an action associated with playing school and say "Pretend [action/object]" (e.g. "Pretend to pass out paper" or "Pretend to give a hall pass") B. "Play pretend school" C. "Play pretend school"	**Response:** A. Individual will imitate the pretend action B. Individual will chain together three pretend actions C. Individual will chain together three plus pretend actions for a longer duration
Data Collection: S^D A: Skill acquisition; S^D B and C: Prompt data (number and type of prompts used)	**Target Criteria:** S^D A: 80% or above for 3 consecutive days across 2 people, S^D B and C: 0 prompts for 3 consecutive days across 2 people
Materials: 2 sets of pretend school items: books, papers, markers, stickers, calendars, marker boards, hall passes, etc. and reinforcement	

Fading procedure

Maintenance Criteria: 2W = 4 consecutive scores of 100% or 0 prompts; 1W = 4 consecutive scores of 100% or 0 prompts; M = 3 consecutive scores of 100% or 0 prompts	**Natural Environment (NE) Criterion:** Target has been generalized in NE across 3 novel naturally occurring activities	**Archive Criteria:** Target, maintenance and NE criteria have been met

Target list

Suggestions for targets and probe results

Suggestions for Targets: Pass out papers, give a test, teach a lesson at board, praise individual with stickers, tell a story from book, hand out hall pass, lead song at circle time, teach calendar at circle time, teach weather at circle time, and have individuals line up for lunch.

Probe Results (targets in repertoire):

Target	Baseline % or Number and Type of Prompts	Date Introduced	Date Criteria Met	*Fading Procedure*		
				Maintenance	Date NE Introduced	Date Archived
1. S^D A: Target 1:						
2. S^D A: Target 2:						

3. S^D A: Target 3:						
4. S^D A: Target 4:						
5. S^D A: Target 5:						
6. S^D A: Target 6:						
7. S^D A: Target 7:						
8. S^D A: Target 8:						
9. S^D A: Target 9:						
10. S^D A: Target 10:						
11. S^D B: Individual chains 3 pretend actions.						
12. S^D B: Individual chains 3 different pretend actions.						
13. S^D C: Target 1: Duration = 2 minutes						
14. S^D C: Target 1: Duration = 3 minutes						
15. S^D C: Target 1: Duration = 5 minutes						
16. Generalize S^D C of 5 minutes to another environment Environment 1:						
17. Generalize S^D C of 5 minutes to another environment Environment 2:						
18. Maintenance: Assess in varied environments				2W 1W M		

Specific tips for running this task analysis

- Ensure pre-requisite skills have been taught for this TA. Examples of pre-requisite skills for pretend play with chained actions include mastering basic pretend play, "Functional Use of Objects," "Parallel Play," "Receptive Instructions (One-Step)" and fine motor and gross motor imitation programs (TAs found in the first book of the Journey of Development ABA Curriculum series).
- If the individual has difficulty learning this TA, then you may want to start this program out with the S^D "Do this" as written in the imitation programs in the first book of the Journey of Development ABA Curriculum series. Once the individual has grasped the imitation of pretend play with S^D "Do this" then move on to S^D "Pretend [action/object]" as written in this TA.
- This curriculum book offers several pretend play TAs; when beginning to teach this to a individual, choose the pretend play scenario that is likely to be the most motivating and interesting to the individual. In addition, if the individual has pretend play props for another pretend play scenario that is not offered in this book (e.g. grocery store), then modify the TA to include the scenario in which there are already props.
- This TA is written so the individual has to "chain" three pretend actions together. In ABA literature, chaining is a method whereby you chain together related behaviors where one behavior acts as a cue for the next behavior. In this example, giving a test may act as a cue to score the test followed by giving individuals stickers for a job well done. The instructor should teach the individual by prompting them to use different related actions to form different chains; this will help expand the individual's pretend play repertoire.

PRETEND PLAY (NO PROPS)

LEVEL: □ 1 □ 2 □ 3

S^D: "Pretend to [action]" for example, "Pretend to eat an apple"	**Response:** Individual will respond by displaying the pretend action
Data Collection: Skill acquisition	**Target Criteria:** 80% or above for 3 consecutive days across 2 people
Materials: Reinforcement	

Fading procedure

Maintenance Criteria: 2W = 4 consecutive scores of 100%; 1W = 4 consecutive scores of 100%; M = 3 consecutive scores of 100%	**Natural Environment (NE) Criterion:** Target has been generalized in NE across 3 novel naturally occurring activities	**Archive Criteria:** Target, maintenance and NE criteria have been met

Target list

Suggestions for targets and probe results

Suggestions for Targets: Drink from a cup, eat an apple, knock on a door, brush your hair, kick a ball, wash your face, climb a ladder, throw a ball, read a book, and put on chapstick.
Probe Results (targets in repertoire):

Target	Baseline %	Date Introduced	Date Criteria Met	*Fading Procedure*		
				Maintenance	Date NE Introduced	Date Archived
1. Target 1:						
2. Target 2:						
3. Targets 1 and 2 random rotation						
4. Target 3:						
5. Target 4:						

6. Targets that met criteria: random rotation						
7. Target 5:						
8. Target 6:						
9. Targets that met criteria: random rotation						
10. Target 7:						
11. Target 8:						
12. Targets that met criteria: random rotation						
13. Target 9:						
14. Target 10:						
15. Targets that met criteria: random rotation						
16. Generalize to another environment Environment 1:						
17. Generalize to another environment Environment 2:						
18. Maintenance: Assess in varied environments				2W 1W M		

Specific tips for running this task analysis

- Ensure pre-requisite skills have been taught for this TA. Examples of pre-requisite skills for "Pretend Play (No Props)" include play/leisure activities in the first book of the Journey of Development ABA Curriculum series and "Pretend Actions Imitation (No Objects Used)" in this curriculum book.
- If the individual has difficulty learning this skill, you may want to use a visual prompt of the actual item (i.e. using a cup when you give the S^D to pretend to drink from a cup). The instructor should then fade the visual prompt.

PRETEND PLAY: SAME ROLE—DANCERS

LEVEL: □ 1 □ 2 □ 3

S^D: Present individual with dress-up dancer clothes and say "Let's pretend to be dancers"	**Response:** Individual will imitate and initiate pretend play actions
Data Collection: Prompt data (number and type of prompts used)	**Target criteria:** 0 prompts for 3 consecutive days across 2 people
Materials: Dress-up dancer clothes, music, maracas, ribbon sticks, dance mats, etc. and reinforcement	

Fading procedure

Maintenance Criteria: 2W = 4 consecutive scores of 0 prompts; 1W = 4 consecutive scores of 0 prompts; M = 3 consecutive scores of 0 prompts	**Natural Environment (NE) Criterion:** Target has been generalized in NE across 3 novel naturally occurring activities	**Archive Criteria:** Target, maintenance and NE criteria have been met

Target list

Suggestions for targets and probe results

Suggestions for Targets: Dress up in dance clothes, turn, walk on tiptoes, walk backwards, jump, partner drills (side step, twirls), kick legs, arm rolls, curtsey, etc.
Probe Results (targets in repertoire):

Target	Baseline: Number and Type of Prompts	Date Introduced	Date Criteria Met	*Fading Procedure*		
				Maintenance	Date NE Introduced	Date Archived
1. Target 1: Individual imitates 5 actions.						
2. Target 2: Individual imitates 4 actions and initiates 1 action.						
3. Target 3: Individual imitates 3 actions and initiates 2 actions.						
4. Target 4: Individual imitates 2 actions and initiates 3 actions.						

5. Target 5: Individual imitates 1 action and initiates 4 actions.						
6. Target 6: Individual initiates 5 actions.						
7. Generalize to another environment Environment 1:						
8. Generalize to another environment Environment 2:						
9. Maintenance: Assess in varied environments				2W 1W M		

Specific tips for running this task analysis

- Ensure pre-requisite skills have been taught for this TA. Examples of pre-requisite skills for "Pretend Play: Same Role—Dancers" include mastering basic pretend play, "Parallel Play," "Receptive Instructions (One-Step)" and fine motor and gross motor imitation programs (TAs found in the first book of the Journey of Development ABA Curriculum series).
- If the individual has difficulty learning this TA, then you may want to start this program out with the S^D "Do this" as written in the imitation programs in the first book of the Journey of Development ABA Curriculum series. Once the individual has grasped the imitation of pretend play with S^D "Do this" then move on to S^D as written in this TA.
- The goal of this TA is to teach pretend play with another person, whereby both individuals are engaging in the same role. Once the instructor teaches this TA, the responses should be generalized to both the instructor and individual acting as a dancer and performing different movements. The skill should also be generalized to the peer group.
- This curriculum book offers several pretend play same role TAs. When beginning to teach this to a individual, choose the pretend play same role scenario that is likely to be the most motivating and interesting to the individual. In addition, if the individual has pretend play props for another pretend play same role scenario that is not offered in this book (e.g. individual's favorite superhero or cartoon character), then modify the TA to include the scenario in which there are already props.
- The S^D associated with this TA can be modified so that the individual will understand that they need to initiate some actions, such as "My turn" and "Your turn."

PRETEND PLAY: SAME ROLE—PIRATES

LEVEL: □ 1 □ 2 □ 3

S^D: Present individual with dress-up pirate clothes and say "Let's pretend to be pirates"	**Response:** Individual will imitate and initiate pretend play actions
Data Collection: Prompt data (number and type of prompts used)	**Target criteria:** 0 prompts for 3 consecutive days across 2 people
Materials: Dress-up pirate clothes, swords, treasure chest, pretend boat, flag, parrot, map, eye patch, telescope, plank, etc. and reinforcement	

Fading procedure

Maintenance Criteria: 2W = 4 consecutive scores of 0 prompts; 1W = 4 consecutive scores of 0 prompts; M = 3 consecutive scores of 0 prompts	**Natural Environment (NE) Criterion:** Target has been generalized in NE across 3 novel naturally occurring activities	**Archive Criteria:** Target, maintenance and NE criteria have been met

Target list

Suggestions for targets and probe results

Suggestions for Targets: Dress up in clothes, wear an eye patch, hold a parrot, have a sword fight, find a buried treasure, open the treasure, look through a telescope, raise a flag, walk the plank, sail a boat, and read a map.
Probe Results (targets in repertoire):

Target	Baseline: Number and Type of Prompts	Date Introduced	Date Criteria Met	*Fading Procedure*		
				Maintenance	Date NE Introduced	Date Archived
1. Target 1: Individual imitates 5 actions.						
2. Target 2: Individual imitates 4 actions and initiates 1 action.						
3. Target 3: Individual imitates 3 actions and initiates 2 actions.						

4. Target 4: Individual imitates 2 actions and initiates 3 actions.						
5. Target 5: Individual imitates 1 action and initiates 4 actions.						
6. Target 6: Individual initiates 5 actions.						
7. Generalize to another environment Environment 1:						
8. Generalize to another environment Environment 2:						
9. Maintenance: Assess in varied environments				2W 1W M		

Specific tips for running this task analysis

- Ensure pre-requisite skills have been taught for this TA. Examples of pre-requisite skills for "Pretend Play: Same Role—Pirates" include mastering basic pretend play, "Parallel Play," "Receptive Instructions (One-Step)" and fine motor and gross motor imitation programs (TAs found in the first book of the Journey of Development ABA Curriculum series).
- If the individual has difficulty learning this TA, then you may want to start this program out with the S^D "Do this" as written in the imitation programs in the first book of the Journey of Development ABA Curriculum series. Once the individual has grasped the imitation of pretend play with S^D "Do this" then move on to S^D as written in this TA.
- The goal of this TA is to teach pretend play with another person, whereby both individuals are engaging in the same role. Once the instructor teaches this TA, the responses should be generalized to both the instructor and individual acting as a pirate and performing different movements. The skill should also be generalized to the peer group.
- This curriculum book offers several pretend play same role TAs. When beginning to teach this to a individual, choose the pretend play same role scenario that is likely to be the most motivating and interesting to the individual. In addition, if the individual has pretend play props for another pretend play same role scenario that is not offered in this book (e.g. individual's favorite superhero or cartoon character), then modify the TA to include the scenario in which there are already props.
- The S^D associated with this TA can be modified so that the individual will understand that they need to initiate some actions, such as "My turn" and "Your turn."

PRETEND PLAY: SAME ROLE—PRINCESSES

LEVEL: □ 1 □ 2 □ 3

S^D: Present individual with dress-up princess clothes and say "Let's pretend to be princesses"	**Response:** Individual will imitate and initiate pretend play actions
Data Collection: Prompt data (number and type of prompts used)	**Target criteria:** 0 prompts for 3 consecutive days across 2 people
Materials: Dress-up princess clothes, crown, wand, jewelry, glass slippers, tea party items, coach, etc. and reinforcement	

Fading procedure

Maintenance Criteria: 2W = 4 consecutive scores of 0 prompts; 1W = 4 consecutive scores of 0 prompts; M = 3 consecutive scores of 0 prompts	**Natural Environment (NE) Criterion:** Target has been generalized in NE across 3 novel naturally occurring activities	**Archive Criteria:** Target, maintenance and NE criteria have been met

Target list

Suggestions for targets and probe results

Suggestions for Targets: Dress up in clothes, twirl or dance, wave like a princess, have a tea party, curtsey, wave the wand, walk in a parade, ride in pretend coach and put on jewelry.
Probe Results (targets in repertoire):

Target	Baseline: Number and Type of Prompts	Date Introduced	Date Criteria Met	*Fading Procedure*		
				Maintenance	Date NE Introduced	Date Archived
1. Target 1: Individual imitates 5 actions.						
2. Target 2: Individual imitates 4 actions and initiates 1 action.						
3. Target 3: Individual imitates 3 actions and initiates 2 actions.						

4. Target 4: Individual imitates 2 actions and initiates 3 actions.						
5. Target 5: Individual imitates 1 action and initiates 4 actions.						
6. Target 6: Individual initiates 5 actions.						
7. Generalize to another environment Environment 1:						
8. Generalize to another environment Environment 2:						
9. Maintenance: Assess in varied environments				2W 1W M		

Specific tips for running this task analysis

- Ensure pre-requisite skills have been taught for this TA. Examples of pre-requisite skills for "Pretend Play: Same Role—Princesses" includes mastering basic pretend play, "Parallel Play," "Receptive Instructions (One-Step)" and fine motor and gross motor imitation programs (TAs found in the first book of the Journey of Development ABA Curriculum series).
- If the individual has difficulty learning this TA, then you may want to start this program out with the S^D "Do this" as written in the imitation programs in the first book of the Journey of Development ABA curriculum series. Once the individual has grasped the imitation of pretend play with S^D "Do this" then move on to S^D as written in this TA.
- The goal of this TA is to teach pretend play with another person, whereby both individuals are engaging in the same role. Once the instructor teaches this TA, the responses should be generalized to both the instructor and individual acting as a princess and performing different movements. The skill should also be generalized to the peer group.
- This curriculum book offers several pretend play same role TAs. When beginning to teach this to a individual, choose the pretend play same role scenario that is likely to be the most motivating and interesting to the individual. In addition, if the individual has pretend play props for another pretend play same role scenario that is not offered in this book (e.g. individual's favorite superhero or cartoon character), then modify the TA to include the scenario in which there are already props.
- The S^D associated with this TA can be modified so that the individual will understand that they need to initiate some actions, such as "My turn" and "Your turn."

PRETEND PLAY: SAME ROLE—RACE CAR DRIVER

LEVEL: □ 1 □ 2 □ 3

S^D: Present individual with dress-up race car driver clothes and say "Let's pretend to be a race car driver"	**Response:** Individual will imitate and initiate pretend play actions
Data Collection: Prompt data (number and type of prompts used)	**Target criteria:** 0 prompts for 3 consecutive days across 2 people
Materials: Dress-up race car driver clothes, pretend car, seatbelt, flag, trophy, gas pump, paper towels and windshield fluid, etc. and reinforcement	

Fading procedure

Maintenance Criteria: 2W = 4 consecutive scores of 0 prompts; 1W = 4 consecutive scores of 0 prompts; M = 3 consecutive scores of 0 prompts	**Natural Environment (NE) Criterion:** Target has been generalized in NE across 3 novel naturally occurring activities	**Archive Criteria:** Target, maintenance and NE criteria have been met

Target list

Suggestions for targets and probe results

Suggestions for Targets: Dress up in race car driver clothes, pretend to drive a car, race around in a circle, pretend to change a tire, pretend to get gas, pretend to wash your window, put on seatbelt, wave a flag, get a trophy.
Probe Results (targets in repertoire):

Target	Baseline: Number and Type of Prompts	Date Introduced	Date Criteria Met	*Fading Procedure*		
				Maintenance	Date NE Introduced	Date Archived
1. Target 1: Individual imitates 5 actions.						
2. Target 2: Individual imitates 4 actions and initiates 1 action.						
3. Target 3: Individual imitates 3 actions and initiates 2 actions.						

4. Target 4: Individual imitates 2 actions and initiates 3 actions.						
5. Target 5: Individual imitates 1 action and initiates 4 actions.						
6. Target 6: Individual initiates 5 actions.						
7. Generalize to another environment Environment 1:						
8. Generalize to another environment Environment 2:						
9. Maintenance: Assess in varied environments				2W 1W M		

Specific tips for running this task analysis

- Ensure pre-requisite skills have been taught for this TA. Examples of pre-requisite skills for "Pretend Play: Same Role—Race Car Driver" include mastering basic pretend play, "Parallel Play," "Receptive Instructions (One-Step)" and fine motor and gross motor imitation programs (TAs found in the first book of the Journey of Development ABA Curriculum series).
- If the individual has difficulty learning this TA, then you may want to start this program out with the S^D "Do this" as written in the imitation programs in the first book of the Journey of Development ABA Curriculum series. Once the individual has grasped the imitation of pretend play with S^D "Do this" then move on to S^D as written in this TA.
- The goal of this TA is to teach pretend play with another person, whereby both individuals are engaging in the same role. Once the instructor teaches this TA, the responses should be generalized to both the instructor and individual acting as a race car driver and performing different movements. The skill should also be generalized to the peer group.
- This curriculum book offers several pretend play same role TAs. When beginning to teach this to a individual, choose the pretend play same role scenario that is likely to be the most motivating and interesting to the individual. In addition, if the individual has pretend play props for another pretend play same role scenario that is not offered in this book (e.g. individual's favorite superhero or cartoon character), then modify the TA to include the scenario in which there are already props.
- The S^D associated with this TA can be modified so that the individual will understand that they need to initiate some actions, such as "My turn" and "Your turn."

PRETEND PLAY: SAME ROLE—TRAIN ENGINEERS

LEVEL: □ 1 □ 2 □ 3

S^D: Present individual with dress-up train engineer clothes and say "Let's pretend to play trains"	**Response:** Individual will imitate and initiate pretend play actions
Data Collection: Prompt data (number and type of prompts used)	**Target criteria:** 0 prompts for 3 consecutive days across 2 people
Materials: Dress-up train engineer clothes, train hat, train tracks, trains, crane, whistle, passengers (i.e. stuffed animals), etc. and reinforcement	

Fading procedure

Maintenance Criteria: 2W = 4 consecutive scores of 0 prompts; 1W = 4 consecutive scores of 0 prompts; M = 3 consecutive scores of 0 prompts	**Natural Environment (NE) Criterion:** Target has been generalized in NE across 3 novel naturally occurring activities	**Archive Criteria:** Target, maintenance and NE criteria have been met

Target list

Suggestions for targets and probe results

Suggestions for Targets: Dress up in train engineer clothes, build a train track, push the trains, crash the trains, use a crane, blow the train whistle, stop for passengers, drive and stop the train, connect the train, turn on train light and yell "all aboard."
Probe Results (targets in repertoire):

Target	Baseline: Number and Type of Prompts	Date Introduced	Date Criteria Met	*Fading Procedure*		
				Maintenance	Date NE Introduced	Date Archived
1. Target 1: Individual imitates 5 actions.						
2. Target 2: Individual imitates 4 actions and initiates 1 action.						
3. Target 3: Individual imitates 3 actions and initiates 2 actions.						

4. Target 4: Individual imitates 2 actions and initiates 3 actions.						
5. Target 5: Individual imitates 1 action and initiates 4 actions.						
6. Target 6: Individual initiates 5 actions						
7. Generalize to another environment Environment 1:						
8. Generalize to another environment Environment 2:						
9. Maintenance: Assess in varied environments				2W 1W M		

Specific tips for running this task analysis

- Ensure pre-requisite skills have been taught for this TA. Examples of pre-requisite skills for "Pretend Play: Same Role—Trains" include mastering basic pretend play, "Parallel Play," "Receptive Instructions (One-Step)" and fine motor and gross motor imitation programs (TAs found in the first book of the Journey of Development ABA Curriculum series).
- If the individual has difficulty learning this TA, then you may want to start this program out with the S^D "Do this" as written in the imitation programs in the first book of the Journey of Development ABA Curriculum series. Once the individual has grasped the imitation of pretend play with S^D "Do this" then move on to S^D as written in this TA.
- The goal of this TA is to teach pretend play with another person, whereby both individuals are engaging in the same role. Once the instructor teaches this TA, the responses should be generalized to both the instructor and individual acting as a train engineer and performing different movements. The skill should also be generalized to the peer group.
- This curriculum book offers several pretend play same role TAs. When beginning to teach this to a individual, choose the pretend play same role scenario that is likely to be the most motivating and interesting to the individual. In addition, if the individual has pretend play props for another pretend play same role scenario that is not offered in this book (e.g. individual's favorite superhero or cartoon character), then modify the TA to include the scenario in which there are already props.
- The S^D associated with this TA can be modified so that the individual will understand that they need to initiate some actions, such as "My turn" and "Your turn."

SWIMMING: LEVEL 1

LEVEL: □ 1 □ 2 □ 3

S^D: A. Give a verbal directive (e.g. kick, bob, blow bubbles with your mouth) B. Give a verbal directive that takes longer to follow (e.g. use kick board for 2 lengths of pool) C. Give a verbal safety directive (e.g. get in and out of the pool safely, put on a life jacket, hold on to wall moving down the pool, etc.)	**Response:** A. Individual will follow the directives B. Individual will follow the directives independently for a longer duration C. Individual will follow the directives
Data Collection: S^D A: Skill acquisition; S^D B and C: Prompt data (number and type of prompts used)	**Target Criteria:** S^D A: 80% or above for 3 consecutive days across 2 people, S^D B and C: 0 prompts for 3 consecutive days across 2 people
Materials: Pool, kick board, life jacket, swim noodle, goggles, floats, diving rings, etc. and reinforcement	

Fading procedure

Maintenance Criteria: 2W = 4 consecutive scores of 0 prompts; 1W = 4 consecutive scores of 0 prompts; M = 3 consecutive scores of 0 prompts	**Natural Environment (NE) Criterion:** Target has been generalized in NE across 3 novel naturally occurring activities	**Archive Criteria:** Target, maintenance and NE criteria have been met

Target list

Suggestions for targets and probe results

Suggestions for Targets: *S^D A*: kick, big arms (straight arms that reach in a circle out of the water), blow bubbles with your mouth, blow bubbles with your nose, bob, float, and get rings. *S^D B*: Use kick board across pool, use kick board 2 lengths of pool, front glide (push off wall on stomach), back glide (push off wall on back), back float for 2 seconds or 5 seconds, simultaneous leg action on front or on back (2 body lengths), simultaneous arm action on front or on back (2 body lengths), arm and leg movements on front (1 or 2 body lengths), arm and leg movements on back (1 or 2 body lengths). *S^D C*: Enter pool using ladder/steps, exit pool using ladder/steps, put on life jacket, hold on to wall while moving down the pool and take off life jacket.
Probe Results (targets in repertoire):

Target	Baseline: Number and Type of Prompts	Date Introduced	Date Criteria Met	*Fading Procedure* Maintenance	Date NE Introduced	Date Archived
1. S^D A: Target 1:						
2. S^D A: Target 2:						
3. Targets 1 and 2 random rotation						
4. S^D A: Target 3:						
5. S^D A: Target 4:						
6. Targets that met criteria: random rotation						
7. S^D A: Target 5:						
8. S^D A: Target 6:						
9. Targets that met criteria: random rotation						
10. S^D B: Target 1:						
11. S^D B: Target 2:						
12. Targets that met criteria: random rotation						
13. S^D B: Target 3:						
14. S^D B: Target 4:						

15. Targets that met criteria: random rotation						
16. S^D B: Target 5:						
17. S^D B: Target 6:						
18. Targets that met criteria: random rotation						
19. S^D C: Target 1:						
20. S^D C: Target 2:						
21. Targets that met criteria: random rotation						
22. S^D C: Target 3:						
23. S^D C: Target 4:						
24. Targets that met criteria: random rotation						
25. S^D C: Target 5:						
26. S^D C: Target 6:						
27. Targets that met criteria: random rotation						
28. Generalize another environment Environment 1:						
29. Generalize another environment Environment 2:						
30. Maintenance: Assess in varied environments				2W 1W M		

Specific tips for running this task analysis

- Ensure pre-requisite skills have been taught for this TA. Examples of pre-requisite skills for "Swimming: Level 1" include mastering "Receptive Instructions (One-Step)" and "Gross Motor Imitation" (TAs found in the first book of the Journey of Development ABA Curriculum series).
- Targets for "Swimming: Level 1" are adapted from the American Red Cross suggestions for learning how to swim. TA can be followed with "Swimming Level 2" and "Swimming Level 3" (TAs found in the third book of the Journey of Development ABA Curriculum series).

SYMBOLIC PLAY

LEVEL: □ 1 □ 2 □ 3

S^D: Give individual an object and direct them to do a symbolic action with the object by saying "Pretend to [action]." For example, hand individual a block and say "Pretend to talk on the phone"	**Response:** Individual will display the symbolic action with an object
Data Collection: Skill acquisition	**Target Criteria:** 80% or above for 3 consecutive days across 2 people
Materials: Objects that represent familiar objects (e.g. banana for a phone, chair for a car, popsicle stick for a person) and reinforcement	

Fading procedure

Maintenance Criteria: 2W = 4 consecutive scores of 100%; 1W = 4 consecutive scores of 100%; M = 3 consecutive scores of 100%	**Natural Environment (NE) Criterion:** Target has been generalized in NE across 3 novel naturally occurring activities	**Archive Criteria:** Target, maintenance and NE criteria have been met

Target list

Suggestions for targets and probe results

Suggestions for Targets: Use a banana for a phone, use a chair for a car, use a box for a crib, use paper towel holder for sword, use pillow for shield, use blanket for fort, use block for train, use popsicle stick for person, use lid for boat and use cotton ball for bear.
Probe Results (targets in repertoire):

Target	Baseline %	Date Introduced	Date Criteria Met	*Fading Procedure*		
				Maintenance	Date NE Introduced	Date Archived
1. Target 1:						
2. Target 2:						
3. Targets that met criteria: random rotation						
4. Target 3:						

5. Target 4:						
6. Targets that met criteria: random rotation						
7. Target 5:						
8. Target 6:						
9. Targets that met criteria: random rotation						
10. Target 7:						
11. Target 8:						
12. Targets that met criteria: random rotation						
13. Target 9:						
14. Target 10:						
15. Targets that met criteria: random rotation						
16. Generalize to another environment Environment 1:						
17. Generalize to another environment Environment 2:						
18. Maintenance: Assess in varied environments				2W 1W M		

Specific tips for running this task analysis

- Ensure pre-requisite skills have been taught for this TA. Examples of pre-requisite skills for "Symbolic Play" include basic pretend play in the first book of the Journey of Development ABA Curriculum series and "Pretend Actions Imitation (No Objects Used)" and "Pretend Play (No Props)" (TAs found in this curriculum book).
- If the individual has difficulty grasping this skill, try using the actual object to teach the behavior followed by immediately using the symbolic object.

TURN-TAKING

LEVEL: □ 1 □ 2 □ 3

S^D: A. Present a toy or activity and say, "My turn" or "Your turn" B. Present a toy/activity without a verbal S^D	**Response:** Individual will take their turn or wait appropriately for their turn ("My turn" is the instructor and "Your turn" is the individual)
Data Collection: Prompt data (number and type of prompts used)	**Target Criteria:** 0 prompts for 3 consecutive days across 2 people
Materials: Simple toys and turn-taking activities, and reinforcement	

Fading procedure

Maintenance Criteria: 2W = 4 consecutive scores of 0 prompts; 1W = 4 consecutive scores of 0 prompts; M = 3 consecutive scores of 0 prompts	**Natural Environment (NE) Criterion:** Target has been generalized in NE across 3 novel naturally occurring activities	**Archive Criteria:** Target, maintenance and NE criteria have been met

Target list

Target	Baseline: Number and Type of Prompts	Date Introduced	Date Criteria Met	*Fading Procedure*		
				Maintenance	Date NE Introduced	Date Archived
1. S^D A: Individual will take 2 turns (Individual's turn and partner's turn = 2 turns).						
2. S^D A: Individual will take 4 turns (Individual's 2 turns and partner's 2 turns = 4 turns).						
3. S^D A: Individual will take 6 turns (Individual's 3 turns and partner's 3 turns = 6 turns).						
4. S^D A: Individual will take 8 turns (Individual's 4 turns and partner's 4 turns = 8 turns).						

5. S^D A: Individual will take 10 turns (Individual's 5 turns and partner's 5 turns = 10 turns).						
6. S^D B: Individual will take 2 turns (Individual's turn and partner's turn = 2 turns).						
7. S^D B: Individual will take 4 turns (Individual's 2 turns and partner's 2 turns = 4 turns).						
8. S^D B: Individual will take 6 turns (Individual's 3 turns and partner's 3 turns = 6 turns).						
9. S^D B: Individual will take 8 turns (Individual's 4 turns and partner's 4 turns = 8 turns).						
10. S^D B: Individual will take 10 turns (Individual's 5 turns and partner's 5 turns = 10 turns).						
11. Generalize to another environment Environment 1:						
12. Generalize to another environment Environment 2:						
13. Maintenance: Assess in varied environments				2W 1W M		

Specific tips for running this task analysis

- Ensure pre-requisite skills have been taught for this TA. Examples of pre-requisite skills for "Turn-Taking" include mastering "Receptive Instructions (One-Step)," "Appropriate Sitting," "Functional Use of Objects," "Giving Objects to Another" (TAs found in the first book of the Journey of Development ABA Curriculum series) and "Waiting" (TA found in this book).
- When first teaching this skill, it may be helpful to use moderately preferred toys or objects, as opposed to highly preferred ones, so the individual may be more willing to release the object for the partner to take a turn. The instructor should then build up to using highly preferred objects and toys.

Chapter 16

TASK ANALYSES FOR ADAPTIVE SKILLS

- Applying Chapstick
- Buttoning and Unbuttoning
- Cleaning Ears
- Dressing and Undressing: Putting on and Taking off Gloves
- Dressing and Undressing: Putting on and Taking off Gym Clothes
- Snapping and Unsnapping
- Systematic Desensitization: Brushing Hair
- Systematic Desensitization: Brushing Teeth
- Unzipping a Zipper
- Waiting
- Walking Backwards
- Wiping Hands and Face
- Zipping a Connected and Unconnected Zipper

APPLYING CHAPSTICK

LEVEL: □ 1 □ 2 □ 3

S^D: Individual's lips are dry, or this skill is placed on the individual's hygiene or work schedule. Alternatively, you can give a verbal S^D "Put on chapstick"	**Response:** Individual will apply chapstick
Data Collection: Prompt data (number and type of prompts used)	**Target criteria:** 0 prompts for 3 consecutive days across 2 people
Materials: Chapstick or lip balm, and reinforcement. Alternative materials: visual schedule	

Fading procedure

Maintenance Criteria: 2W = 4 consecutive scores of 0 prompts; 1W = 4 consecutive scores of 0 prompts; M = 3 consecutive scores of 0 prompts	**Natural Environment (NE) Criterion:** Target has been generalized in NE across 3 novel naturally occurring activities	**Archive Criteria:** Target, maintenance and NE criteria have been met

Target list

Target	Baseline: Number and Type of Prompts	Date Introduced	Date Criteria Met	*Fading Procedure*		
				Maintenance	Date NE Introduced	Date Archived
Forward Chaining Procedure						
1. Target 1: Individual will retrieve chapstick						
2. Target 2: Individual will pull off lid of chapstick.						
3. Target 3: Individual will apply chapstick along upper lip.						
4. Target 4: Individual will apply chapstick along lower lip.						
5. Target 5: Individual will rub lips together.						

6. Target 6: Individual will put cap back on chapstick.						
7. Target 7: Individual will put chapstick away.						
8. Generalize to another environment Environment 1:						
9. Generalize to another environment Environment 2:						
10. Maintenance: Assess in varied environments				2W 1W M		

Specific tips for running this task analysis

- Ensure pre-requisite skills have been taught for this TA. Examples of pre-requisite skills for "Applying Chapstick" include progress made toward "Receptive Instructions (One-Step)" and attending programs (TAs found in the first book of the Journey of Development ABA Curriculum series). In addition, the individual has the ability to engage in the fine motor skills required for this task, such as removing and replacing the cap.
- This TA uses a forward chaining procedure whereby the TA is taught in the order in which they occur naturally until all steps are completed independently. Thus, for Target 1, the individual displays the target behavior then is prompted through the remaining steps. For Target 2, all steps are prompted except for the previous Target 1. For Target 3, all steps are prompted except for the previous Targets 1 and 2. Continue to follow this procedure until independent mastery of entire chain.
- This forward chain requires using a chapstick that the lid pulls off. Be sure to generalize to other types of chapstick or lip balm, such as one that the lid unscrews.
- Use chapstick flavors that the individual likes or will tolerate.
- It is best to practice this skill during naturally occurring times (when the individual's lips are dry).

BUTTONING AND UNBUTTONING

LEVEL: □ 1 □ 2 □ 3

S^D: A. Present an item to button and say "Button" B. Present an item to unbutton and say "Unbutton"	**Response:** Individual will independently button or unbutton the item
Data Collection: Prompt data (number and type of prompts used)	**Target criteria:** 0 prompts for 3 consecutive days across 2 people
Materials: Items with buttons of various sizes and reinforcement; alternative teaching materials: doll with clothes that button or a lapboard	

Fading procedure

Maintenance Criteria: 2W = 4 consecutive scores of 0 prompts; 1W = 4 consecutive scores of 0 prompts; M = 3 consecutive scores of 0 prompts	**Natural Environment (NE) Criterion:** Target has been generalized in NE across 3 novel naturally occurring activities	**Archive Criteria:** Target, maintenance and NE criteria have been met

Target list

Target	Baseline: Number and Type of Prompts	Date Introduced	Date Criteria Met	*Fading Procedure*		
				Maintenance	Date NE Introduced	Date Archived
"Button"						
1. Target 1: Final step of chain: Individual pushes entire button through buttonhole.						
2. Target 2: Step 5 of chain: Individual pushes button through three quarters of buttonhole.						
3. Target 3: Step 4 of chain: Individual pushes button through half of buttonhole.						
4. Target 4: Step 3 of chain: Individual pushes button through final one quarter of buttonhole.						

5. Target 5: Step 2 of chain: Individual puts button underneath button hole.						
6. Target 6: Step 1 of chain: Individual lines up buttons to put underneath buttonhole.						
7. Generalize to buttoning clothes on self.						
8. Generalize to another environment Environment 1:						
9. Generalize to another environment Environment 2:						
10. Maintenance: Assess with various buttons in varied environments.				2W 1W M		
"Unbutton"						
11. Target 1: Final step of chain: Individual pushes entire button out of buttonhole.						
12. Target 2: Step 3 of chain: Individual pushes three quarters of button out of buttonhole.						
13. Target 3: Step 2 of chain: Individual pushes half of button out of buttonhole.						
14. Target 4: Step 1 of chain: Individual pushes one quarter of button out of buttonhole.						
15. Generalize to unbuttoning clothes on self.						
16. Generalize to another environment Environment 1:						

17. Generalize to another environment Environment 2:						
18. Maintenance: Assess with various buttons in varied environments.				2W 1W M		

Specific tips for running this task analysis

- Ensure pre-requisite skills have been taught for this TA. Examples of pre-requisite skills for "Buttoning and Unbuttoning" include progress made toward "Receptive Instructions (One-Step)" (TA found in the first book of the Journey of Development ABA Curriculum series). In addition, the individual should have the ability to engage in the fine motor skills required of this task such as holding on to buttons and pushing buttons into or out of holes.
- This program is designed to teach the individual how to button/unbutton clothes and other items with buttons using the backward chaining procedure. The TA is taught in reverse order (last step first) until all steps are completed independently. Thus, for Target 1 in S^D A, prompt the individual through all steps of the chain with the exception of the last step. For Target 2, prompt the individual through all steps with the exception of the final step and Step 5. For Target 3, prompt the individual through all steps with the exception of the final step, Step 5 and Step 4. Continue to follow this procedure until independent mastery of entire chain has been achieved.
- It is suggested that you begin teaching this TA using large buttons. When the individual achieves success then introduce smaller buttons.
- It is also suggested that you begin teaching buttoning/unbuttoning off the body then generalize the skill to buttoning/unbuttoning on the body.

CLEANING EARS

LEVEL: □ 1 □ 2 □ 3

S^D: This skill is placed on the individual's hygiene or work schedule; alternatively, you can hand the individual a cotton swab while giving verbal S^D "Clean your ears"	**Response:** Individual will clean their ears
Data Collection: Prompt data (number and type of prompts used)	**Target criteria:** 0 prompts for 3 consecutive days across 2 people
Materials: Cotton swabs and reinforcement	

Fading procedure

Maintenance Criteria: 2W = 4 consecutive scores of 0 prompts; 1W = 4 consecutive scores of 0 prompts; M = 3 consecutive scores of 0 prompts	**Natural Environment (NE) Criterion:** Target has been generalized in NE across 3 novel naturally occurring activities	**Archive Criteria:** Target, maintenance and NE criteria have been met

Target list

Target	Baseline: Number and Type of Prompts	Date Introduced	Date Criteria Met	*Fading Procedure*		
				Maintenance	Date NE Introduced	Date Archived
Forward Chaining Procedure						
1. Target 1: Individual will retrieve two cotton swabs.						
2. Target 2: Individual will hold cotton swab in dominant hand.						
3. Target 3: Individual will run the cotton swab along the inside of their right ear lobe.						
4. Target 4: Individual will throw away cotton swab.						
5. Target 5: Individual will retrieve the second cotton swab.						

6. Target 6: Individual will run the cotton swab along the inside of their left ear lobe.						
7. Target 7: Individual will throw away cotton swab.						
8. Generalize to another environment Environment 1:						
9. Generalize to another environment Environment 2:						
10. Maintenance: Assess in varied environments				2W 1W M		

Specific tips for running this task analysis

- Ensure pre-requisite skills have been taught for this TA. Examples of pre-requisite skills for "Cleaning Ears" include progress made toward "Receptive Instructions (One-Step)" (TA found in the first book of the Journey of Development ABA Curriculum series). In addition, the individual should have the ability to engage in the fine motor skills required in this task such as holding the cotton swab and placing swab in their ear.
- This TA uses a forward chaining procedure whereby the TA is taught in the order in which they occur naturally until all steps are completed independently. Thus, for Target 1, the individual displays the target behavior then is prompted through the remaining steps. For Target 2, all steps are prompted except for the previous Target 1. For Target 3, all steps are prompted except for the previous Targets 1 and 2. Continue to follow this procedure until independent mastery of the entire chain has been achieved.
- This TA does not require the individual to clean their inner ear as it is difficult to teach the appropriate pressure to use for some individuals. If working with an individual that can discriminate light vs. heavy pressure, include these steps in the TA.
- Some individuals may find it beneficial to practice on dolls, if looking in the mirror is too difficult.
- To improve safety with teaching this skill, use the cotton swabs made for young children that have a thick collar (safety head) that prevents cotton swab from going into the ear too far.

DRESSING AND UNDRESSING: PUTTING ON AND TAKING OFF GLOVES

LEVEL: □ 1 □ 2 □ 3

S^D: A. Say "Take off your gloves" B. Present individual with their gloves and say "Put on your gloves"	**Response:** Individual will put on/take off their gloves
Data Collection: Prompt data (number and type of prompts used)	**Target criteria:** 0 prompts for 3 consecutive days across 2 people
Materials: Gloves and reinforcement	

Fading procedure

Maintenance Criteria: 2W = 4 consecutive scores of 0 prompts; 1W = 4 consecutive scores of 0 prompts; M = 3 consecutive scores of 0 prompts	**Natural Environment (NE) Criterion:** Target has been generalized in NE across 3 novel naturally occurring activities	**Archive Criteria:** Target, maintenance and NE criteria have been met

Target list

Target	Number and Type of Prompts	Date Introduced	Date Criteria Met	*Fading Procedure* Maintenance	Date NE Introduced	Date Archived
Backwards Chain—Taking off Gloves						
1. S^D A: Target 1: Last step of chain: Using their dominant hand, individual will pull off glove on the nondominant hand (peeling off glove).						
2. S^D A: Target 2: Step 5 of chain: Individual will open nondominant hand						
3. S^D A: Target 3: Step 4 of chain: Individual will place thumb of dominant hand inside glove located on nondominant hand.						
4. S^D A: Target 4: Step 3 of chain: Using their nondominant hand, individual will pull off the glove.						

5. S^D A: Target 5: Step 2 of chain: Individual will open dominant hand.						
6. S^D A: Target 6: Step 1 of chain: Individual will place thumb of nondominant hand inside glove located on the dominant hand.						
7. Generalize to another environment Environment 1:						
8. Generalize to another environment Environment 2:						
9. Maintenance: Assess in varied environments				2W 1W M		
Backwards Chain—Putting on Gloves						
1. S^D B: Target 1: Last step of chain: Adjust glove on hand.						
2. S^D B: Target 2: Step 9 of chain: Insert fingers in finger holes.						
3. S^D B: Target 3: Step 8 of chain: Insert ungloved hand in glove while pulling glove towards self.						
4. S^D B: Target 4: Step 7 of chain: Hold glove hanging open.						
5. S^D B: Target 5: Step 6 of chain: Pick up other glove with gloved hand.						
6. S^D B: Target 6: Step 5 of chain: Adjust glove on hand.						
7. S^D B: Target 7: Step 4 of chain: Insert fingers in finger holes.						
8. S^D B: Target 8: Step 3 of chain: Insert hand into glove while pulling glove towards self.						

9. S^D B: Target 9: Step 2 of chain: Hold glove hanging open.						
10. S^D B: Target 10: Step 1 of chain: Pick up first glove.						
11. Generalize to another environment Environment 1:						
12. Generalize to another environment Environment 2:						
13. Maintenance: Assess in varied environments				2W 1W M		

Specific tips for running this task analysis

- Ensure pre-requisite skills have been taught for this TA. Examples of pre-requisite skills for "Dressing and Undressing: Putting On and Taking Off Gloves" include mastering the dressing and undressing programs for shirts and pants (TAs found in the first book of the Journey of Development ABA Curriculum series). In addition, the individual should have the fine motor skills necessary for putting on and taking off gloves.
- It is best to run this program at naturally occurring times, such as putting on/taking off gloves immediately prior to going outside or coming inside.
- This program is designed to teach the individual how to put on and take off gloves using the backward chaining procedure. The TA is taught in reverse order (last step first) until all steps are completed independently. Thus, for Target 1 in S^D A, prompt the individual through all steps of chain with the exception of the last step. For Target 2, prompt the individual through all steps with the exception of the final step and Step 5. For Target 3, prompt the individual through all steps with the exception of the final step, Step 5 and Step 4. Continue to follow this procedure until independent mastery of the entire chain has been achieved.

DRESSING AND UNDRESSING: PUTTING ON AND TAKING OFF GYM CLOTHES

LEVEL: □ 1 □ 2 □ 3

S^D: A. Tell individual "Get undressed." Using backward chaining, prompt individual through task analysis B. Present individual with their gym clothes and say "Get dressed" Using backward chaining, prompt individual through task analysis	**Response:** Individual will independently put on/take off their shorts and shirt. Then get dressed in their gym clothes
Data Collection: Prompt data (number and type of prompts used)	**Target criteria:** 0 prompts for 3 consecutive days across 2 people
Materials: Gym clothes (shirt and shorts) and reinforcement	

Fading procedure

Maintenance Criteria: 2W = 4 consecutive scores of 0 prompts; 1W = 4 consecutive scores of 0 prompts; M = 3 consecutive scores of 0 prompts	**Natural Environment (NE) Criterion:** Target has been generalized in NE across 3 novel naturally occurring activities	**Archive Criteria:** Target, maintenance and NE criteria have been met

Target list

Target	Number and Type of Prompts	Date Introduced	Date Criteria Met	*Fading Procedure*		
				Maintenance	Date NE Introduced	Date Archived
Backwards Chain—Taking off gym clothes (shorts and shirt)						
1. S^D A: Target 1: Last step of chain: Individual will put shorts in bag.						
2. S^D A: Target 2: Step 10 of chain: Individual will step second leg out of shorts.						
3. S^D A: Target 3: Step 9 of chain: Individual will step one leg out of shorts.						
4. S^D A: Target 4: Step 8 of chain: Individual will pull down shorts.						

5. S^D A: Target 5: Step 7 of chain: Individual will unzip shorts (if applicable).						
6. S^D A: Target 6: Step 6 of chain: Individual will unbutton shorts (if applicable).						
7. S^D A: Target 7: Step 5 of chain: Individual will put shirt in bag.						
8. S^D A: Target 8: Step 4 of chain: Individual will pull second arm out of shirt.						
9. S^D A: Target 9: Step 3 of chain: Individual will pull one arm out of shirt.						
10. S^D A: Target 10: Step 2 of chain: Individual will pull shirt over their head.						
11. S^D A: Target 11: Step 1 of chain: Individual will pull shirt up to head.						
12. Generalize to another environment Environment 1:						
13. Generalize to another environment Environment 2:						
14. Maintenance: Assess in varied environments				2W 1W M		
Backwards Chain—Putting on Gym Clothes						
1. S^D B: Target 1: Last step of chain: Individual will adjust shorts onto hips.						
2. S^D B: Target 2: Step 10 of chain: Individual will pull shorts.						
3. S^D B: Target 3 Step 9 of chain: Individual will place leg into second shorts leg.						

4. S^D B: Target 4: Step 8 of chain: Individual will place leg into first shorts leg.						
5. S^D B: Target 5: Step 7 of chain: Individual will hold open their shorts.						
6. S^D B: Target 6: Step 6 of the chain: Individual will grab shorts.						
7. S^D B: Target 7: Step 5 of chain: Individual will pull shirt down to waist.						
8. S^D B: Target 8: Step 4 of chain: Individual will place second arm into sleeve.						
9. S^D B: Target 9: Step 3 of chain: Individual will place first arm into sleeve.						
10. S^D B: Target 10: Step 2 of chain: Individual will pull shirt over their head.						
11. S^D B: Target 11: Step 1 of chain: Individual will form hole with neck on shirt to prepare to pull over head.						
12. Generalize to another environment Environment 1:						
13. Generalize to another environment Environment 2:						
14. Maintenance: Assess in varied environments				2W 1W M		

Specific tips for running this task analysis

- Ensure pre-requisite skills have been taught for this TA. Examples of pre-requisite skills for "Dressing and Undressing: Putting On and Taking Off Gym Clothes" include mastering the dressing and undressing programs for shirts and pants (TAs found in the first book of the Journey of Development ABA Curriculum series). In addition, the individual should have the fine motor skills necessary for putting on and shirt and shorts.
- It is best to run this program at naturally occurring times, such as before and after gym class.
- This program is designed to teach the individual how to put on and take off their gym clothes using the backward chaining procedure. The TA is taught in reverse order (last step first) until all steps are completed independently. Thus, for Target 1 in S^D A, prompt the individual through all steps of the chain with the exception of the last step. For Target 2, prompt the individual through all steps with the exception of the final step and Step 10. For Target 3, prompt the individual through all steps with the exception of the final step, Step 10 and Step 9. Continue to follow this procedure until independent mastery of the entire chain has been achieved.

SNAPPING AND UNSNAPPING

LEVEL: □ 1 □ 2 □ 3

S^D: A. Present an item to unsnap and say "Unsnap" B. Present an item to snap and say "Snap"	**Response:** Individual will snap and unsnap the item
Data Collection: Prompt data (number and type of prompts used)	**Target criteria:** 0 prompts for 3 consecutive days across 2 people
Materials: Items with snaps and reinforcement	

Fading procedure

Maintenance Criteria: 2W = 4 consecutive scores of 0 prompts; 1W = 4 consecutive scores of 0 prompts; M = 3 consecutive scores of 0 prompts	**Natural Environment (NE) Criterion:** Target has been generalized in NE across 3 novel naturally occurring activities	**Archive Criteria:** Target, maintenance and NE criteria have been met

Target list

Target	Baseline: Number and Type of Prompts	Date Introduced	Date Criteria Met	*Fading Procedure*		
				Maintenance	Date NE Introduced	Date Archived
"Unsnap"						
1. Target 1: Final step of chain: Pull material attached to top snap upward.						
2. Target 2: Step 2 of chain: Hold down material attached to bottom of snap.						
3. Target 3: Step 1 of chain: Grab on to both sides of material near the snaps.						
4. Generalize to another environment Environment 1:						
5. Generalize to another environment Environment 2:						

6. Maintenance: Assess in varied environments				2W 1W M		
"Snap"						
7. Target 1: Final step of chain: Apply pressure to bring the snaps together						
8. Target 2: Step 2 of chain: Line the snaps up						
9. Target 3: Step 1 of chain: Grab on to both sides of material near the snaps						
10. Generalize to another environment Environment 1:						
11. Generalize to another environment Environment 2:						
12. Maintenance: Assess in varied environments				2W 1W M		

Specific tips for running this task analysis

- Ensure pre-requisite skills have been taught for this TA. Examples of pre-requisite skills for "Snapping and Unsnapping" include progress made toward "Receptive Instructions (One-Step)" (TA found in the first book of the Journey of Development ABA Curriculum series). In addition, the individual should have the ability to engage in the fine motor skills required in this task such as being able to manipulate small objects.
- This program is designed to teach the individual how to snap/unsnap clothes and other items with snaps using the backward chaining procedure. The TA is taught in reverse order (last step first) until all steps are completed independently. Thus, for Target 1 in S^D A, prompt the individual through all steps of the chain with the exception of the last step. For Target 2, prompt the individual through all steps with the exception of the final step and Step 2. For Target 3, prompt the individual through all steps (since this TA only contains 3 steps).
- Be sure to generalize this skill to different materials with snaps such as snaps on a coat, shirt, dressing board, bag, etc. Also, generalize to various sizes of snaps.
- It is suggested that you begin teaching this TA using large snaps. When the individual achieves success then introduce smaller snaps.
- It is also suggested that you begin teaching snapping/unsnapping off the body then generalize the skill to snapping/unsnapping on the body.

SYSTEMATIC DESENSITIZATION: BRUSHING HAIR

LEVEL: □ 1 □ 2 □ 3

S^D: Have hairbrush in hand and follow targets within the TA, and say "It is time to brush your hair"	**Response:** Individual will increase their tolerance toward brushing their hair by completing the systematic desensitization plan/hairbrushing chain listed below
Data Collection: Prompt data (number and type of prompts used)	**Target Criteria:** 0 prompts for 3 consecutive days and no problem behaviors or anxiety observed during the procedure
Materials: Hairbrush and reinforcement; optional materials: timer, pictures of each step in the plan and first/then board	

Fading procedure

Maintenance Criteria: 2W = 4 consecutive scores of 0 prompts; 1W = 4 consecutive scores of 0 prompts; M = 3 consecutive scores of 0 prompts	**Natural Environment (NE) Criterion:** Target has been generalized in NE across 3 novel naturally occurring activities	**Archive Criteria:** Target, maintenance and NE criteria have been met

Target list

Target	Baseline: Number and Type of Prompts	Date Introduced	Date Criteria Met	*Fading Procedure*		
				Maintenance	Date NE Introduced	Date Archived
1. Target 1: Place a hairbrush 5 feet away from instructor and individual (work on other tasks).						
2. Target 2: Instructor stands next to individual with hairbrush for a few seconds.						
3. Target 3: Instructor brushes individual's hair one time at the ends.						
4. Target 3: Instructor brushes individual's hair one time from root to ends.						
5. Target 4: Instructor brushes individual's hair 2 times at the ends.						

6. Target 5: Instructor brushes individual's hair 2 times from root to ends.						
7. Target 6: Instructor brushes individual's hair 3 times from root to ends.						
8. Target 7: Instructor brushes individual's hair 5 times from root to ends.						
9. Target 8: Instructor brushes individual's hair 10 times from root to ends.						
10. Target 9: Instructor brushes all of individual's hair.						
11. Generalize to another environment Environment 1:						
12. Generalize to another environment Environment 2:						
13. Maintenance: Assess in varied environments				2W 1W M		

Specific tips for running this task analysis

- Systematic desensitization is a type of behavioral therapy that involves classical conditioning (just like ABA). It essentially means to gradually expose an individual to the stimuli that causes them anxiety. It involves developing a desensitization hierarchy designed to incrementally increase an individual's ability to tolerate an offending stimulus (this hierarchy has been developed within this TA). The initial steps in the hierarchy involve very brief or distant exposure to the offending stimulus, followed immediately by an opportunity to engage in a relaxing, self-selected reinforcing activity. It is essential during the initial phases that the individual be removed from the aversive stimuli before they can become agitated. This will help prevent a cycle of behavior in which the individual's reaction becomes associated with escaping the feared stimulus and thereby the behavior becomes reinforcing. You want to ensure the individual does not learn that a problem behavior or extreme reaction can be used to escape the feared stimuli. If the individual is successful in escaping the stimuli, their problem behavior can be inadvertently reinforced. When the individual experiences the stimuli without reacting to it, the association between the offending stimuli and the problem behavior is lessened and alternative behaviors can be taught.
- After each step of this systematic desensitization plan, ensure the individual is given a reinforcing activity to engage in for tolerating the offending stimulus.
- Once individual completes this TA, you should immediately implement the "Brushing Hair" TA found in the third book of the Journey of Development ABA Curriculum series.
- Consider using some form of conditioner to make the process less painful. This could include leave-in (spray) conditioner, detangler and using a great amount of conditioner after shampooing hair when bathing.
- To help alleviate some anxiety of getting hair brushed, show individual pictures of age-related individuals getting their hair brushed. Talk through the picture with individual. This could be done as a preliminary step before implementing Step 1 of this TA.

SYSTEMATIC DESENSITIZATION: BRUSHING TEETH

LEVEL: □ 1 □ 2 □ 3

S^D: Say "Let's play with a toothbrush"	**Response:** Individual will increase their tolerance toward brushing teeth as evidenced by completing the systematic desensitization plan/teeth-brushing chain listed below
Data Collection: Prompt data (number and type of prompts used)	**Target Criteria:** 0 prompts for 3 consecutive days and no problem behaviors/anxiety observed during the procedure
Materials: Toothbrush and reinforcement; optional materials: timer, pictures of each step in the plan, and first/then board	

Fading procedure

Maintenance Criteria: 2W = 4 consecutive scores of 0 prompts; 1W = 4 consecutive scores of 0 prompts; M = 3 consecutive scores of 0 prompts	**Natural Environment (NE) Criterion:** Target has been generalized in NE across 3 novel naturally occurring activities	**Archive Criteria:** Target, maintenance and NE criteria have been met

Target list

Target	Baseline: Number and Type of Prompts	Date Introduced	Date Criteria Met	*Fading Procedure*		
				Maintenance	Date NE Introduced	Date Archived
1. Target 1: Individual will touch the toothbrush.						
2. Target 2: Individual will hold the toothbrush for 5 seconds						
3. Target 3: Individual will hold the toothbrush for 10 seconds						
4. Target 4: Individual will touch the toothbrush to their mouth.						
5. Target 5: Individual will touch the toothbrush to their teeth.						
6. Target 6: Individual will swipe toothbrush across teeth 1 time.						

7. Target 7: Individual will swipe toothbrush across teeth 2 times.						
8. Target 8: Individual will brush teeth for 5 seconds.						
9. Target 9: Individual will brush teeth for 10 seconds.						
10. Generalize to another environment Environment 1:						
11. Generalize to another environment Environment 2:						
12. Maintenance: Assess in varied environments				2W 1W M		

Specific tips for running this task analysis

- Systematic desensitization is a type of behavioral therapy that involves classical conditioning (just like ABA). It essentially means to gradually expose an individual to the stimuli that causes them anxiety. It involves developing a desensitization hierarchy designed to incrementally increase an individual's ability to tolerate an offending stimulus (this hierarchy has been developed within this TA). The initial steps in the hierarchy involve very brief or distant exposure to the offending stimulus, followed immediately by an opportunity to engage in a relaxing, self-selected reinforcing activity. It is essential during the initial phases that the individual be removed from the aversive stimuli before they can become agitated. This will help prevent a cycle of behavior in which the individual's reaction becomes associated with escaping the feared stimulus and thereby the behavior becomes reinforcing. You want to ensure the individual does not learn that a problem behavior or extreme reaction can be used to escape the feared stimuli. If the individual is successful to escaping the stimuli, their problem behavior can be inadvertently reinforced. When the individual experiences the stimuli without reacting to it, the association between the offending stimuli and the problem behavior is lessened and alternative behaviors can be taught.
- After each step of this systematic desensitization plan, ensure the individual is given a reinforcing activity to engage in for tolerating the offending stimulus.
- Once individual completes this TA, you should immediately implement the "Brushing Teeth" TA found in the third book of the Journey of Development ABA Curriculum series.

UNZIPPING A ZIPPER

LEVEL: □ 1 □ 2 □ 3

S^D: Say "Unzip your coat"	**Response:** Individual will independently unzip their coat
Data Collection: Prompt data (number and type of prompts used)	**Target Criteria:** 0 prompts for 3 consecutive days across 2 people
Materials: Coat and reinforcement	

Fading procedure

Maintenance Criteria: 2W = 4 consecutive scores of 0 prompts; 1W = 4 consecutive scores of 0 prompts; M = 3 consecutive scores of 0 prompts	**Natural Environment (NE) Criterion:** Target has been generalized in NE across 3 novel naturally occurring activities	**Archive Criteria:** Target, maintenance and NE criteria have been met

Target list

Target	Baseline: Number and Type of Prompts	Date Introduced	Date Criteria Met	*Fading Procedure*		
				Maintenance	Date NE Introduced	Date Archived
1. Target 1: Step 1 of chain: Individual will grasp the bottom of the coat with their nondominant hand.						
2. Target 2: Step 2 of chain: Individual will grasp the pull tab with dominant hand.						
3. Target 3: Step 3 of chain: Individual will unzip zipper using the pull tab.						
4. Target 4: Last step of chain: Individual will disengage zipper from the retainer box.						
5. Generalize to another environment Environment 1:						
6. Generalize to another environment Environment 2:						

7. Maintenance: Assess in varied environments				2W 1W M		

Specific tips for running this task analysis

- Ensure pre-requisite skills have been taught for this TA. Examples of pre-requisite skills for "Unzipping a Zipper" include progress made toward "Receptive Instructions (One-Step)" (TA found in the first book of the Journey of Development ABA Curriculum series). In addition, the individual should have the ability to engage in the fine motor skills required in this task such as grasping the pull tab and holding the edge of the coat.
- This program is designed to teach the individual how to unzip a zipper using the forward chaining procedure whereby the TA is taught in the order of completion. Thus, Target 1 requires the individual to become independent with the first step while being prompted (least to most prompting) through the remaining steps. For Target 2, the individual should complete Step 1 and Step 2 independently while being prompted through the remaining steps. Continue to follow this procedure until independent mastery of the entire chain has been achieved.
- Generalize to other zippers (winter coat, spring coat, rain coat and/or zippered sweatshirt, pants, book bag, suitcase, boots/shoes).
- It is best to practice this skill during naturally occurring times (after coming inside, undressing, etc.).

WAITING

LEVEL: □ 1 □ 2 □ 3

S^D: A. Present individual with preferred object and say "Wait" B. Present individual with preferred activity and say "Wait" C. Set up a contrived situation (e.g. mother on telephone), give individual preferred object or activity and say "Let's go show [x]" (e.g. Mom). Have person in contrived situation tell individual "Wait"	**Response:** Individual will sit or stand appropriately (quiet mouth, quiet body) and wait for 2 minutes to receive preferred object, activity or person's attention
Data Collection: Skill acquisition	**Target Criteria:** 80% for 3 consecutive days across 2 people
Materials: Preferred objects and activities, and reinforcement	

Fading procedure

Maintenance Criteria: 2W = 4 consecutive scores of 100%; 1W = 4 consecutive scores of 100%; M = 3 consecutive scores of 100%	**Natural Environment (NE) Criterion:** Target has been generalized in NE across 3 novel naturally occurring activities	**Archive Criteria:** Target, maintenance and NE criteria have been met

Target list

Suggestions for targets and probe results

Suggestions for Targets: *Preferred Objects*: Any object that the individual finds moderately reinforcing such as bubbles, trains, musical instrument, etc.
Preferred Activities: Any activity that the individual finds moderately reinforcing such as computer time, CD player, board game, etc.
Contrived Situations: Instructor talking on the telephone, adults engaging in conversation, instructor making dinner or instructor engaging in a household chore.

Probe Results (targets in repertoire):

Target	Baseline %	Date Introduced	Date Criteria Met	*Fading Procedure*		
				Maintenance	Date NE Introduced	Date Archived
Waiting for Preferred Object						
1. Target 1: 2 seconds						
2. Target 2: 5 seconds						

3. Target 3: 10 seconds						
4. Target 4: 20 seconds						
5. Target 5: 30 seconds						
6. Target 6: 45 seconds						
7. Target 7: 60 seconds						
8. Target 8: 90 seconds						
9. Target 9: 2 minutes						
10. Generalize to another environment Environment 1:						
11. Generalize to another environment Environment 2:						
12. Maintenance: Assess in varied environments				2W 1W M		
Waiting for Preferred Activity						
1. Target 1: 2 seconds						
2. Target 2: 5 seconds						
3. Target 3: 10 seconds						
4. Target 4: 20 seconds						
5. Target 5: 30 seconds						

6. Target 6: 45 seconds						
7. Target 7: 60 seconds						
8. Target 8: 90 seconds						
9. Target 9: 2 minutes						
10. Generalize to another environment Environment 1:						
11. Generalize to another environment Environment 2:						
12. Maintenance: Assess in varied environments				2W 1W M		
Waiting for Attention in Contrived Situations *Contrived Situation Number 1:*						
1. Target 1: 2 seconds						
2. Target 2: 5 seconds						
3. Target 3: 10 seconds						
4. Target 4: 20 seconds						
5. Target 5: 30 seconds						
6. Target 6: 45 seconds						
7. Target 7: 60 seconds						
8. Target 8: 90 seconds						

9. Target 9: 2 minutes						
10. Generalize to another environment Environment 1:						
11. Generalize to another environment Environment 2:						
Waiting for Attention in Contrived Situations *Contrived Situation Number 2:*						
12. Target 1: 2 seconds						
13. Target 2: 5 seconds						
14. Target 3: 10 seconds						
15. Target 4: 20 seconds						
16. Target 5: 30 seconds						
17. Target 6: 45 seconds						
18. Target 7: 60 seconds						
19. Target 8: 90 seconds						
20. Target 9: 2 minutes						
21. Generalize to another environment Environment 1:						
22. Generalize to another environment Environment 2:						

Waiting for Attention in Contrived Situations *Contrived Situation Number 3:*						
1. Target 1: 2 seconds						
2. Target 2: 5 seconds						
3. Target 3: 10 seconds						
4. Target 4: 20 seconds						
5. Target 5: 30 seconds						
6. Target 6: 45 seconds						
7. Target 7: 60 seconds						
8. Target 8: 90 seconds						
9. Target 9: 2 minutes						
10. Generalize to another environment Environment 1:						
11. Generalize to another environment Environment 2:						
12. Maintenance: random rotation of all contrived situation targets—assess in varied environments				2W 1W M		

Specific tips for running this task analysis

- Ensure pre-requisite skills have been taught for this TA. Examples of pre-requisite skills for "Waiting" include progress made toward "Receptive Instructions (One-Step)" (TA found in the first book of the Journey of Development ABA Curriculum series).
- It is suggested in this TA to use moderately preferred activities as it may be much more difficult to have an individual wait for a highly preferred object or activity, which can lead to problem behaviors and a risk of reinforcing those problem behaviors.

WALKING BACKWARDS

LEVEL: □ 1 □ 2 □ 3

S^D: Present a line and say "Walk backwards"	**Response:** Individual will walk backwards staying on the line
Data Collection: Prompt data (number and type of prompts used)	**Target criteria:** 0 prompts for 3 consecutive days across 2 people
Materials: Various lines to walk on (tape on the floor, chalk line, foam mats, etc.) and reinforcement	

Fading procedure

Maintenance Criteria: 2W = 4 consecutive scores of 0 prompts; 1W = 4 consecutive scores of 0 prompts; M = 3 consecutive scores of 0 prompts	**Natural Environment (NE) Criterion:** Target has been generalized in NE across 3 novel naturally occurring activities	**Archive Criteria:** Target, maintenance and NE criteria have been met

Target list

Suggestions for targets and probe results

Suggestions for Targets: Walk 2 feet without a line, walk 4 feet without a line, walk 6 feet without a line, walk 10 feet without a line, walk 10 feet along a mat, walk 10 feet along tape line, walk 10 feet along a chalk line, walk 10 feet along a sidewalk crack, walk 10 feet down the middle of a hall.

Probe Results (targets in repertoire):

Target	Baseline: Number and Type of Prompts	Date Introduced	Date Criteria Met	*Fading Procedure*		
				Maintenance	Date NE Introduced	Date Archived
1. Target 1:						
2. Target 2:						
3. Target 3:						
4. Target 4:						

5. Target 5:						
6. Target 6:						
7. Targets that met criteria: random rotation						
8. Generalize to another environment Environment 1:						
9. Generalize to another environment Environment 2:						
10. Maintenance: Assess in varied environments				2W 1W M		

Specific tips for running this task analysis

- Ensure pre-requisite skills have been taught for this TA. Examples of pre-requisite skills for "Walking Backwards" include mastering the attending skills programs and fine and gross motor imitation programs (TAs found in the first book of the Journey of Development ABA Curriculum series).
- Prompts of holding the individual's hand can be used as a teaching strategy.
- When using a line, you can have starting and stopping points so the individual knows how far they have to walk (e.g. start at the green dot and stop at the red dot).
- You can also teach the individual the safety measure of looking over their shoulder as they walk backwards. This should be targeted later once the individual masters walking backward without a line.

WIPING HANDS AND FACE

LEVEL: □ 1 □ 2 □ 3

S^D: "Wipe your hands and face"	**Response:** Individual will respond by independently wiping their hands and face
Data Collection: Prompt data (number and type of prompts used)	**Target Criteria:** 0 prompts for 3 consecutive days across 2 people
Materials: Cloth or paper towel and reinforcement	

Fading procedure

Maintenance Criteria: 2W = 4 consecutive scores of 0 prompts; 1W = 4 consecutive scores of 0 prompts; M = 3 consecutive scores of 0 prompts	**Natural Environment (NE) Criterion:** Target has been generalized in NE across 3 novel naturally occurring activities	**Archive Criteria:** Target, maintenance and NE criteria have been met

Target list

Target	Baseline: Number and Type of Prompts	Date Introduced	Date Criteria Met	*Fading Procedure*		
				Maintenance	Date NE Introduced	Date Archived
Backwards chaining procedure						
1. Target 1: Final step of chain: Throw away or replace paper or cloth towel.						
2. Target 2: Step 6: Wipe the back of dominant hand using paper or cloth towel.						
3. Target 3: Step 5: Wipe the front of dominant hand using paper or cloth towel.						
4. Target 4: Step 4: Wipe the back of nondominant hand using paper or cloth towel.						

5. Target 5: Step 3: Wipe the front of nondominant hand using paper or cloth towel.						
6. Target 6: Step 2: Using both hands, wipe mouth and chin with paper or cloth towel.						
7. Target 7: Step 1: Grab paper or cloth towel with dominant hand.						
8. Generalize to another environment Environment 1:						
9. Generalize to another environment Environment 2:						
10. Maintenance: Assess in varied environments				2W 1W M		

Specific tips for running this task analysis

- This program is designed to teach the individual how to wipe their face and hands using the backward chaining procedure whereby the TA is taught in reverse order (last step first) until all steps are completed independently. Thus, for Target 1, prompt individual through all steps of the chain with the exception of the last step. For Target 2, prompt individual through all steps with the exception of the final step and Step 6. For Target 3, prompt individual through all steps with the exception of the final step, Step 6 and Step 5. Continue to follow this procedure until independent mastery of the entire chain has been achieved.
- If generalizing this skill to a wet wipe in a package be sure to add steps that require the individual to tear open the packet and open the wet wipe.
- You can also use an S^D, "Wipe your face and hands," paired with a gesture towards their hands and face, to teach this skill initially. If this is done, work to fade your verbal S^D to a gesture only so that the individual does not become reliant on hearing the verbal S^D and will begin to use the sensation of a messy mouth or hands as the natural S^D.

ZIPPING A CONNECTED AND UNCONNECTED ZIPPER

LEVEL: □ 1 □ 2 □ 3

S^D: A. Connected zipper: After the individual has put on their coat, connect the zipper and say "Zip your coat" B. Unconnected zipper: After the individual has put on their coat say "Zip your coat"	**Response:** Individual will independently zip their coat
Data Collection: Prompt data (number and type of prompts used)	**Target Criteria:** 0 prompts for 3 consecutive days across 2 people
Materials: Coat and reinforcement	

Fading procedure

Maintenance Criteria: 2W = 4 consecutive scores of 0 prompts; 1W = 4 consecutive scores of 0 prompts; M = 3 consecutive scores of 0 prompts	**Natural Environment (NE) Criterion:** Target has been generalized in NE across 3 novel naturally occurring activities	**Archive Criteria:** Target, maintenance and NE criteria have been met

Target list

Target	Baseline: Number and Type of Prompts	Date Introduced	Date Criteria Met	*Fading Procedure*		
				Maintenance	NE Date Introduced	Date Archived
Backward chain—zipping connected zipper						
1. S^D A: Target 1: Last step of chain: Individual will zip zipper using the pull tab.						
2. S^D A: Target 2: Step 2 of chain: Individual will grasp the pull tab with dominant hand.						
3. S^D A: Target 3: Step 1 of chain: Individual will grasp under the slider with their nondominant hand.						

4. Generalize to another environment Environment 1:						
5. Generalize to another environment Environment 2:						
Backward chain—zipping unconnected zipper						
1. S^D B: Target 1: Last step of chain: Individual will zip zipper using the pull tab.						
2. S^D B: Target 2: Step 4 of chain: Individual will grasp the pull tab with dominant hand.						
3. S^D B: Target 3: Step 3 of chain: Individual will grasp under the slider with their nondominant hand.						
4. S^D B: Target 4: Step 2 of chain: Individual will place the insertion pin into the slider.						
5. S^D B: Target 5: Step 1 of chain: Individual will grasp the bottom of each side of the zipper (insertion pin and slider).						
6. Generalize to another environment Environment 1:						
7. Generalize to another environment Environment 2:						
8. Maintenance: Assess in varied environments.				2W 1W M		

Specific tips for running this task analysis

- Ensure pre-requisite skills have been taught for this TA. Examples of pre-requisite skills for "Zipping a Connected and Unconnected Zipper" include progress made toward "Receptive Instructions (One-Step)" (TA found in the first book of the Journey of Development ABA Curriculum series). In addition, the individual should have the ability to engage in the fine motor skills required in this task such as grasping the pull tab.

- This program is designed to teach the individual how to zip a connected and unconnected zipper using the backward chaining procedure whereby the TA is taught in reverse order (last step first) until all steps are completed independently. Thus, for Target 1, prompt the individual through all steps of the chain with the exception of the last step. For Target 2, prompt individual through all steps with the exception of the final step and Step 2. Continue to follow this procedure until independent mastery of the entire chain has been achieved.
- Generalize to other connected zippers (winter coat, spring coat, rain coat and/or zippered sweatshirt, pants, book bag, suitcase, boots/shoes).
- It is best to practice this skill during naturally occurring times (before leaving and going outside, dressing, etc.).

References

American Red Cross (undated) Learn to Swim Levels 1–6. Available at www.yourswimmingspace.com/skills-checklist.html, accessed 30 January 2014.

Bondy, A. and Frost, L. (2002) *The Picture Exchange Communication System.* Newark DE: Pyramid Educational Products.

Bracken, B.A. (2006) *Bracken Basic Concept Scale, Expressive.* Bloomington, MN: Pearson Education, Inc.

Cooper, J.O., Heron, T.E., and Heward, W.L. (2007) *Applied Behavior Analysis* (2nd Edition). New Jersey: Pearson.

Leaf, R. and McEachin, J. (1997) *A Work In Progress: Behavior Management Strategies and a Curriculum for Intensive Behavioral Treatment of Autism.* New York, NY: DRL Books, LLC.

Lovaas, O.I. (2003) *Teaching Persons with Developmental Disabilities: Basic Intervention Techniques.* Austin, TX: Pro-ed.

Partington, J.W. (2006) *The Assessment of Basic Language and Learning Skills – Revised (The ABLLS-R).* Pleasant Hill, CA: Behavior Analysts, Inc.